Drawings by J. FRANKLIN WHITMAN, JR.

I FOUGHT WITH GERONIMO

By Jason Betzinez with Wilbur Sturtevant Nye

University of Nebraska Press
Lincoln and London

Copyright © 1959 by the Stackpole Company
All rights reserved
Manufactured in the United States of America

First Bison Book printing: 1987
Most recent printing indicated by the first digit below:
                 4   5   6   7   8   9   10

Library of Congress Cataloging in Publication Data
Betzinez, Jason.
  I fought with Geronimo.

  Reprint. Originally published: Harrisburg, Pa.:
Stackpole, 1959.
  Includes index.
  1. Apache Indians — Wars, 1883–1886 — Personal narratives.
2. Betzinez, Jason. 3. Geronimo, Apache chief, 1809–
1909. 4. Apache Indians — Biography. I. Nye, Wilbur
Sturtevant, 1898–   . II. title.
E83.88.B48 1987   973.8′4′0924   87-10839
ISBN 0-8032-1204-6
ISBN 0-8032-6086-5 (pbk.)

Reprinted by arrangement with Stackpole Books

∞

FOREWORD

This is the autobiography of an Apache Indian who has been virtually a part of the Stone Age and the Atomic Era. As a boy Jason Betzinez hunted with bow and arrow within sight of the New Mexico flats where, eighty years later, the first atomic blast was fired. As savages he and his tribe fought their enemies through deserts and mountains where giant missiles are tested today. The careers of few if any living persons offer such striking contrasts and unique features.

Now nearly a hundred years old Jason has been, successively, on the warpath with his cousin and lifelong associate, Geronimo, the "Human Tiger" of the southwestern frontier; a prisoner of war in an ancient Spanish fort in Florida; a student at the Carlisle Indian School; a steelworker in Pennsylvania, and a blacksmith and farmer in Oklahoma. His wife was a white missionary; she is of pure Dutch descent, related to the House of Orange. Both Mr. and Mrs. Betzinez are devout Christians and active church workers. In an accident at the age of 90 Jason suffered injuries that would have finished most of us. Then, if that were not enough, six years later he underwent serious abdominal surgery. Nothing keeps him down! In 1958, alone and on crutches, and with failing vision and hearing, he made his first trip by air, with several changes of plane, to Pennsylvania to visit his "old stomping grounds." A week later he made another transcontinental flight to New York to participate in the TV show "I've Got a Secret."

Jason Betzinez inherited the toughness of his fiber from his mother, who lived 112 years. When he was a "wild" Indian he could travel on foot up to 75 miles a day through the burning desert and over lofty, rugged mountains. Later, in Pennsylvania, he played baseball, was a wrestler, and a fullback on a steelworks football team. Had his background and education been more favorable, Jason could well have made his mark in the public life of the nation, for he is strong mentally and spiritually as well as physically. He braved the enmity of his own people to advocate a course of action contrary to their wishes, where he saw that they were ruining themselves. He sought and gained the assistance of high U. S. officials to promote the welfare of the tribe.

Though Jason is inflexible when he is convinced that he is on the side of wisdom and righteousness, he has a friendly, tolerant attitude, with a broad understanding and forgiveness even for those who have used his people shamefully. Those who cling to the myth that the Indian is stoical, taciturn, and gruff, would open their eyes at meeting Jason with his robust sense of humor, hearty laugh, and emotional, voluble nature. He has hundreds of warm friends—a fact which he cherishes above all else in life.

This is not a dialect story. Jason speaks and writes English, not pidgin English. He wrote his own account; but appreciating that his education had been shortened, he asked that the manuscript be rigorously edited. This has been done by rearranging much of the material and by paraphrasing where necessary. It is not, however, an "as told to" type of work except where some information has been added which was furnished in conversation, correspondence, or tape recordings. Since it represents personal knowledge gained from his experiences and those of close associates, Jason's book is *source* material—there can be no bibliography.

The author furnished many of the photographs, the editor a few. Others are from the Smithsonian Institution and the National Archives. The author drew maps and sketches to illustrate his wanderings. This information was transferred to a map drawn by the editor based on a modern chart obtained from the U.S. Coast and Geodetic Survey and checked against old maps in the Library of Congress and Gen. George Crook's scrapbook (Army War College). The pen-and-ink sketches were drawn in 1852 by John Russell Bartlett. The other drawings are by Mr. J. Franklin Whitman, Jr. of Lebanon, Pennsylvania.

The author and the editor take this occasion to thank the many persons who have extended assistance and encouragement. Special acknowledgment is made to Major General Thomas E. de Shazo, Commanding General, The U.S. Army Artillery and Missile School, and Major General Max Johnson, Commandant The Army War College, for the use of photographic and other material in their official collections; to Mr. Gillett Griswold, Director of the Fort Sill Museum, for tireless efforts on our behalf; and to Mrs. Rose Weiss of the Army Map Service and Mrs. Margaret C. Blaker of the Smithsonian Institution, for advice and assistance.

W. S. NYE
Harrisburg, Pennsylvania

January, 1959

CONTENTS

Chapter		Page
1	REVENGE AT RAMOS	1
2	FURTHER TREACHERY	10
3	MY MOTHER IS CAPTURED	18
4	PRIMITIVE LIFE	26
5	OUR TROUBLES BEGIN AGAIN	38
6	OUTBREAK	47
7	INTO THE WILDERNESS	56
8	TRAGEDY IN MEXICO	67
9	ON THE WARPATH WITH GERONIMO	81
10	EXPEDITION AGAINST GALEANA	93
11	WE INVADE SONORA	97
12	PROPHECIES OF DISASTER	110
13	SURRENDER	116
14	THE LAST OUTBREAK	126
15	PRISONERS OF WAR	140
16	GOLDEN DAYS	149
17	FOLLOWING A TRADE	160
18	THE APACHES ARE MOVED TO FORT SILL	165
19	WORKING FOR MY PEOPLE	175
20	THE PROMISED LAND	185
21	OUR CAPTIVITY IS ENDED	189
22	A HOME AT LAST	200
	INDEX	211

ILLUSTRATIONS

The capital letters in parentheses in the following list of illustrations refer to the sources shown below, to which credit is due:

(A) Army War College, Carlisle Barracks, Pennsylvania
(B) John R. Bartlett
(E) Bureau of American Ethnology
(N) National Archives
(S) Fort Sill, Oklahoma
(W) J. Franklin Whitman, Jr.

	Page
SANTA RITA DEL COBRE (B)	2
APACHE WARRIORS (E)	5
MEXICAN VILLAGE WITH CHURCH AND PLAZA (B)	7
DILTHCHE'S CROSSING SITE (B)	12
JANOS (B)	16
GUADALUPE PASS (B)	19
NAH-THLE-TLA	22
TYPICAL APACHE SHELTER AND FAMILY GROUP (N)	29
APACHE HUNTER STALKING ANTELOPE (W)	31
CHIEF LOCO OF WARM SPRINGS APACHE BAND (E)	32
CHIRICAHUA MOUNTAINS (B)	39
MICKEY FREE AS AN ADULT (E)	40
COCHISE'S STRONGHOLD (N)	42
MAP 1. THE MOVE FROM WARM SPRINGS TO SAN CARLOS	45
THE SAN CARLOS AGENCY, WITH APACHE CAMPS (E)	48
VICTORIO (N)	51
ALBERT STERLING AND HIS APACHE SCOUTS (N)	57
LILLIAN KAZSHE IN COSTUME FOR WOMANHOOD CEREMONY, MADE BY NAH-THLE-TLA	59
MAP 2. FLIGHT FROM SAN CARLOS TO MEXICO	64
CAVALRY IN BOX CANYON TYPICAL OF SITE OF FIGHT NEAR STEINS (N)	65
APACHE ROUTE TO MEXICO (B)	66
MAP 3. GERONIMO'S ROUTE SOUTH OF THE BORDER	71
GERONIMO IN MEXICO (E)	76
NEAR CASAS GRANDES (B)	79
MAP 4. ROUTE OF APACHES IN SUMMER AND FALL OF 1882	82
APACHE CAMP PACKED READY TO MOVE (E)	84
NEAR OPUTO (B)	90
GALEANA (B)	94

	Page
MAP 5. FIGHT NEAR GALEANA	96
MAP 6. RAID INTO SONORA	98
SOME OF THE ENEMY WERE KILLED (W)	101
MAP 7. RAID BELOW URES	103
NEAR URES (B)	104
OUR WARRIORS PREPARED AN AMBUSH (W)	106
CHATTO (E)	108
MAP 8. BATTLE OF THE CANYON AND RAID TOWARD CHIHUAHUA	112
SOME OF THE MEN DROVE IN CATTLE (W)	114
APACHE HIDEOUT IN THE HEART OF THE SIERRA MADRES (N)	117
TSO-AY (PEACHES), GUIDE TO GENERAL CROOK (N)	119
CHARLIE McCOMAS, WHITE CAPTIVE KILLED BY APACHES (N)	120
MAJOR GENERAL GEORGE CROOK (A)	124
JASON PLANTS SOME BARLEY (W)	125
NAH-DE-GAH-AH, APACHE DESPERADO KILLED NEAR FORT APACHE (N)	127
GERONIMO ON THE LAST WARPATH (E)	132
SURRENDER CONFERENCE BETWEEN GENERAL CROOK AND GERONIMO, MARCH 25, 1886 (N)	134
SOME OF GERONIMO'S BAND AT TIME OF FINAL SURRENDER (N)	136
LEAVING FORT BOWIE ON WAY TO CAPTIVITY (N)	139
THE TRAIN TRIP (E)	142
OLD WARRIOR'S CLUB	147
ARRIVAL AT CARLISLE (A)	151
CIVILIZING INFLUENCE OF THE SCHOOL	152
JASON BETZINEZ AT NEWTOWN, PENNSYLVANIA	157
STEEL MILL FOOTBALL TEAM	162
APACHE VILLAGE NEAR FOUR MILE CROSSING, FORT SILL (S)	168
THE APACHES ARE TAUGHT TO WORK	169
APACHE MISSION AT FORT SILL	171
CHRISTIAN ENDEAVOR SOCIETY	172
CAPT. FARRAND SAYRE AND HIS APACHE TROOP AT FORT SILL (S)	178
JASON IN HIS BLACKSMITH SHOP (W)	180
LAWTON, OKLAHOMA SHORTLY AFTER THE OPENING OF THE COUNTRY IN SEPTEMBER, 1901 (S)	186
APACHE POW-WOW AT FORT SILL	196
GERONIMO'S GRAVE (S)	197
LAST ROUNDUP	201
JASON REPAIRING HIS CORNBINDER	202
APACHE FARMERS—THE BETZINEZ "TEAM"	204
JASON AND ANNA AT HOME (S)	206

Chapter 1

REVENGE AT RAMOS

To the Indian it is a curious thing that white people accept as fact only that which is written on paper, whereas events retold by word of mouth, even if of greater importance, are disparaged as being mere folklore. For example, I have read that a slaughter of Apaches at Santa Rita del Cobre in 1837 and another at Janos twenty years later were notable occurrences in the history of my people. Actually these were only two of a series of treacherous attacks made upon us by whites or Mexicans. We have little remembrance of what happened at Santa Rita, and the affair at Janos is noted mainly because my cousin Geronimo's family were killed there, thus setting his hand against the Mexicans forever. So far as we are concerned the ghastly butchery of our families at Ramos and the terrific revenge raid which followed constitute the greatest and bloodiest conflict in which Apaches were ever involved. You will, nevertheless, search the libraries in vain for some mention of it. I believe I am here telling the story in public for the first time.

Northern Chihuahua—A Dread Area

In 1850, as today, the Mexican town of Ramos stood in a level plain eighty miles south of the present site of Columbus, New Mexico. The land was dry, and bare except for scattered tufts of buffalo grass and a few weeds, with occasional cottonwoods along the sandy stream bed near Ramos. To the northwest were the blue ridges of the Guadalupe Mountains, in the northeast and east only several small conical hills of gravel. East of Ramos flowed the San Miguel River, normally shallow and clear. Along its course were little fields of corn, beans, and other vegetables, while elsewhere on the plain small flocks of sheep and some longhorn cattle nuzzled among the soapweeds for forage.

A wagon road came north from Casas Grandes through Ramos to Janos, being a portion of the former supply route running on to the copper mines at Santa Rita. Janos was a garrison town with a presidio and a company or two of Mexican soldiers.

Ramos, or Kintal (wide-walled houses) as we called it, was then a fairly large town as compared with the other settlements in northern Chihuahua. It had a population of eight hundred or a thousand people living in the usual flat-roofed adobe houses clustered about a large church. There was no wall around the town, and it was built on flat ground.

The Warm Springs Apaches of the Black Mountains area in southwest New Mexico and eastern Arizona had been on good terms with most Mexicans since the time of the great, peace-loving Chief Mah-ko. They liked to visit towns such as Ramos to barter animal hides and furs for brightly-colored cloth, knives, ornaments, and other things of value. These friendly relations, however, were not always shared by other Indian groups. Our Chihenne Apaches, having only infrequent contact with other bands, did not always know of their warlike activities. What was more to the point, the Chihennes felt no responsibility for the atrocities committed by other Indians, and were not aware that the Governor of Chihuahua had set a bounty on the head of every man, woman, and child of the whole tribe. They did not realize that at this time it was unsafe

SANTA RITA DEL COBRE

to visit Mexican villages, even where the inhabitants appeared to be friendly.

Treachery

So in the summer months of 1850 quite a few families of Warm Springs Apaches went south to camp along the river near Ramos, as had been their custom in the past. During the days they traded in the town, while the evenings were spent in camp—singing, storytelling, dancing, and gambling.

One day a runner came through the camps calling out that everyone was to go to town. The "hospitable" Mexicans had just distilled a large supply of mescal and were pouring out drinks for all comers. The liquor was absolutely free, all Indians could drink as much as they wanted in the cantinas, then could carry some back to camp. The mad scramble which followed this announcement left the camp deserted except for people too old or too young to walk. The Apache could always be baited, by means of intoxicating liquor, to enter any trap. Even the enticing smell of aguardiente dulled his native caution.

The Apaches had a wild time in Ramos that day, not noticing in their carousing that the streets were empty of Mexican women and children and that only the mangy dogs and wallowing pigs were still sleeping there in the sunshine. The revelry continued in camp far into the night. The Apache never drinks in moderation. He keeps at it until the supply is exhausted or he is unconscious. So it was this time. Not long after midnight nearly everyone was lying in a drunken stupor. The camp was quiet except for barking dogs, which barked all the time anyway.

Just before the first light, Mexican soldiers and villagers slipped into the Indian camp. They carried ready muskets, spears, knives, and clubs. At a sudden signal violent firing broke out. Following this first ragged volley the stabbing and hacking and the clubbing of recumbent forms commenced. There were curses in Spanish, thuds, grunts, a few screams, and the whimpering of a child. Here and there a rustle told where some more alert Indian managed to steal away in the semidarkness. But there were few such. In a short time most of the Indians were lying in their blood, dead or dying. The Mexicans fell to work with sharp knives, wrenching off the gory trophies for which they would receive gold and silver from their authorities. It is said that two hundred pesos was the price paid for the scalp of a man, with lesser amounts for those of women and children.

A few days later several survivors straggled into the main camps of the Indians near Warm Springs, west of the Rio Grande. They told the rest of the band what had happened. For many days and nights continuous wailing could be heard in the tepees and on top of the surrounding hills at daybreak each day. There was scarcely a family group that had not lost one or more of its members.

Apache Vengeance

The chiefs considered for a long time the action which they should take to pay back the Mexicans of Ramos. The problem was too serious to be decided without consultation and deliberation. But the desire for vengeance burned more fiercely as the days and weeks passed. Finally Baishan, the principal chief of the Warm Springs Apaches, called a council of the chiefs of several bands. Among those who responded were Cochise, Chief of the Chiricahuas, our close relatives from the Chiricahua Mountains southwest of us, Mangas Colorado of the Mimbrenos, who lived near Santa Rita, and others whose names I do not recall. Baishan, whose name means Knife, is known in written history by his Mexican nickname, Cuchillo or Cuchillo Negro. Several terrain features in our part of the country are named for him today. He took the lead in the planning and in the expedition against Ramos.

The decision having been made to attack Ramos, and the plans agreed upon, the chiefs announced that a great war dance would be held. Everyone in camp was invited to witness this exciting spectacle, whose purpose was to recruit volunteers for the expedition and to stir up a fighting spirit.

A bonfire was built at night in the center of a large cleared circle around which were gathered the onlookers. Ten paces west of the fire sat four or five men who thumped tom-toms and pounded a sheet of stiff rawhide, meanwhile singing a highpitched weird chant which may remind white people of bagpipe music—being both martial and stimulating. From time to time they would call out the name of some prominent warrior, who would then step forth from the crowd and walk around the fire while the singers praised his bravery and deeds in battle. This was the signal for other Indians who wished to take the warpath to join this man in the promenade and later to serve under his leadership during the raid.

Finally, when it seemed likely that all brave and eligible fighters had joined the war party, the men would form a line on the opposite side of the circle from the drummers then advance toward the latter in a succession of leaps, zig-zagging as if in a real assault. Brandish-

APACHE WARRIORS

ing their weapons they would approach the musicians then stop, yell, and shoot their guns or bows and arrows over the heads of the singers. It was realistic and exhilarating, especially to young boys who, just as today's children, loved to stage sham battles in imitation of their elders.

Following the dance the warriors commenced preparing for the invasion of Mexico. New bows and arrows were made, ammunition procured for the few available firearms, and extra moccasins and food supplies prepared. In those days before the Civil War in the United States guns were scarce. They could be obtained only in fights with Mexican soldiers or attacks on gold seekers and settlers who were crossing the mountains on their way to California. The Indians still relied mainly on the lance and the bow and arrow.

Many times as a boy have I watched men making spears and bows and arrows. The lances were generally tipped with the blades of sabers taken from the cavalry, while arrowheads were likewise filed from bits of steel or iron. In my time stone arrowheads had not been made for generations. Bows were fashioned from mulberry wood which was cut from second-growth trees found along the base of the hills. After having been dried for a long time the wood was worked down to the right size, being as thick as man's wrist in the center and tapering to the ends. Bowstrings were of twisted sinew. Arrow shafts were made of the straight stalks of some bush, the name of which I do not know. The arrows were usually fletched with the feathers of the turkey. Eagle feathers were prized, of course, but were hard to get even in the old days. The bow and arrow was an effective weapon in the hands of a grown man, for he had practised with it since childhood. Many men could drive an arrow clear through a large animal. In later years I often saw men like Nanay and Chief Loco slaughter a steer in this manner on issue day at the Warm Springs agency.

Several months elapsed before everyone was ready to start. The people in Ramos must have decided that all danger was past, that the Indians had either been cowed by their defeat, or that too few warriors survived to make a return raid practicable. If they had known the truth they would have left their town and gone far south for safety.

The great war party contained one hundred and seventy-five full-fledged warriors plus a large number of young apprentices. The latter would not take part in the actual fighting but would assist the fighting men in other ways, looking after their horses and equipment and cooking their food enroute. This was an exceptionally large expedition, the strength of which can be appreciated if the reader considers that in the eighties Geronimo, Victorio, and Nanay managed to frustrate, for several years, several thousand U. S. and Mexican troops. Geronimo never had more than seventy-five, Victorio about sixty, and Nanay twenty or thirty men. In this case the outlook for the people of Ramos was grim indeed.

The expedition started south early one morning in the late fall. The weather was clear and cool, which enabled the men to go straight through to the vicinity of Ramos in only two or three days. If this seems incredible, the reader should know that the old-time Apache warriors could travel up to seventy-five miles a day—on foot and over rough country. Officers of the United States Army, veterans of the Civil War and of the Indian campaigns, and some of them observers of nineteenth century wars in Europe, have stated that in this respect the Apache was the greatest fighter the world has ever seen.

Having made their evening rendezvous at a waterhole north of Ramos, the Apaches observed the town from a distance, scanning the area for signs of soldiers. They saw none. That night the medicine men made their prophecies, all of which were favorable. Chief

Baishan then gave instructions for the attack to take place on the following day, telling each subgroup just where they were to make their advance, in what direction they would attack, and at what signal. He made sure that every man understood his part.

Before entering battle the Apache warrior always took off his shirt and placed it folded under his belt so that it wouldn't be lost during the action. I have always understood that our men did this so as to be able to distinguish friends from enemy, the latter being clothed or in uniform. It is possible, too, that this helped men to conceal themselves while advancing through rocks or crawling on the ground, as the color of their skin would blend better with the red and brown earth. On this particular morning, as the sky turned blood red, the men stripped down to their breechcloths and moccasins. Then they waited impatiently until it was light enough to see for at least a hundred paces to the front.

When Baishan gave the word the men advanced rapidly and silently toward Ramos. Soon the buildings loomed up through the vanishing morning mists. At the sight of the hated place, thoughts of dead kinfolk crowded into the mind of every man. Almost with one voice the warriors burst forth in their battle cry and then rushed

MEXICAN VILLAGE WITH CHURCH AND PLAZA

forward. All plans and orders were forgotten. They poured through the narrow streets and fanned out into the central plaza or square. Here they were met by thirty or forty armed Mexicans who, tumbling out of the buildings at the first war cry, were trying to form a line in front of the church.

The Indians received a blast of musket fire practically in their faces. There must have been soldiers in the town! Or at least some home guards. A number of Apaches fell as a result of this fire. Among them was Chief Baishan, struck dead by a dozen balls. At once the fighting was hand to hand. More and more Mexicans appeared. They resisted desperately, knowing well that no mercy would be shown on either side. There was none. As the Mexican line melted and little groups began to pull back into the alleys and rear courtyards, the Indians were after them like tigers. The plaza was filled with the white smoke clouds from the old-fashioned black powder. In the fog and confusion some Indians were struck down by others. The air was filled with arrows flicking in all directions and glancing off the buildings. As the Mexicans gave way, those Indians who were mounted galloped after them and impaled them in the back with lances.

Before long the fighting was all over except for Indians hunting through the dark houses for hidden refugees. No captives were taken. And no scalps, for scalping was not practiced by the Apaches, despite many untrue stories to the contrary.

The victory was complete. The Indians said that few Mexicans managed to get away. The Apaches remained in Ramos only briefly to loot, lest troop reinforcements be coming from Janos and Casas Grandes. They loaded their wounded on horses and withdrew as rapidly as they could, thus burdened and with many injured limping along. But their spirits were high, they exulted greatly. The men who took part in this battle, especially those who were my kinsmen, later told me that everyone agreed that this was the greatest of Apache victories. The losses had included a number of famous men in addition to Baishan. Their names are now forgotten, for that is the Apache custom.*

The return to the home camps in New Mexico was a happy one, except for the crying over those who did not come back. The whole

---

*When an Apache dies his name is never used again. If the name is also that of some object or animal, as is usually the case, then a new word for this has to be invented. Thus over a period of years the language changes radically, so that old Indians can scarcely understand the younger ones, and vice versa. Jason only recently has disclosed the name "Baishan," and it must be remembered that he is one Indian who has made unusual efforts to rid himself of old superstitions.

tribe were tremendously proud of their fighting men and for years thereafter loved to hear the stories of the battle retold. Among those who increased their reputations in the battle were Cochise, Mangas Colorado, Benito, my cousin Goyakla (Geronimo), and my grandfather, Tudeevia. As a result of this and because of his outstanding qualities, Tudeevia* was chosen to succeed Baishan as principal chief of the Warm Springs Apaches. This band, which we called Chihennes, never recognized Mangas Colorado as their chief.

Our people felt that the Mexicans of Ramos had been repaid in full for their treacherous attack on us, but they never slackened in their bitter hatred of the Mexicans from that day thenceforth.

---

*Jason says that Tudeevia was not known to the white people, as he died before any substantial number of Americans arrived in his area. He was known to the Mexicans, however. It seems possible, however, that Tudeevia (or Dudeevia) was the Warm Springs chieftain known to such early writers and explorers as Bartlett and Cremony as *Delgadito*. This deduction is made from the fact that Chief Loco later told Lieut. Britton Davis that Delgadito was the Indian who succeeded Cuchillo as Chief of the Warm Springs band.

Chapter 2

FURTHER TREACHERY

Primitive Indians, like most wild creatures, are supposed to be wary of traps with which they have had previous experience. Unfortunately this was not true of the Apaches. The bitter memory of Ramos did not prevent them from becoming victims of further treacherous attacks, some almost identical with that at Ramos. Usually this was a result of the Indians' craving for liquor. They never seemed to learn. In a series of such affairs a number of my kinsfolk were killed, wounded, or captured. In a final one I was involved personally, so I know whereof I speak.

Dilchthe's Adventure

Old Aunt Dilchthe was the heroine of the aftermath of one of the massacres which followed Ramos. I have often heard her tell her story. Dilchthe wasn't actually my aunt, being only a relative of my mother. But it was the Indian custom to refer to an older person in the family group as "aunt" or "uncle," these being terms of great respect. Similarly cousins were called "brothers" or "sisters," and they were very close to one another.

Dilchthe's account indicates some of the terrors and hardships our people experienced during those days when the hand of every man was set against us. It illustrates also the amazing resourcefulness, endurance, and courage of the old-time Apache. I am proud to believe, too, that it shows why others of my bloodline, such as Geronimo, my mother, and I, have lasted so long. Geronimo was over ninety when he died; my mother passed on at the age of one hundred and twelve; and I am still going strong at ninety-nine!

A year or so after the Battle of Ramos our band began visiting the Mexican town of Esqueda, south of the present site of Douglas, Arizona to trade and to get liquor. As usual the apparent friendliness of the Mexicans didn't last long. They plied the Indians with méscal or aguardiente, then, when the Apaches were dead drunk, slaughtered the men and took the women and children to such towns as Chihuahua to be sold as slaves. This cold-blooded treachery happened twice over a period of some months resulting, the second time, in the capture of a great many women and children of our band. Some of the prisoners were driven southwest through the cactus and briars for at least two hundred miles until they came to the Gulf of California. Here they were shipped across to some penal colony on Lower California where they were forced to labor as slaves. Among this group was Aunt Dilchthe, then a middle-aged woman who had a daughter and some grandchildren back in the Indian camps in our Black Mountains of southwestern New Mexico.

Most of the Indian captives died in this prison camp, probably because the climate and the altitude, as well as other conditions, were so different from that to which they were accustomed.

Under the able leadership of Dilchthe a few survivors managed one night to escape. They started out on foot to return to their distant homeland. Being unable to recross the Gulf they decided to make their way up the coast of Lower California to Arizona. They knew full well that the trip would involve great hardship and danger, that maybe none of them would succeed in getting back. But so great was their misery as captives, and so slight was their chance of survival in the prison camp, that they were willing to risk everything in the attempt. Their courage and determination were inspiring to those of us who later heard this true story retold around our campfires.

After they had walked along the coast for nearly three hundred miles the Apache women met a kind Mexican who told them that they would have to cross the Colorado River before they could turn inland at the head of the Gulf, but that he knew where there was a ford. The place he described was at the juncture of the Gila River with the Colorado, where Yuma, Arizona, now stands.

Though the country was strange to them, and they had never traveled this route before, the women continued bravely on. Their feet were cut, bleeding, and sore, and they were hungry all the time, having subsisted only on such grasses, weed seeds, insects, and dead animals as they could find along the way. Many miles of unknown, forbidding country still stretched out ahead of them.

After weeks of hard, continuous travel they came to the Colorado and shortly afterwards to its confluence with the Gila. Some of them asked, despairingly, "Is it possible, as the Mexican said it was, to wade across this wide and deep river? No, it is impossible!"

Dilchthe felt that with caution they could accomplish it. She took the lead, wading out into the river just where the Mexican had advised them to. The water got deeper and deeper but never above her armpits. Soon her feet touched a sand bar. Shortly after-

DILTHCHE'S CROSSING SITE
Confluence of Colorado and Gila Rivers, site of present city of Yuma, Arizona

wards the whole party crossed safely to the south bank of the Gila. Their hearts were full of gratitude to their god and to the kind old Mexican who had told them where to cross.

After resting awhile the women resumed their journey eastward along the shallow Gila.

On the third night after they had left the Colorado the women began to quarrel among themselves. Some wanted to turn north toward the mountains, while Dilchthe and several others were determined to follow the almost dry Gila through the desert. They knew that its headwaters were in their own Black Mountains. While they were disputing the choice of a route the women were attacked by strange Indians, possibly Mojaves or Yumas. One woman was captured, while all but two of the rest were killed. The one who was carried off as a captive later was returned to her people. Dilchthe and one other were the two who escaped.

These two survivors now faced perhaps the hardest part of their trip. In this waterless, empty land, beyond the site of Phoenix, no food was to be found. Starvation seemed sure. Almost overcome by hunger and thirst, damaged feet, weariness, and loneliness, the two women were carried forward only through the unswerving determination of Dilchthe. They prayed to their god to have pity on them, that in some way food would be found. As if in answer to their prayer they began to find a few freshly-killed birds. Beginning with the smallest birds these got successively larger, up to the size of an eagle. Then they found larger and larger dead animals, desert rats, rabbits, and finally a coyote. This the other woman refused to eat. The Apaches have such a strong superstition against the coyotes that they will not even handle them. In vain Dilchthe begged her companion to eat.

From that moment they found no more dead birds or animals. Starvation was at hand. They straggled on for another day or two, being now nearly four hundred miles from the Colorado and northeast of the present town of Safford, Arizona. Too weak to go farther they sat down on the side of a mountain and gazed longingly and with despair toward the north. As the morning haze lifted they saw a heartshaped mountain in the distance.

"I know of only one place," cried Dilchthe, "where there is a mountain shaped like that one—in our own home country!"

Joint by joint but with great rejoicing Dilchthe got up and looked around for materials with which to build a smoke signal. This is how Indians who do not have matches or flint and steel make a fire: they cut, as Dilchthe did, a round, hard stick of wood which they twirl between their palms, the rounded end bearing in a little cup-shaped hollow made in a flat, softer piece of wood. The trick is in cutting a little notch in the end of the round stick, so that the friction quickly generates heat to cause the soft piece to smolder. The little wood shavings then glow, and when blown upon burst into flame. Of course the Indian has already prepared a little heap of dry materials to which the flame is applied. In this manner a fire can be started in a few moments.

The Apaches used smoke on mountaintops mainly as signals of distress. The smoke meant, "There is some kind of trouble here. Come and investigate." The investigating party would approach carefully, and keeping under cover. They always suspected a trick. Today we see cartoons telling how Indians carry on a regular conversation by means of smoke signals. From my experience that is all nonsense. I never saw signal fires or smokes that conveyed more than the simple message I have indicated. I am always surprised at the absurdities written and played on the screen concerning Indians, especially when the truth is so easy to learn and just as interesting as what is invented.

In the case of Dilchthe some Indian in the distance, seeing her smoke signal, came to investigate. He found the two women almost dead from starvation. Dilchthe was his own mother-in-law.

Now the Apaches, like some other western tribes, have a custom or a taboo whereby a man is forbidden to look his mother-in-law in the face or even to speak to her. So strong is this rule that anyone who violates it accidentally is deeply ashamed and, when the fact becomes known, is severely criticized in the tribe. Criticism is something that most Indians cannot tolerate. This will be made clear later in my story with reference to Geronimo, whose worst outbreak started partly as a result of criticism of him in official circles.

In the case of Dilchthe and her son-in-law the taboo was forgotten. They embraced joyfully. The young warrior gave the two women some deer meat and when they had recovered some of their strength he conducted them north to his base camp. Here Dilchthe was reunited with her daughter and grandchildren. The reception was a warm one, for in accordance with tribal custom she had long since been given up as dead. All her belongings had been burned and her name "forgotten," never to be used again.

From a study of modern maps I estimate that from Esqueda back to the Black Mountains by the way of Lower California Dilchthe must have walked at least a thousand miles. She had no map, she had never been through that part of the country, and she had no weapons or supplies. She was a strong, muscular woman but she must also have had an iron will.

Slaughter of Geronimo's Family

Mah-ko, the great chief of the Bedonkohe Apaches, was the grandfather of my mother and of Goyahkla* who were, therefore, first cousins. They grew up together as children, living with their parents in the vicinity of their birthplace, the site of the present town of Clifton, Arizona. During their childhood these cousins came under the strong influence of their grandfather and grandmother, which was good—for Mah-ko and his wife were powerful in the tribe and of good repute among the Mexicans who then inhabited that country. Mah-ko was a unique Apache being a man of peace and a successful rancher. He raised much corn and good horses and traded with the Mexicans, who respected him and admired his business ability. Although he never led his people in war Chief Mah-ko was greatly loved by them for his generosity. He stored in caves much dried beef and venison as well as corn, then issued it to them free when winter came on and the improvident Indians had nothing to eat. He also hired quite a few men as ranch hands, to whom he gave horses, saddles, bridles, and firearms—the weapons being used by these people to hunt deer and other game. No emergency ever arose

---

*Geronimo was the name by which he was known to the Mexicans and whites.

during Mah-ko's time which caused the Bedonkohes to fight the Mexicans.

Conditions got bad after Mah-ko died. The first white people seen in the area had been early Mormon homeseekers, whom the Indians called Wide-brimmed Hat People. They caused no trouble but they were followed by other whites who dispossessed the Indians of their land around Clifton and drove them away.

When my mother and Goyahkla were in their teens Mah-ko's family group was visited by a cousin from the band of untamed Apaches who lived in the high sierras of Old Mexico. This youth's name was Juh, which means Long Neck.* We generally called the band to which he belonged the *Netdahe*. They were outlaws recruited from other bands, and included in their membership a few Navajoes as well as Mexicans and whites who had been captured while children and who had grown up as savages. We Warm Springs Apaches regarded the Netdahe as being true wild men, whose mode of life was quite different from that of the reservation Indians, being devoted entirely to warfare and raiding the settlements. Nevertheless some of them, like Juh, were our blood relatives or had some connection with us by marriage.

I fear that Juh, who even as a boy displayed a mischievous nature, influenced Goyahkla away from the more peaceful teachings of Mah-ko and his wife. Eventually the two became associated on the warpath, Goyahkla, or Geronimo, as the Mexicans called him, acquiring an even worse reputation than Juh.

During Juh's boyhood visit to the Bedonkohes he used to go out into the woods with a few other young men to tease the girls who were gathering acorns. One of their tricks was to wait until the girls had done a lot of hard work, then take the acorns away from them. This came to the attention of the wife of Chief Mah-ko, who told her grandson Goyakla and some of his friends to waylay Juh and give him and his gang a good whipping.

After Juh had matured and become a man of good standing among the Bedonkohes he married one of Goyakla's cousins, one of the same girls whom he formerly had tormented. After living among her people for a number of years he took her back to his own region in Mexico. There he became a noted leader of the Netdahe, spending most of his time preying on the Mexicans and hiding in the almost inaccessible mountains of northern Chihuahua and Sonora.

---

*Jason pronounces the name "Who," but spells it "Whoa," as do some other Apaches. The spelling used here conforms with that of published accounts of the Apache wars.

JANOS

Some years after Juh returned to Mexico, Goyakla lost his father, who had succeeded Mah-ko as chief of the Bedonkohes. Both he and his mother were so grief stricken that they decided to take their immediate family group on a visit to the strange land of Old Mexico, which they had never seen, and renew their acquaintance with Chief Juh. The trip was a difficult one because of the lack of water and their own ignorance as to the location of the infrequent waterholes. After several days of hard travel they reached the rugged mountains south of the border, where they expected to find the camps of Juh's people. But they saw no white objects in the distance, no trails leading toward an Indian camp or from one creek or spring to another, no fires by night or smoke by day. They heard no barking camp dogs and did not see where Indian horses had been tethered. This was because the wild Indians were accustomed to conceal their tracks, hide their camps, and pasture their horses at a distance. Nevertheless after a tiresome search lasting several days Goyakla located Juh's camp.

Here they were given a courteous welcome by the Netdahe and a hearty one by Juh and his wife, the niece of Goyakla's mother.

While living with the Netdahe Goyakla fell in love with a young woman of the band. They were married and had three children, of whom they were very proud.

The Netdahe were then at peace, or thought they were, with the Mexicans of the State of Chihuahua but considered the inhabitants of Sonora, to the west, to be their enemies and fair game. The Indians did not appreciate that all Mexicans were citizens of one nation. So they made frequent raids into Sonora to get cattle for food, horses and mules to ride or carry their camp gear, or cloth and other drygoods to wear. They had numerous small fights with civilians and soldiers in Sonora, to whom Goyakla gradually became well and unfavorably known.

In 1858 the men of the Netdahe were in the "friendly" town of Janos in northern Chihuahua, drinking whisky and having a gay time. While this was going on, soldiers from Sonora* attacked their camp, not far from Janos, killing many of the women and children. Among the victims were Goyakla's mother, wife, and children. When Goyakla and his friends returned from their drinking spree in Janos they found the slaughtered bodies of their families. Almost crazy with grief and filled with an undying hatred of the Mexicans, Goyakla went north. He lived among the Chiricahuas for a time, where he acquired another wife, a very handsome young woman by whom he had two children neither of whom is living today. After his children were grown Goyakla, or Geronimo, as even the Indians were beginning to call him, came to live among our band of Warm Springs Apaches.

---

*Under a General Carasco.

Chapter 3

MY MOTHER IS CAPTURED

Geronimo was not the only grandchild of the Great Chief Mah-ko who had trouble with the Mexicans. His cousin Nah-thle-tla (who was to become my mother) had suffered greatly at their hands some three years before Geronimo's family was butchered at Janos.

Nah-thle-tla must have been born about 1823, as she was thought to be twelve years old when Halley's Comet appeared in 1835. One of her early memories was of "The Night the Stars Fell," an awesome shower of meteors which greatly frightened the Indians in the summer of 1832.* She lived for at least one hundred and twelve years, at the time of her death being known as the oldest mother in the United States. Perhaps I inherited from her some of this quality. Certainly she taught me much, for my father came to a tragic end before he had much lasting influence on my character.

When Nah-thle-tla reached womanhood she fell in love with an Apache named Shnowin and he with her. Like all young Indians in love, Shnowin was full of love songs which he sang early in the morning and late in the evening. In spite of the intensity of his affection the young man was too bashful to tell Nah-thle-tla about it, while she, because of tribal tradition, could not show in the slightest that she was aware of his feelings or that she returned them.

Shnowin had to obtain the consent of his parents to his marriage. They in turn had to call on Nah-thle-tla's parents to secure their agreement and to bargain with them over the marriage price, which usually consisted of one or more good horses. During this formal conference in the lodge of the girl's parents Shnowin was obliged to sit outside peeping in through the entrance while his sweetheart sat sedately behind her mother. Neither was permitted to say a word. And after the marriage was arranged the young people still were kept apart and the coming ceremony was not disclosed to the rest of the tribe. Meantime a strict watch was kept over the girl lest her reputation be tarnished.

---

*Many white people were frightened, too, as is attested by old newspaper accounts which speculated that the end of the world was near.

[18]

Nah-thle-tla's first marriage was a happy one, two children being born to the couple. I should add that I was not a child of this first marriage, my father being Nah-thle-tla's second husband. But Nah-thle-tla and Shnowin lived contentedly together until the spring of 1855 when he went on the warpath with other warriors of the band. They were joined in Mexico by Juh and some of his outlaws and the combined forces attacked the Mexicans near Namiquipa, far south of Casas Grandes. The fight was a severe one but because of Juh's brilliant leadership resulted in a victory for the Apaches. Unfortunately Shnowin was killed.

The Mexicans Retaliate

While her husband was on the raid Nah-thle-tla was living with his parents in a camp in the mountains south of the present site of Lordsburg, New Mexico. As a result of the treaty following the war between the United States and Mexico the troops of the respective nations were not supposed to cross the border in pursuit of hostile Indians except under previously-made and specific agreement at governmental level. Therefore the Apaches felt safe in their camps, which were probably not far from the old border post of Fort Cummings, then garrisoned by United States troops. When the Indians saw a body of men approaching their camp they did not realize that these were Mexican soldiers, but thought that they were their own warriors returning from the raid.

No preparations were made to flee. No men of fighting age were

GUADALUPE PASS

in camp and no one had any firearms. Therefore the camp was virtually defenseless. Following the first burst of fire from the enemy the camp was quickly overrun. The Mexicans again without mercy killed indiscriminately—women, children, old men, and boys. The survivors were seized as prisoners, among these being Nah-thle-tla and her two small children.

While some of the Mexicans were rounding up the captives others were destroying all the Indian belongings except for some dried venison which they carried off as rations for themselves and their prisoners. The Mexicans had been guided to this locality by an Apache woman who had lived with them for years and who knew the country and the Indian habits perfectly. She now urged them to depart before the ever-present shadow of Apache vengeance should become a reality. The Mexicans needed little urging, having experienced Indian savagery before. So they hustled off through the Guadalupe Pass herding their prisoners with them.

The Long Trip Into Slavery

Nah-thle-tla told me in later years that during the march toward Chihuahua the Mexican commander, whom she described as being a general, was kind to most of his prisoners. He was a bit harsh with one Indian woman who boasted that her husband was one of the fighters who had made the recent raid to Namiquipa. The general forced this woman to walk all the way to Casas Grandes, a distance of a hundred miles, instead of riding a horse or a mule like the other captives. He didn't realize that such a hike was no hardship to an Apache woman.

At each night's camp the soldiers guarded the women so closely that they had no chance to escape. At Casas Grandes the column halted for two days to rest. Then the Indians were loaded into two-wheeled carts and started off southeast for Galeana, still under guard. This stage of the journey, though only twenty-five miles long, required two days because of the slow pace of the carts. The route continued southeast up the Santa Maria River some sixty miles to Namiquipa. Here the inhabitants, still in a fury over the recent Indian attack, urged that the general turn over to them his prisoners to be slaughtered. The commander refused, so as the column pulled out, the Mexican women ran alongside the vehicles screaming curses and throwing rocks.

Chihuahua, a hundred miles southeast of Namiquipa, was reached after several more days of travel. At this point the captives, who had been well treated, were turned over to various Mexican families in the city. Nah-thle-tla's children were taken from her and she never saw them again. But on the whole the captives were treated kindly even being taken on sightseeing walks through the town. After several months spent in working as a slave for a Mexican family Nah-thle-tla was sold to a wealthy Mexican from Santa Fe, New Mexico. She and another young Apache woman were loaded into an oxcart for the long journey north to her owner's home. The cart, webbed up with rope like a cage, was drawn by four oxen who moved quite slowly. Tied to a pole at the front of the cart trotted a large, mean dog to assist in preventing the escape of the prisoners.

The Mexican and his column traveled the main road due north to Juarez, where they crossed the Rio Grande. El Paso then consisted of a small village with a few additional adobe farmhouses along the river. From there the route ran north to Rincon then over the hills to the plains northeast of the mountains and on toward Albuquerque. At one stage they were passing through the country of the Warm Springs Apaches, the band to which my mother belonged. The other young woman began to cry.

"What are you crying for?" asked Nah-thle-tla. "Don't you know that we are close to our homeland, that if we should manage to escape we would find our own people? Cheer up!" But they found no chance to slip away.

Several days later they reached Albuquerque, tired but in good health. After two days of rest the journey was continued to Santa Fe. They were well received by the wife and children of the wealthy señor but Nah-thle-tla's companion was sent to some other family. Thereafter the two girls seldom saw each other.

The Escape

Nah-thle-tla did her best to be a good houseworker, grinding corn for tortillas, and doing the cooking and laundry for the family. The whole family were kind to her. For example they often gave her some kind of fruit for breakfast. One day, not receiving fruit, she asked for it. The man replied that it was all gone but since she liked it so much he would make a trip of some four days over the mountains to obtain a new supply. Fruits in those days were mostly imported from Sonora. After he was gone the young people of the household held a big dance which lasted nearly the whole night. The second night they slept so soundly that Nah-thle-tla saw a chance to escape. She wrapped in a cloth some food and other things which she would need, climbed through a window to the wall surrounding the house and garden, and lowered herself by a rope to the ground. Then she fled to the outskirts of the town.

NAH-THLE-TLA

Photo Made at Fort Sill When Jason's Mother
Was Over 100 Years Old

As it was beginning to get light she concealed herself under a pile of brush where some woodcutters had been at work, to wait through the day until darkness. No one disturbed her and her only danger came from dogs sniffing around where she was. After dark she started south, heading toward the mountains as the Apaches always did when in flight. At first she traveled only at night, hiding during the daytime. Several times she saw Mexican *vaqueros* riding near her place of concealment but she was not found. Finally in the high mountains she felt that it was safe to travel during the daytime. Though her only weapon was a butcher knife and there were wolves, mountain lions, and grizzlies in the range, she was not afraid. Once she saw the tracks of a large bear at a waterhole, the rocks still wet from water he had splashed, but never met any creature large enough to be dangerous.

After her initial food supply was exhausted Nah-thle-tla found enough piñon nuts, seeds, and berries to keep her alive.

She was a wiry, well-built young woman, accustomed to walking long distances. The trip over steep mountains, cliffs, canyons, and rough lava beds was tiring but she stood up well under the hardships. After eight or nine days she came to the top of a ridge from which she was able to gaze far off to the south and southwest. She recognized the distinctive shape of one of the high peaks of the Magdalena Mountains, perhaps Mt. Baldy. Then at last she began to cry, for the first time since she had been captured, months before. But it was for gladness that soon she might see her mother again.

At sunset Nah-thle-tla started down the ridge toward the Rio Grande, somewhere near the Isleta pueblo. When she came to its banks in the darkness she was afraid to cross, not knowing how deep the water might be. She moved back a few yards and hid in the weeds. About noon the next day she saw some Mexicans fording the river on foot, which showed her where it was possible to cross. After dark when she was sure that the Mexicans in the nearby farmhouse were asleep, she waded down into the water, holding her bundle on her head. In its deepest place the river came up to her armpits but it was a half mile wide.

On the other side she found a lone pony grazing in a cornfield. She made a bridle of the rope which she had with her, stole the horse, and rode it southward across the plains until she came to the mountains. On the third day after crossing the Rio Grande, while resting on a hilltop, she saw three men walking not far below. She was afraid that they might be Navajoes, with whom the Warm Spring Apaches were not friendly at that time. As the strangers came nearer she saw, from their clothing and the bands around their hair, that they were Apaches. She called out to them whereupon they at once vanished. Since hostile Indians often used women as decoys, these Apaches would not show themselves unless they were sure that no danger existed. So she called out more loudly, giving her name and telling that she had just escaped from Mexican captivity. As the Apaches moved cautiously in her direction, with great joy Nah-thle-tla recognized one of them as Loco, chief of her own subgroup! With the other two men, he said, he had been out hunting; their camp was not far away. Probably some of her own relatives were there.

An even more wonderful surprise awaited Nah-thle-tla. In the camp was her mother as well as other relatives.

During this amazing flight my mother had covered at least two hundred and fifty miles mostly on foot and in very rough country. To see for yourself what a remarkable feat that was, drive your own car today from Las Cruces north over US 85 to Santa Fe, taking some side trips into the mountains and desert on either side.

Nah-thle-tla Is Again Married and Again Captured by Mexicans

Two years after Nah-thle-tla returned to her people she married Tudeevia, son of the chief of the same name—the one who had succeeded Baishan after the Battle of Ramos. Chief Tudeevia had died before his son was old enough to succeed him, so our Warm Springs Apaches had elected Victorio and Loco as dual leaders of the band. Both were experienced fighters, very able men, Victorio being the more warlike of the two. I became well acquainted with both of them. Victorio of course had an Indian name but as usual it is "forgotten." I think it was something resembling "Beduiat" and it may be that the Mexicans made Victorio out of that.

Not long after her marriage to Tudeevia, Nah-thle-tla was captured again by Mexicans—this time, fortunately, by people with whom we were to become good friends. The new captors took her to their town of Monticello, which is in our Warm Springs country of southwestern New Mexico some twenty miles northwest of the present site of Elephant Butte Dam on the Rio Grande. They sent her to tell Chief Loco that they would like to make peace with the Indians. Loco, always peaceably inclined, was quite willing. The resulting "treaty" between our band and Monticello was never broken not even during the reigns of terror which resulted successively from the outbreaks of Cochise, Victorio, Nanay, Chatto, and Geronimo.

The Warm Springs Reservation

At about the same time our band made peace with the people of Monticello, Chiefs Loco and Victorio, and perhaps Mangas and others, were negotiating with authorities of the United States Government. Councils were held at Fort Craig, the ruins of which are still standing thirty miles north of Elephant Butte Dam, and at Fort McRae which was just east of the present dam site. After the meeting at the latter post and while our people were still camped near the fort, some Mexican troops from south of the border attacked them. But the Apaches were rescued by U. S. troops, who arrested the Mexicans, held them at the fort for a time, then sent them home.

The government now established the Warm Springs Reservation for us. This reservation, which lay just northeast of our native Black Mountains, extended for twenty-five miles in a north-south direction and fifty miles east and west. An agency garrisoned by a troop of Negro cavalry was built after the Civil War in the northwest corner not far from the everliving warm springs which gave the region its name.

We loved this beautiful land with its pine-covered hills, upland meadows, clear streams, and abundant wild fruit, nuts, and berries as well as game—all of which supplied us with food. The hot springs were a source of pleasure to us especially for wintertime bathing. The colored soldiers also liked them. Southeastward through the reservation ran a creek which the Mexicans called the Alamosa. In those days it was clear, cold, and full of rainbow trout. At that time we paid no attention to fish, on account of an Apache taboo against anything that lived under the water.

Between about the year 1858, when the Government granted us this reservation "forever," and 1876, when the same Government took it away from us forever so that white men seeking gold might have it, we lived there in peace and contentment. We hunted the deer, antelope, and turkeys, gathered fruit, nuts, and berries, and traded with the friendly Mexicans of nearby Monticello. For a short time life was to be a happy one. But it was to be a very short time.

Chapter 4

PRIMITIVE LIFE

Early in the summer of 1860 Tudeevia and his wife Nah-thle-tla came down from the Warm Springs reservation to camp just outside the village of Monticello. They had been invited to visit a Mexican family with whom they were on good terms. During their pleasant stay at Monticello I was born in my parents' tepee, being the first child of this couple. Two years later my sister Ellen was born in the same locality on the occasion of a subsequent visit which my father and mother made to Monticello. Since our family often stopped here to see our Mexican friends, my sister and I frequently played with their children. When I revisited Monticello in 1911 I was happy to find some of this Mexican family still living there. One old lady recognized me and embraced me with warm affection.

When I was a baby my mother wrapped me in an Apache cradle which she tied to her back with a strong buckskin strap. When she rode a horse she fastened this strap so that the carrier would hang on the side of the animal. When I was just beginning to walk mother made for me a buckskin jacket to which was sewed a strong carrying strap. This saved my life on at least one occasion when we were under attack. When I was about two years old part of our band, having wandered south of the Black Range on a hunting expedition, were camped a little north of the present site of Duncan, Arizona. Early in the morning the camp was attacked by some troops from one of the nearby frontier posts, the soldiers evidently mistaking us for hostile Indians. Having no firearms, and realizing that bows and arrows were no match for the weapons of the troops, our people scattered and fled into the hills. My mother, who could always ride like a cowboy, ran to where our horses were tethered and flung herself on a pony while I was still toddling out of our tent. At that moment father galloped up, swung down to grab me by the strap on my jacket, and lifted me to a safe place in front of mother. Then he wheeled his horse and went toward the sound of the firing, to cover our escape.

After we had dashed through the rocks and cactus for several miles mother and I were overtaken by father, who was a little weak from loss of blood. He had been shot in the fleshy part of his back but not seriously injured. All our people succeeded in getting away. From the hill tops we could see the soldiers destroying everything in our camp. They also drove off our livestock. The loss of our animals and camp equipment was a disaster. Most of the Indians would now have to walk back to Warm Springs, crossing several ranges of mountains some of which were nine thousand feet high. For the able-bodied this was nothing but for the very young and the very old it was an appalling prospect. Nevertheless we made it.

Although father recovered quickly from his wound it left him with a slight limp. The tribe soon began calling him Nonithian (The Limper) instead of Tudeevia.

Peaceful Interlude

In my time the Apaches had not yet reached the same degree of civilization as the white man, who seemingly had learned how to avoid war for as long as four or five years at a time. We were almost continuously fighting our enemies and if none such were available we fought among ourselves just as the white Americans were doing on a somewhat larger scale during the next few years following my birth. This diversion left us practically undisturbed, for even the Mexicans stayed within their own borders. Our Warm Springs band, normally peacefully inclined, enjoyed a quiet period which, unfortunately, was to be broken soon enough.

My earliest memories concerned the way we lived in those primitive days. Although we were hardened to moving through the desert and to surviving in a harsh land of intense heat and no water, we were primarily a mountain people. We loved the high ranges where we were safe among the cool pine forests and upland meadows and where there was always plentiful game as well as supplies of edible nuts and berries. Formerly the Apaches had used animal hides for clothing and shelter but by my time cloth was obtainable from the Mexicans as well as from the few American traders who were beginning to appear in the Southwest. Our women liked to make long, bright-colored shirts for their men, these garments, except for a breechcloth and high moccasins, forming our sole clothing. Indians who lived around the agencies, especially those who served the Army as scouts, sometimes wore trousers and even coats. We weren't feathered Indians, but usually wore a bandanna or a strip of red cloth around the head to keep the hair from the face. A few Apaches got hats from Mexicans or others. Our women wore long, full dresses which were similar in pattern to those worn today by Navajoes. The most important single item of clothing for men, women, and children was the moccasin. Apache moccasins were different from those of most other Indians in that they were a combination legging and shoe but of one piece except for the sole. This type of footgear offered protection from the thorns and rocks through which we had to travel, especially at night when it was impossible to avoid running into cactus, yucca, and other sharp-pointed vegetation.

All Apache men knew how to make moccasins, it being necessary to repair or replace the footgear often while on a raid. Consequently each warrior always carried an awl and some sinew thread and perhaps a tough piece of sole leather and soft buckskin for the upper and legging. The moccasin was made quite simply. A piece of thick, tough cowhide was buried in damp earth overnight to make it pliable. Then the outline of the foot was drawn on the hide, about a quarter of an inch larger than the outside of the foot. A sheet of soft buckskin was laid over the foot and around the leg then cut to fit. The upper was sewed to the sole by pulling twisted sinew through awl holes, the edge of the seam being turned up slightly as the sinew was drawn tight. Some moccasins were made with plain toes, others had the toe turned up an inch or two. This was a matter of style and individual preference, the turned-up toe having no particular value except perhaps as slightly added protection in moving through rocky soil.

An incident typical of childhood marked the making of the first pair of moccasins that I can remember. My mother had just made me a fine new pair and had told me to take care of them, when one of the neighboring women came over to our tepee for a visit. My mother lifted me to the back of the woman's horse, saying, "Ride this horse down to the creek and water it. Don't get off while he is drinking."

So, very proud of my new moccasins, I rode the half mile to the waterhole. As the horse stood in the stream drinking, I became fascinated by the way the successive rings widened in the water from his muzzle. I kept leaning farther and farther forward until I toppled over his neck into the creek. All my pride melting away I ran crying back to our lodge. A group of women were sitting there laughing at me. Instead of whipping me for getting my new moccasins wet my mother slipped them from my feet, took me in her arms, and comforted me.

TYPICAL APACHE SHELTER AND FAMILY GROUP

We used a form of shelter which was rather primitive as compared to the tents of the prairie tribes and certainly far less advanced than the adobe dwellings of the Pueblo Indians. It was, however, well adapted to our wandering kind of life and especially to the fact that we frequently had to move in a great hurry and to abandon our camps to our enemies. We didn't carry lodge poles about with us but simply made a rude framework of sticks, saplings, or brush, and threw over it whatever we had available. In early times the covering was animal hides, in later years we were able to obtain muslin or other cloth from the Mexicans. Sometimes the tent was covered mostly with brush. It had one entrance, a low one which always faced to the east. Fires were built in the center in a little scooped-out place, the smoke escaping through a hole in the roof. I shall refer to the Apache tent as a tepee, as that word is familiar to more readers than "wickiup," which is the name used by more scientific writers.

In front of this low, igloo-like tepee there might be built a brush windbreak. Inside the men generally sat on piles of bedding or pine needles while the women occupied places on the ground. Visitors announced their presence at the entrance before entering, as the sole means of avoiding violation of family privacy.

While we were living in the Warm Springs area we were able to obtain plenty of wild game and other food materials in the vicinity of our camps. White-tailed deer were abundant both in the plains and the upland regions while black-tailed (mule) deer as well as elk were to be found in the mountains. Antelope grazed mostly on the plains south of the Chiricahua Mountains and from there far on down into Old Mexico. We hunted them generally by means of an organized drive in which a large number of Indians would surround a herd and keep narrowing it down until we could get within shooting distance. In the woods, both in the hills and on the plains, were flocks of wild turkeys. Despite some statements to the contrary we Apaches liked to eat turkey but did not often get a chance to do so. Turkeys then as now were very wary. We could only get within shooting range with the bow and arrow by creeping up on their roosts on moonlight nights. Rifle and shotgun ammunition was too hard to get and too expensive to waste in shooting at turkeys.

The Apache was a successful hunter because he studied wildlife from his earliest childhood. He knew all their habits, what they fed upon and where, and how to track and stalk each species. As a boy I was taught to shoot a bow as soon as I was strong enough and like all my playmates I practiced constantly. We greatly enjoyed hunting small animals such as rabbits, squirrels, grouse, and prairie chickens.

We played war games a good deal of the time, too, just as other children do today. We would make clay forts and soldiers then throw mud balls at them or shoot arrows into them from a distance and make our final charge just as real warriors would do in battle. We also learned to ride, wrestle, and play Indian shinny. This last is a rough game which often ended in a number of casualties. I became a very good wrestler, as I inherited a powerful frame and strong muscles; this stood me in good stead many years later when I often tussled with white friends in the steel plant where I worked near Harrisburg.

APACHE HUNTER STALKING ANTELOPE

When I was about ten years old my parents sent me for a long visit with my aunt, Nonithian's sister, who lived with her husband and children some fifteen miles from our camp. My uncle, who was a skilled hunter, let me go with him on several occasions when he was after deer for the family meat supply. His method was to stalk the game until he got within a few paces thus giving him a sure shot at a selected buck. To do this he slipped over his head and shoulders the tanned head of a doe, disguising himself as a deer. Today with so many amateur hunters in the woods this probably would mean sure death but in those times it was safe enough. And very effective, too. From a distance, concealed behind a tree, I would watch my uncle approach the herd on all fours, moving like an animal and imitating the motions of a doe. Now and then the deer would gaze at him curiously before resuming their feeding. Deer do not see too well but depend more on hearing and sense of smell. Finally my uncle would get close to the game then fit an arrow and quickly drive it into a large buck.

I remained with my aunt's family for several weeks until I began to get homesick for my father, whom I loved greatly. After awhile my aunt, fearing that I would be sick, sent for my father to come for me. How glad I was to see him coming! I ran to jump into his arms as I always did, from which habit he had given me my boyhood name of Nah-delthy-ah, which means The Runner or Going-to-Run. Father stayed overnight with my aunt and uncle. The next day we rode home, I being on the horse behind my father. On the

CHIEF LOCO OF WARM SPRINGS APACHE BAND

way a large bear crossed the trail in front of us. My father immediately gave chase meanwhile fitting an arrow into his bow. When close enough, and with the beast turning to give fight, he drove an arrow deep into the bear's side killing it almost instantly.

Instead of skinning the bear we recovered the arrow without touching the carcass and rode home quickly, not looking back. The Apaches had a strong superstition concerning the bear. Several Indian tribes which are supposed to have drifted down from the far north over a period of centuries have this same taboo concerning the bear. As I understand it there is an old legend to the effect that the bear was some kind of an ancestor. Though we have no tradition of it, scientists think that the Apaches were once a northern race; possibly that is where we got this superstitious fear of the bear.

Numerous bears—brown, black, and silvertip—infested our country in those days. We usually gave them a wide berth especially the grizzlies, which would attack without provocation sometimes. Women and young girls gathering berries or fruit in the woods were often in danger from bears and the grizzly was to be encountered even on the plains. The Apache warrior fought the grizzly when he had to. He did not care to show cowardice by running from a bear, in spite of the awe with which he regarded the animal. His courage can therefore be appreciated all the more when you consider the inadequate weapons with which he faced this formidable opponent. Old Man Loco, the subchief of our band, once had to fight a grizzly single handed and armed only with a knife. The bear tore him badly, damaging his left eye and scarring his cheek. When you see a photograph of an old-time Indian wearing a necklace of bear claws you will know that he killed the animal himself, probably with his hunting knife.

Although buffalo once roamed all over what is now the United States, Southern Canada, and northern Mexico, when I was a boy they had largely disappeared from the mountain area and were vanishing from the plains, too. On rare occasions we traveled eastward to find them. I was on one such expedition when I was ten years old. It is queer how clearly I can recall happenings of my early days, yet quite recent events escape my memory. Perhaps those were the exciting days!

I had heard stories about buffalo for so long a time that in my imagination they had grown to monstrous size. So it was with a feeling of mixed dread and anticipation that I looked forward to the buffalo hunt. For a week or more I watched with great interest while the men reinforced their bows with rawhide and sharpened their spears and arrowpoints. All preparations being complete we rode for several days towards the Great Plains, accompanied by a few women who would prepare our food and take care of the buffalo meat and hides which we hoped to get. We crossed successively the Rio Grande and the Pecos River. I recall the latter because its water was so salty that we couldn't drink it. We camped east of the Pecos, where it was expected that buffalo herds would be sighted. The first night the chiefs made plans for the hunt to take place on the following day.

In the morning small parties were sent out in several directions to scout for buffalo. Finally the main herd was seen in the distance whereupon we all converged and rode rapidly in that direction. I was up behind my father on his gray horse. As we got within striking distance the chase began. It was wildly exciting and dangerous, too, for if your horse stumbled and fell you stood a good chance of being trampled or gored by the stampeding buffalo. Suddenly we were right among the great beasts, riding full tilt, the men spearing or shooting the quarry with their knees practically against the lumbering bison. When enough buffalo had been killed to supply all our wants the leaders called off the chase.

The Apaches were delighted with the success of the hunt, for there was sufficient meat and hides to supply all our families through the winter. The women already were busy here and there over the prairie skinning and cutting up the great carcasses. The meat was sliced in sheets about a half-inch thick then strung up to dry in the sun like laundry on the line. After a few days, when the meat was thoroughly "jerked" in this manner and would keep indefinitely, we packed up for the homeward journey. As we rode westward toward the Rockies we all were singing happily. There would be no hunger in the tepees that winter.

We Apaches did not have a triumphal buffalo dance like the prairie Indians, so on our return to Warm Springs the women got busy right away in tanning and decorating the hides. First the skins were pegged out in the sun to dry. After they were flint-hard they were scraped with elk-horn scrapers shaped like small hoes, thus removing all surplus fat and flesh. If any of you have ever tried this you know what a back-breaking job it is. Then the hide would be softened by working into it a mixture of animal brains and tallow and possibly by scraping it some more, after which it was again stretched out to dry. Now the hide was ready to be painted. Each woman had her own design, such as a picture of the sun, a rainbow, a war shield, lightning, continued-stepping spirit advancement, or minor small objects. I have been asked what is meant by continued-stepping spirit advancement. My aunt explained it to me somewhat as follows. She said, "Son, here is the record of my life, each step representing some event." So I suppose you might call it a sort of diary, though there is something a little mystic about it, too.

Walnut bark furnished the brown color, while from earth and minerals we made paint in colors of red, yellow, blue-gray, green, and black. To the woman who painted them the designs were sacred, having special significance to her or her family. She regarded them with as much reverence as if they were religious ordinances. In some cases, however, the patterns were purely for decoration.

Decorated buffalo hides were truly beautiful as well as useful for bedding and other purposes. But sad to tell, they were all destroyed when the owner died. At such times the whole tepee and all that was in it had to be burned. Even after the Apaches had come under a civilizing influence they continued this superstitious practice through fear of tribal criticism and ridicule for not conforming to old customs.

The Apaches were not wholly dependent on meat for food. They knew of many sources of food in the desert and mountains where white men would have starved. These natural foods included sunflower and other weed seeds, wild grasses, wild onions, the fruit of the cactus and similar desert plants, as well as various berries and nuts which were obtainable in season in the high mountains. The women ground acorns, hackberry and mesquite beans or seeds, as well as other berries not edible in the raw state, and baked a crude type of bread from the paste. They preserved the fruits of the cactus and yucca by drying them.

One of the most interesting and useful wild plants in Arizona and New Mexico was the mescal, sometimes called agave or century plant. Apache women worked hard in gathering and cooking the head of the mescal. It was baked for twenty-four hours or more in a pit of heated stones, the whole being covered with damp grass and earth. When this large, artichoke-like plant was thoroughly cooked it was uncovered from the firepit, the petals peeled off and eaten then, the heart sliced like cheese and dried for later use. The cooked heart of the mescal was sweet and nutritious.

Superstition and Witchcraft

Superstition rode the Indian's back like a witch, producing fear which turned to suspicion and hatred. The Apaches continued to believe in witchcraft for many years after the white race had largely given up such fancies. As with all races the Indians practiced witchcraft in its most brutal forms accompanied sometimes by torture and death.

Apaches, ignorant of medicine and surgery, relied on incantation and magic for the cure of injury and sickness. A medicine man or woman was called in to treat the patient, being tendered a horse or something else of value in payment for his services. If by howling, dancing, and beating a tom-tom he failed to drive away the evil spirit which had caused the trouble, the witch doctor had to seek some excuse which would foist off the indignation of the relatives to someone beside himself. The usual method was to claim that some old Indian, usually a woman, was a witch who had cast a spell on the ailing person. The medicine man would take a pinch of ashes from the fire in the tepee of the sick Indian and scatter it about the lodge of the supposed witch meanwhile muttering magic words. If this didn't work, the family was persuaded to punish the "witch" or even, in extreme cases, to hang that innocent person. Of course this always started a fight between the families, for the Indians never forgave anyone for any wrong. This was one of the most serious flaws in the Apache character, which only Christianity could cure.

Another common superstition was the belief that an owl is the ghost of your grandmother or some other close relative. The Apaches dreaded the call of the owl, claiming that it was saying, "I am your grandmother," and that a death in the family group was imminent. Aside from the foolishness of thinking that a small, harmless bird probably calling to its mate was the spirit of a deceased Indian or foretold a death they might have asked themselves "What language is the owl speaking?" The Kiowas and other tribes as well as the Mexicans have the same belief. It is a bit difficult to accept that the owl was able to converse in so many diverse tongues. Furthermore some of my white friends tell me that this superstition concerning the owl goes back to Roman times, maybe earlier. I have only one additional comment: The Apaches, when they heard the eerie cry of the owl, got up and sprinkled ashes around their beds for protection. Maybe if some other superstitious people would take the same action they would sleep better.

I am not sure that it is charitable to poke fun at other people's superstitions. All races have them and in many cases borrow from one another. We Apaches certainly had our share of whimsies. One of them, as I have described, was the taboo against touching a dead bear. Another was a prohibition against eating anything that lived under the water. Those of us who were later imprisoned at St. Augustine, Florida got over that one pretty well. In fact I even learned to eat oysters.

I also rid myself of the traditional Apache fear of touching dead snakes and coyotes. At Fort Sill subsequent to 1900 I used to kill snakes and coyotes and skin them, much to the dismay of my fellow tribesmen. Even the former Carlisle students, who should have known better, used to protest, "How do you dare do that?"

The Apache notion was that if you handled a dead coyote you would develop some bad habit such as twitching your mouth, jerking your head, or even going crazy. If you touched a snake the skin would peel off your hands. I assured the Indians that there was nothing to such ideas and proved it to them by skinning plenty of snakes and coyotes.

In this connection I recall an Apache theory that if you met a snake in your path you should mark a cross on the ground in front of you. Perhaps this came to us from the Mexicans. I am sorry to admit that there is no truth in the story that the old-time Indians had a secret remedy for snake bites. Many an Apache died from the effects of a rattlesnake or copperhead bite. Beating a tom-tom and burning feathers did no good.

Chapter 5

OUR TROUBLES BEGIN AGAIN

Apaches possessed many virtues such as honesty, endurance, loyalty, love of children, and sense of humor. They also had at least two serious faults. One of these was drunkenness and the other a fondness for fighting among themselves, these often going hand in hand. Sometimes hard feeling between two men would start over a minor disagreement then grow until finally a regular battle would break out between family groups. I understand that some white tribes, notably the Scotch clans and some of their descendants in the Kentucky hills, have had the same problem.

My own father fell victim to a combination of those two vicious practices, too much liquor and fighting. One day when I was about twelve years old two of my father's half-brothers got into a drunken fight. Nonithian, my father, was a kindhearted man with a pleasant disposition. His great popularity in the Warm Springs band stemmed from his everready willingness to help those who were in trouble or distress. So on this occasion, when the people of the camp were standing around watching these two drunken men snarling and tearing at each other like dogs, Nonithian stepped in to try to stop it. Someone from the crowd fired a shot which felled my father. This was replied to by someone from his family, killing a person in the group which had fired the first shot. My kinsfolk, in grief and rage over Nonithian's death, couldn't tell who had shot him so were preparing to attack the whole group from which the fatal shot had come.

Just then an old woman stepped out in front. "No more shooting," she insisted. "One of each side has been killed. Let that end it."

I had worshipped my father. His death grieved me deeply.

I now began to appreciate how much a father's love and guidance means to a growing boy. The raising of my sister and myself, including both our support and our training, fell entirely on my mother. Though she had to work very hard to obtain enough food and clothing for us she saw to it that we were never in want. Also she had strong principles of conduct which she impressed on us.

Very likely these had been passed down to her from her grandfather, old Mah-ko. At any rate she taught us to be truthful, obedient, respectful to our elders, and above all to be industrious. In the tradition of Mah-ko as well as from the example of my father, she taught us to be kind and friendly.

But before we could become tame Indians we had to go through twenty-five years of intermittent warfare against the whites and the Mexicans.

The Chiricahuas Go To War

Southwest of our Black Mountain homeland were the high and rugged peaks of the Chiricahua Mountains, which were the home of our close kinsmen the Chiricahua Apaches. The latter were more warlike than our Warm Springs band and had been fighting more or less continually with the Mexicans as well as some of the white settlers. Under their chief, Cochise, they had, however, been observing somewhat "correct" relations with the U. S. authorities particularly the military. Cochise, whose fame is preserved even today through a television serial, was a noted warrior in the middle of the last century. My grandfather Tudeevia was associated with him during the campaign against the Mexicans at Ramos and I knew him slightly myself. Had I been older and had Cochise lived longer it is likely that I would have been well acquainted with him because

CHIRICAHUAS MOUNTAINS

one of his sons, Naiche, later became the hereditary chief of our own band, the Chihennes. Cochise's outbreak and desperate war against the U. S. troops marked the end of our decade of peace and the beginning of troubles for us all which were to end only with the final surrender of Geronimo in 1886.

While I was still a small boy Cochise and his band were living in and around what is known as Apache Pass, a canyon just west of old Fort Bowie, which was then probably only a temporary camp. An officer of the post acting, perhaps, under instructions from one of the Indian agents was attempting to secure the return of some half-breed boy captured by San Carlos Indians. This officer, Lieu-

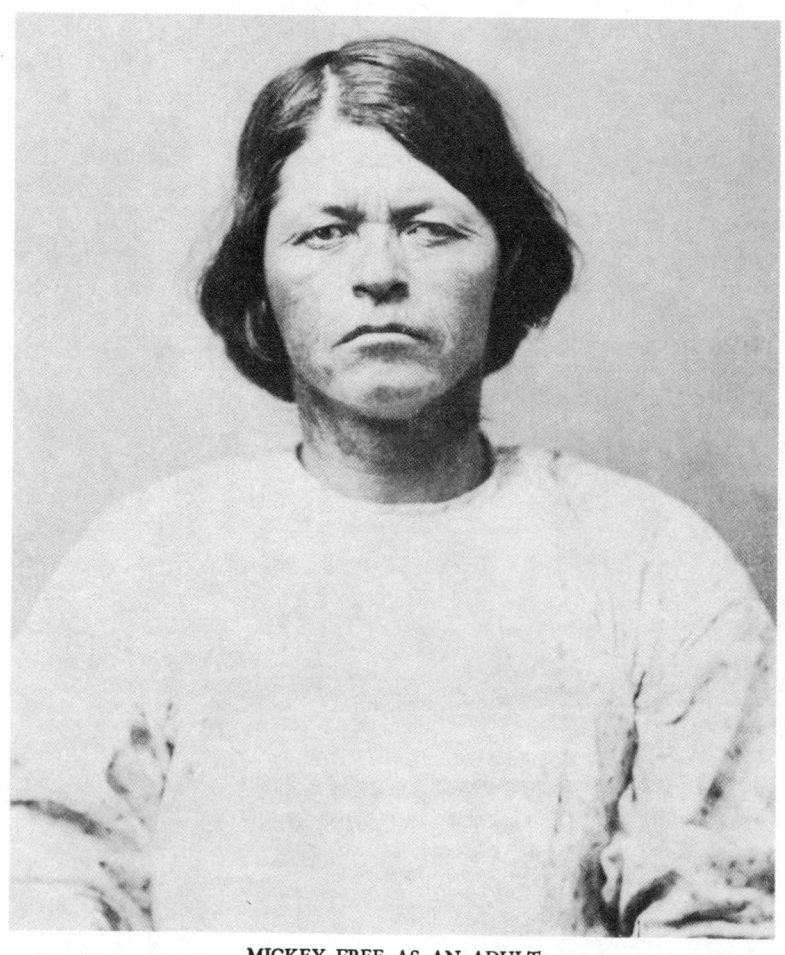

MICKEY FREE AS AN ADULT

tenant Bascom, sent an invitation to Cochise to meet with him in a conference in the pass.

Not expecting any trouble and not being conscious of having committed any offense against the Government, Cochise and his subchiefs prepared to go to the meeting. They had their women give them a good scrubbing, comb their hair, paint their faces, and otherwise make them presentable for such an honored occasion.

At the meeting the officer in command of the troop detachment accused the Indians of having in captivity a small white boy named Mickey Free.* Cochise replied that he had never heard of this case, which was quite true. The officer didn't believe him.

After the meeting was over, the officer told the chiefs to go into a tent where a fine dinner had been prepared for them. When they were all inside, the soldiers surrounded the tent and attacked. All the Indians except three were captured. One of those who escaped was Cochise. Evidently he reacted more quickly than the others for he sprang to the side of the tent, slashed it open with his knife, and with two others dashed out into the brush, making good his escape. This affair became known to the Apaches as "Cut Through the Tent." On account of the circumstances it aroused much indignation and interest even on the part of the Apaches of bands distant from the Chiricahua country. I have heard my parents as well as others discuss it many a time.

On their return to the rest of the tribe Cochise and his companions told the story of this act of treachery on the part of the white officer. Under Cochise's leadership the warriors established road blocks or ambushes on the wagon road leading through the pass, interrupting traffic both to the east and west. They captured a number of teamsters and other travelers. Then Cochise sent a messenger to Lieutenant Bascom offering to exchange his prisoners for the Apaches held by the military. The officer refused. A day or so afterwards Cochise and his men found these Indians hanging from trees where the soldiers had executed them. The Indians sadly took down the bodies of their friends and buried them. Then they hung all their white captives to the same trees. This affair changed a prominent, highly-thought-of chief and his band from Indians who had been friendly and cooperative with the Government to a bitterly hostile group. The warfare which was set off lasted as long

---

*The officer was Lieut. George N. Bascom, a man new to the West, inexperienced in dealing with Indians, and poorly informed as to the facts at issue. His accusation made at this time was without basis. Mickey Free, said to be half-Irish half-Mexican, had been taken by the San Carlos tribe; later he became an official interpreter with the Army.

COCHISE'S STRONGHOLD

as Cochise lived and cost the lives of many people.

A year after the "Cut Through the Tent" affair, soldiers attacked some Indians—not hostiles—who with their families were moving through Apache Pass. My mother told me that the soldiers fired cannon at the Apaches causing them to flee in great fright into the rocks while the shells burst over their heads. In this fight, the first in which the Apaches can remember being attacked by artillery, no one was hurt by the firing.

Cochise established a stronghold in the Dragoon Mountains west of Fort Bowie in what is now part of the Coronado National Forest. The enemy were never able to dislodge him from this high, rocky fastness. At length, however, he died or was killed. This occurred when I was about sixteen years old but I cannot give particulars. The Chiricahuas kept secret the circumstances of Cochise's death and his burial place. I feel sure that some of the Chiricahuas, however, know the true story.

By this time the Chiricahuas, tired and discouraged, had been driven out of their stronghold and most of their ablest warriors killed. They saw no other course except surrender to the United States troops. So they came back to the Chiricahua reservation and remained peaceably near Fort Bowie until, like all the other Apaches, they were forced to move to the San Carlos reservation.

Other Causes of Apache Outbreaks

East of our Warm Springs reservation, across the Rio Grande, lay the reservation of our kinsfolk the Mescalero Apaches. Whenever these Indians had trouble among themselves or with the Mexicans or white people they would drift into our reservation for refuge. Sometimes they drove in stolen stock. When this was identified by the owners or the authorities we frequently got the blame. Much of our later grief could have been avoided if these other Indians had never been admitted to our reservation. Another cause of trouble was the fact that mineral deposits, believed to be valuable, lay under our land. Some of our people, particulary Mangas and his group, had found a little gold and silver which they had beaten into ornaments or traded with Mexicans and whites. This aroused the greed of the latter and caused them to petition their government to get us all off the reservation to some less desirable region.

The first American officials who visited the Southwest have universally testified that the Indians initially showed a sincere desire to be friendly with the whites. This could not last. There were robbers, killers, and criminally-minded on both sides. Atrocities soon started, wherein Indians weren't always at fault initially though of course in the long run they were savage enough to satisfy anyone who enjoys bloodshed. Our Warm Springs area could not long remain peaceful.

Just over the mountains to our south there used to be a mining town, the name of which I cannot recall. The Apaches in this area were Mimbrenos under Mangas Colorado. They had been living at peace with the people of this town, often camping along the creek nearby and going into town to trade. Now and then the Indians found a nugget of gold along the streams in their country, which they brought into town.

One day the friendly attitude of the town people changed suddenly and for no reason at all so far as the Indians could tell. They attacked and killed quite a few of the Apaches. The reason was simply a greed for the gold which they thought was to be found in the Indian country. They immediately laid the blame for the fighting on the Apaches, sending false reports to Washington and to the nearby Army posts demanding that the Indians be removed from their reservation.

"Indian uprising!" they screamed. "We are in danger! Hurry! Send help!"

There was absolutely nothing to such reports. It was merely an expression of the miners' and prospectors' greedy selfishness, which so many times had put the Indians in trouble or had forced them from their homelands. I speak from personal experience.

Added to all this was the fact that various acts of treachery on both sides had stirred up the warlike instincts and spirit of revenge among many Apaches, which had resulted in various outbreaks and raids on settlers in Arizona. The Warm Springs Apaches were responsible for few if any of these raids but of course the white settlers made no distinction between the various bands. Therefore we came in for our share of the blame. By 1876 the pressure on the Indian agents had reached a point where they had decided to drive all Apaches on to one reservation. San Carlos, worthless to whites and Indians alike, was selected.

Early in the spring of that year we were living contentedly at Warm Springs, the agency being garrisoned by a troop of Negro cavalry with whom we were on friendly terms. One day another colored troop accompanied by Indian scouts from San Carlos arrived at our agency. We felt that something unpleasant was about to happen but we didn't know what or why. Still, we remained quiet and gave no trouble.

Moved to San Carlos

On a beautiful clear morning a few days later messengers came to all our camps ordering us to assemble at the agency. Having gathered there we were lined up and searched for weapons by the scouts. No one was overlooked—not a man, woman, or child. Everything was taken from us, even our butcher knives. We opened our eyes in great surprise. What had we done to be treated in such a rude manner?

No explanation was made then or later. But in spite of our resentment we remained quiet and orderly. We young boys and the women and children were ordered back to our camps as were most of the men. Victorio, Loco, Nanay, Geronimo, and practically all of the able-bodied men were directed to report to the agency blacksmith shop where iron chains were put on their wrists and ankles. In a day or two they were loaded in wagons and started off under military guard for some unknown destination. The rest of us remained in our camps, fearful and sad.

Within a couple of days word was passed for us to pack up our belongings. We were formed into a column and started off toward the west. Some of the Indian scouts from San Carlos, who seemed to be a little friendly, hinted that the Government, under the urging of the white settlers, was about to take our beloved reservation away from us. The column pulled out sorrowfully, some of us on foot, a

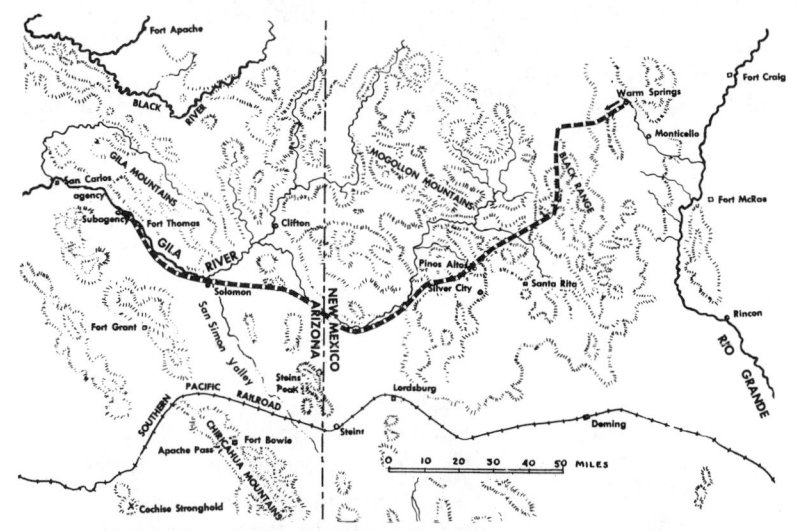

Map 1. THE MOVE FROM WARM SPRINGS TO SAN CARLOS

few on horses or mules, these being mostly women or old people too feeble to walk. Ahead of us marched the Negro troopers, in rear were the Indian scouts. The latter, proud of their status, acted as if they were a guard of honor, which failed, however, to improve our spirits.

After a fifteen-mile march we camped for the night among the hills on the far edge of the reservation. The following day we moved southwest over the lofty and rugged Black Mountains reaching their southern edge after a tiring trip. The next day we passed through the area north of Silver City, where some mining was being conducted. While some of us were trading in the little mining town* several Indians who had wandered near one of the mines were fired upon. Several were killed and others wounded. We were entirely without arms so had no way of fighting back or even of protecting ourselves. Our escort did nothing about it.

From this point we took an old road toward Silver City, stopping northwest of the town for a few days of rest. The women and children who were on foot were developing sore feet. While in this camp some of the women visited Silver City to trade for cloth and other goods. They brought back to the tribe the dreadful disease, smallpox, though we didn't realize this until later.

The halt here was not only to let us rest, it was for the purpose of allowing the wagon train carrying the chiefs and warriors, which

---

*Probably Pinos Altos.

[45]

had taken a more roundabout, but level, route around to the east and south of the mountains, to overtake us. We were happily surprised and overjoyed to see these wagons approaching though disturbed to find that our men were still in chains. At this point, however, their shackles were removed.

We were led westward toward the Gila River in the vicinity of which we camped for the night. That night's camp would have been a pleasant one except that some of the Negro soldiers got to gambling with the Indian scouts, during which a fight developed. The scouts overpowered the somewhat panicky troopers. The latter, our supposed guards, fled to our camp for safety.

In the morning we took the dirt wagon road (now a portion of US 70) along the Gila River, at that time of the year scarcely more than a dry, sandy stream bed. We now felt the scorching power of the desert sun. No longer did we see the pine-covered slopes of the mountains and the upland pastures of our old homeland. Our route now ran through arid valleys bordered by jagged, rocky peaks bare of vegetation. After a time we passed through the Mexican village of Solomon, there being no town of Safford at that time. We saw no horses, cattle, or sheep, for the land would scarcely support any living creature. The land looked parched, barren, and unproductive —quite different from our beautiful Warm Springs reservation.

After a sweaty, dusty march we came to Fort Thomas, a few miles west of which stood an old house which was to be our subagency, today known as the settlement of Geronimo, Arizona. The main agency of the reservation was San Carlos, twenty miles farther west, near the junction of the Gila and San Carlos Rivers. We were completely downcast over the prospect of having to live in this hot, desolate country.

Another unpleasant surprise awaited us. Many other bands of Apaches had been driven in to this reservation, including the Chiricahuas and Juh's group of outlaws from Mexico. Even had all these bands been on good terms with one another, which they were not, we still would have been unhappy over the inhospitable attitude of the San Carlos Indians. Each of our bands would much have preferred to settle on a separate reservation.

I well remember our feeling of indignation and helplessness over this ill turn in our fortunes.

Chapter 6

OUTBREAK

Shortly after we had settled down along the Gila River smallpox broke out in some of the camps. Our people were terrified, for that affliction had always proved deadly to the Indians. Many Apaches were seriously sick, some died. Those who did not at once contract the disease moved their camps into the mountains to the north hoping that the higher altitude would be more healthy. Those who remained along the river took care of themselves as best they could without any help from the agency.

Many of our tribe, especially the wilder ones from Mexico, had never learned to practise self control or to live with their misfortunes. This together with the dissatisfaction with the surroundings built up among the Netdahe and Chiricahuas an increasing restlessness which spread to all the bands. Even the usually peaceful Warm Springs Apaches were affected. The older people wished to return to their home country. The younger men began to talk of going on the warpath. After considerable confusion and argument the more warlike spirit prevailed. The day came when many warriors began stealing and buying guns and ammunition and otherwise preparing for conflict.

The Chiricahuas Break Out

The Chiricahuas had been in the Gila Valley for nearly two years. Now, under Juh, who with Geronimo was taking a leading part in encouraging an outbreak, a considerable number of the warriors and their families left the reservation and went to Mexico, back to Juh's old stomping grounds.

That summer Geronimo and his family had been camping in the mountains north of Fort Thomas in order to escape the terrific heat of the Gila Valley. One day just about the time of the outbreak Geronimo was scolding his nephew, for no reason at all. This disturbed the nephew so much that he killed himself. This all happened while they were drinking intoxicating liquor. Geronimo, blaming himself for his nephew's death, left the reservation and joined Juh's group which intended to flee to Mexico. He took with him his own family, he now having two wives as well as another young woman who later also became his wife and the mother of his only surviving son, Robert Geronimo. Since Geronimo was now the senior member of our family group, mother, sister, and I were under compulsion to go with him.

At this time our Warm Springs band had been moved from the Fort Thomas area to a point nearer San Carlos. That afternoon my mother and I heard that the outbreak had occurred back at the subagency. This was a shock to us because my sister, then about fifteen years old, was visiting some relatives near the subagency.

Mother cried, "We must go up there and see if sister has gone with the war party!"

I got my rope, butcher knife (my only weapon), and sheet, we bid our kinsfolk and friends farewell, and started on foot to the subagency fifteen miles to the east. We made such speed that it didn't take us long to get there. We went to the camp of an Indian nearby who told us that sister had gone with the war party. One of the older men who had remained informed us that his son had also gone with the war party and that he was going to bring him back. He said that he would "get Nah-thle-tla's daughter also."

If sister didn't return soon my mother and I intended to steal two horses and follow the war party. With great anxiety we waited until

THE SAN CARLOS AGENCY, WITH APACHE CAMPS

midnight when we heard someone speaking to us outside the tent. It was the man bringing in his son and my sister. What joy there was when sister ran into my mother's arms!

So I narrowly escaped going on the warpath at the age of sixteen. Instead we returned to San Carlos.

The war party, meantime, headed straight for Mexico. On the way the Chiricahuas, who were now under the leadership of Juh and Geronimo, intercepted a wagon train. They killed the poor drivers, who could not defend themselves, not being prepared and probably being unaware that the Indians had broken out of the reservation. After feasting on captured food the war party continued south toward the Sierra Madre Mountains. Some troops overtook them north of the border but the Indians, being well armed by now, were able to hold off the soldiers. The warriors from good cover behind rocks shot back at the soldiers at long range. After some of this skirmishing, one real old Apache, a veteran warrior, came up behind the firing line to shout that they would never win by such tactics. So, with this old fellow in the lead, the Apaches sprang out to charge the troops. The fire from the enemy was so severe, however, that the Chiricahuas finally retreated back to where their families were waiting in the hills. After some further skirmishing the Indians fled on down across the border where they were safe from U. S. troops, at least for the time being. From a hideout in the Sierra Madres they soon resumed their raids into Sonora.

Some years ago the National Geographic Society published a map with some explanatory matter which purported to show the campaigns of Geronimo during the period 1879-1880. This was an error. It is true that Geronimo was off the reservation part of that time, and with Juh in Mexico. But the raids referred to by the National Geographic were in fact the work of Victorio and his assistants Nanay, Kaahtenny, and others, as I will relate later in this chapter. Geronimo's career was sufficiently bloody but he has been credited with many outrages which he never committed.

Victorio's Outbreak

Victorio and Loco were the principal chiefs of the Warm Springs band at the time of which I speak. Some time after the Chiricahua outbreak most of us decided to go back to our old reservation. So, under the leadership of Victorio and Loco, we slipped away. Some Indians of other bands, seeing us go, reported it to the authorities. Soon a few soldiers and Indian scouts from Fort Thomas were on our trail.

The pursuers, overtaking us, captured several families whom they took back to San Carlos. The rest of us continued toward Warm Springs under intermittent attack from the San Carlos scouts. But the Indian scouts, sympathizing with us, stopped and permitted us to go back to our old reservation without further molestation. We lived there in peace for two years more.

Then in 1879 the soldiers and scouts again were sent to return us to San Carlos. We were assembled for a conference at which this decision was announced. Chief Loco was willing to go but Victorio and Nanay were not.

"No!" Victorio protested. "This country belongs to my people as it did to my forefathers. A few years ago the Government set aside for us the Warm Springs Reservation. Now the white people want it. If you force me and my people to leave it, there will be trouble. Leave us alone, so that we may remain at peace."

Nevertheless the agent set a day for us to be ready to move west again.

At that, Victorio and Nanay, together with forty warriors and some women and children, slipped away from the reservation and went on the warpath, most of them never to return.

I had known both these chiefs since my earliest childhood. They had fought under Chief Roan Shirt (Mangas Colorado). Victorio, together with Loco, had succeeded to the chieftainship of the Warm Springs band. In our opinion he stood head and shoulders above the several war chiefs such as Mangas, Cochise, and Geronimo who have bigger names with the white people. At the time of this outbreak both Victorio and Nanay were well along in years, Nanay being quite an old man. But together they caused more fear among the settlers and killed more people in a shorter time than any other Apaches.

I don't know much about Victorio's background but am well informed concerning Nanay, for he was my father's first cousin and they grew up together. In his youth Nanay was a tall, well-built man, so strong that he could shoot an arrow clear through a steer. I have seen him do it on the Warm Springs reservation even after he was old. He had been a proud, fearless warrior under Mangas and Victorio, a fighter who was able to stand up against anyone who tried to overpower him. He also had a friendly nature being well liked by our Mexican neighbors near Warm Springs as well as by his own people. Like most of the Warm Springs band he was inclined by nature to be peaceful. This all changed when he went on the warpath with Victorio in 1879. He was filled with a bitter hatred

VICTORIO

of his enemies which transformed him into a perfect tiger, overcoming his infirmities of age and muscular stiffness.

At first Victorio and his party hid in the Black Mountains south of the Warm Springs reservation. Once in awhile a few of them would skirmish with the San Carlos scouts thus obtaining a few additional guns and ammunition. This permitted them gradually to extend the radius of their activities. Soon they were sallying from the mountains to attack ranches, travelers, and others—initially for the main purpose of completing the arming of the warriors. Then they were ready for more far-reaching operations. They extended their range east to the Rio Grande, killing every human being they encountered. For a time they kept returning to the vicinity of the Warm Springs reservation but soon they headed into the desert and from there south into Mexico.

While in Mexico Victorio's group attacked everyone they saw just as they had in the United States. When pursued by Mexican troops they turned eastward between Chihuahua and Ciudad Juarez, from the latter area moving north across the river into southwestern Texas thence westward again into New Mexico. As they went they were fighting almost every day, killing dozens of people, leaving a trail of blood. Occasionally they lost a warrior, so that the band was gradually shrinking.

Victorio had a fight with U. S. troops south of Alamogordo, another in the desert to the southwest. Then they fought soldiers in in the San Andres Mountains, west of White Sands, New Mexico. From this affair they escaped into the desert called Jornado del Muerto, or Journey of the Dead Man. The Indians knew where to find water in such country where others would perish. When their enemies were in hot pursuit these Apaches simply withdrew into this apparently waterless country.

But they found no rest, no safety. United States troops and Indian scouts kept on their heels, driving them south again into Mexico. In that country it was just the same—no peace nor rest anywhere. The band had to keep on the move day and night. They never thought of surrender, for in addition to the disgrace of such an act they now knew that their killings would never be forgiven. This made them fight even more desperately, with a continued shedding of the blood of many people.

Becoming more dead weary from their continued exertions, Victorio and his men now withdrew into the mountains east of Galeana. While in the vicinity of Casas Grandes and Galeana they had to move with special caution because of the past battles they had had in that area with the Mexicans. They knew that the people of this region were particularly bitter in their hatred of the Apaches. In spite of their stealth they had several encounters with the result that some of their bloodiest fighting now occurred. As they marched east contact with the enemy was broken. Soon they were moving along without alarm beginning to think that they were out of danger.

They had not, however, shaken off Mexican pursuit. Mexican troops were concealed in the hills watching for Victorio and his band, the local inhabitants having informed them that the Indians were headed across the mountains east of Casas Grandes.

Victorio's party was moving in three groups. In advance were the customary scouts, perhaps two or three. Then came the main body, now down to less than thirty, with some women and children in addition. Far to the rear were Nanay, Kaahtenny, and a few others who were acting as rear guard. All the Apaches were moving along confidently toward their appointed rendezvous for the day, unaware that a trap lay ahead.

They approached their campsite in a box canyon some time in the afternoon, a place where there was a welcome pond of water surrounded by rocks and crevices in the cliffs. The advance party reached this spot undisturbed only to be fired upon by the Mexicans lying in ambush on the surrounding heights. Instead of fleeing as they should have done the Indians made a stand. At the same time the main body, closing up, was attacked. Neither party was able to join and reinforce the other. The Indians had no chance of escape. Both groups were surrounded. The firing lasted all afternoon and on into the night. The rear party coming up was unable to cut through to help their comrades hence they were forced to watch the final act of the tragedy from a distance. Some time after dark the Apaches had fired all their cartridges. A captive Mexican boy with them slipped away and told the enemy that the Indians were out of ammunition. The Mexicans stealing closer threw dynamite into the pockets and crevices where the Indians had concealed themselves. Soon all had been destroyed.

I got my account of this fight from James Kawaykla, the last surviving eyewitness, who is still living as a retired scout near Apache, Oklahoma. James, together with his mother and father, was with Victorio on this last campaign. His father was killed during some of the fighting in New Mexico but he and his mother were in the rear guard group with Nanay at the time of the final battle. He was then about four years old. His mother later married Kaahtenny; he himself married Dorothy Naiche, granddaughter of Cochise. According to his story, which he of course got partly from memory and partly from his mother and stepfather, Victorio's death occurred at a place which the Indians call Twin Buttes.*

After Victorio's death Nanay took the lead of the small surviving party. He continued fighting so fiercely that he threw the greater part of southwestern New Mexico, northern Mexico, and a strip of Texas into a frenzy of fear and frustration. He had only about

---

*Paul I. Wellman, in the excellent history, ***Death in the Desert*** (New York: Macmillan Co., 1935), places this as being in the Tres Castillos Mountains, 125 miles due east of Galeana.

twenty men, some of them Navajoes, some Apaches. But they were topnotch fighters.

After several months of successful fighting Nanay joined the Netdahe in Mexico. He surrendered to General Crook in the spring of 1883.

We Return to San Carlos

When Victorio's last outbreak occurred in 1879 the rest of us went back to the San Carlos reservation under the chieftainship of Old Man Loco, in accordance with the demand of the Government. Instead of locating us near Fort Thomas the authorities made us camp three miles east of the San Carlos agency between the San Carlos and Gila Rivers.* An aide to General Crook has said that Fort Thomas had the reputation of being the worst Army post in the United States but that San Carlos was even more undesirable. We Apaches agree. The agency consisted of a few adobe buildings situated on the gravelly flat between the two streams, with a few scraggly cottonwoods offering the only shade in a temperature which often reached 110 degrees or higher. Dust storms were common the year round and in all seasons except the summer the locality swarmed with flies, mosquitoes, gnats, and other pesky insects. The place was almost uninhabitable but we had to stay there.

Our only source of contentment was that we were untroubled by attacks of enemies, and the Government did feed us after a fashion. Quite a bit of strong language both in official reports and in later reminiscences has been written by Army officers concerning the way we Indians were cheated of our rations by unscrupulous or careless agents, so I will not dwell on that phase. We were issued rations once a week and as we were not allowed to wander away to hunt game we were entirely dependent on this issue. The agency was across the river from us. Since if we were not present at the issue, our rations would be given to someone else, we had to get there even when the water was high. Our method of crossing under such circumstances was to make cottonwood rafts and have swimmers pull these across by tow ropes clenched in their teeth.

The great disadvantage to this kind of life was that we had nothing to do. It is true that many Indians were lazy so far as farming was concerned, but who could farm in that desolate country? If they had been set at some activity in which they were interested or experienced they would have been happy and would have exhibited great exertion. This is shown by the zeal in which some of our

---

*Today the site is covered by San Carlos Lake, which has been formed by the Coolidge Dam, 25 miles southeast of Globe, Arizona, and a few miles south of US 70.

Apaches enlisted as scouts and went off with the troops to hunt down their fellow tribesmen. They were as happy as bird dogs turned loose in a field full of quail.

But the rest of the time they lay around their camps, gambling and, when they could get away with it, making and drinking a strong Indian beer made out of fermented corn mash.

My mother kept my sister and me busy in taking long, fast hikes to keep our muscles like iron, our feet tough, and our hearts and wind in good condition. She knew full well how important that might be if troubled times descended upon us again. She was right!

One of our more enjoyable occupations in those idle days was listening to stories told by the older people. Since the Indians had no written language they kept alive their tribal history, and especially tales of their personal exploits, by recounting these stories over and over again. I think that many white people have the false notion that Indians are silent, taciturn. Nothing could be more erroneous. The Indians, or at least the Apaches, are great talkers.

I recall especially one such session of story telling while we were at San Carlos, because this marked the end of our peaceful days for many moons.

It was a mild evening in April of 1882. We had sat up until long after midnight listening to mother and one of her friends exchanging reminiscences. Suddenly we heard a horse approaching on the path leading to our tent. It trotted up to the front of our lodge and stopped. Outside someone spoke in Apache asking for Gil-lee, a member of our Chihenne band. Since Gil-lee lived about five hundred yards southwest of us I ran out to tell the stranger where his tepee was. As he rode away in the darkness the man said, "Don't be alarmed. We only want to see Gil-lee."

But we *were* alarmed. From his accent, the fact that he was not known to any of us, and from what I had seen of his clothing in the light from our tepee, we knew that the man was a wild Indian from Mexico—a Netdahe. This made us afraid, for we knew that these outlaws had not come for any peaceful purpose. The very fact that this man had sneaked into the reservation and to our camp after dark was ominous. For that is the way of Apaches on the warpath. They avoid being seen. They cover their tracks or disguise them to look like something else.

We talked over this threatening visit for some time after the man had gone, wondering what we ought to do or what was going to happen. The next morning we found out!

Chapter 7

INTO THE WILDERNESS

Just as the sun was beginning to shine on the distant mountain tops, promising a hot day, we heard shouts along the river. Running out of our tepee we saw a line of Apache warriors spread out along the west side of camp and coming our way with guns in their hands. Others were swimming horses across the river or pushing floating logs ahead of themselves. One of their leaders was shouting, "Take them all! No one is to be left in the camp. Shoot down anyone who refuses to go with us! Some of you men lead them out."

The suddenness of this attack, its surprise effect, and the inhuman order from one of the chiefs calling for the shooting of people of his own blood threw us all into a tremendous flurry of excitement and fear. We did everything they told us to do. We were given no time to look for our horses and round them up but were driven from our village on foot. We weren't allowed to snatch up anything but a handful of clothing and other belongings. There was no chance to eat breakfast.

The Netdahe Carry Us Away

Geronimo, who seemed to be one of the main leaders of the outlaws, was out in front guiding us east along the foot of the hills north of the Gila River. Some of the warriors of the invading party stayed behind as a rear guard in case any of the U. S. Indian Scouts from the agency came up. We had only gone a short distance when we heard shooting break out behind us. The chief of the San Carlos Indian scouts and some fifteen of his scouts had ridden up to our deserted camp to investigate the commotion. Some Chiricahuas ambushed the scouts, killing the chief, Mr. Sterling, and one of his men. One of the warriors brought back Sterling's boots. This made me feel badly, because Sterling had been a good friend of ours. He had often visited our camp and once taught me how to make a little wooden wagon.

None of our Warm Springs Apaches had weapons. This, with the brutal shooting of the two scouts, convinced us that we were helpless in the hands of the Netdahe. We told ourselves that our safety de-

ALBERT STERLING AND HIS APACHE SCOUTS

pended on keeping quiet and not trying to escape. We were filled with gloom and despair. What had we done to be treated so cruelly by members of our own race?

Our outlook was all the blacker because we realized that the officers at the agency would blame us for the killings which had occurred there and probably would think that we ran away of our own accord. We felt that we could not safely return to the agency even if we could get away from the wild Indians. So the future held for us only hard flight through mountains and desert under constant pursuit by troops. If we had known what was to happen in the next week or so we would have felt even worse. Many of our friends were not to live very long.

After hustling east along the river for several miles our column turned northeast into the Gila Mountains. Apaches on the warpath, especially when accompanied by women and children, move high up in the mountain ranges whenever they can. This way they can see troops approaching and they avoid many combats by following routes which the soldiers dislike. Troops generally carry their ammunition and supplies by wagon, therefore they follow the flat country. It was only when General George Crook chased the Indians with a column supplied by mule pack trains that the Apaches had a hard time staying out of reach.

Also the Apaches moved mostly in the mountains because they knew of springs and water holes there which were not to be found elsewhere. The Apache knows the secret of how to find water in a dry country where most of the year the stream beds are dry sand.

He does not go to a line of green cottonwoods along a creek or river bed to dig for water, for he knows that it is down too deep. In the mountains, especially in a rock basin at the foot of a dry waterfall, he can usually find a little water near the surface by digging with his hands.

When we reached the mountains we were overtaken by the warriors who had been in the fight at the agency. As we climbed higher and higher up the rough slopes, over the steep escarpment, many members of our band began to tire out. My sister, my mother, and I were still feeling strong. We were in good shape because of the physical conditioning which mother had been giving us for the past few years.

Near sunset we reached a spring just on the other side of the first range where the warriors called a halt to let us rest and have some water. But there was nothing to eat. We had had no food since the night before.

After a short rest the leaders told us that a night march lay ahead of us. Soon we were again moving east, this time along the ridge. About midnight we came to another spring known to Geronimo, who had been there with his family when they had fled from the reservation in 1878. It now began to be clear to me that Geronimo was pretty much the main leader although he was not the born chief of any band and there were several Apaches with us, like Naiche, Chatto, and Loco, who were recognized chiefs. But Geronimo seemed to be the most intelligent and resourceful as well as the most vigorous and farsighted. In times of danger he was the man to be relied upon.

During the midnight halt the leaders sent several volunteers to a distant sheepherder's camp to get some sheep for us. They were to meet us later at some assembly point farther along our route. So we took up the march, this time along the southern slopes of the Gila range parallel to the Gila River. We came to the rendezvous near the river shortly after sunrise. Here we met the men who had gone after sheep. Since we had been without food for two nights and a day and had made a hard trip we surely were glad to see that our foragers had driven in several hundred sheep. We were allowed to camp here for two days gorging ourselves on good roast mutton and resting up for the next stage of the journey. An Apache kills a sheep by grabbing it by the legs, throwing it on its back, and cutting its throat. Then he throws the carcass, skin and all, on a brush fire. This barbecues the meat while the hide protects it from dirt. Simple; but that roast meat sure tastes good!

Our leaders talked over the question as to what route to follow

LILLIAN KAZSHE IN COSTUME FOR WOMANHOOD
CEREMONY, MADE BY NAH-THLE-TLA

next. They wanted to avoid combat with the U.S. troops that they knew would be out looking for them. Also it was realized that the band would have to make better time somehow if they wanted to escape into Mexico. Therefore several men were sent north along the San Francisco River to raid a ranch for some horses and mules which the women and children could ride. The warriors themselves were accustomed to make from fifty to seventy-five miles a day on foot! When in a hurry they would trot part of the way, then walk awhile, then take up the dogtrot again.

Those of us who were too young to be warriors, as well as the women and children, waded across the Gila River and climbed up on the plateau on the south bank. There we waited for the men who had gone off to the north. After awhile we saw a dust cloud coming from that direction. Presently here they came driving several head of livestock. We spent another day or two in this place while the men broke the animals to be ridden bareback or with improvised saddles. Apaches made temporary saddles by wrapping cloth or skins around bundles of tules or reeds and tying them over the backs of the animals.

We took up the march east along the river for several miles, when we recrossed and headed north toward a ranch where the men hoped to get some more horses. The rest of us circled around to the north of the ranch houses where we would be out of sight behind a little hill while the attack was going on.

A Curious Interruption

Now a curious thing happened. One of the girls with us reached womanhood, so right away her parents arranged the traditional ceremony in her honor, even while the shooting was heard on the other side of the hill. Since this is one of the most important events in a woman's life the ceremony is never neglected, not even at a time such as this.

This girl was a member of the White Mountain Apaches, who with her parents had been living with us at San Carlos and who had been caught in this raid of the Netdahe. I think that her father had become a member of our band by marrying a Chihenne woman. The ceremony of reaching womanhood marks the time when a girl is ready for marriage. Of course all girls look forward to it eagerly even though if they look around them they should realize that all marriages do not turn out happily.

Before the ceremony begins the parents are very excited, trying to decide who should be the sponsor and who should conduct the ceremony. The sponsor is a close friend of the family, either a man or a woman, and to be selected as such is a mark of real affection. The person who conducts the ceremony is some respected old woman of the tribe who is experienced in such matters. To the sponsor the parents present an eagle feather, something all Indians value. The old woman who conducts the ceremony spreads out a rug or blanket on the ground, marks four footprints leading away from it toward a point about fifty yards away to the east, where the feather is placed on the ground in a dish or plate.

The girl who is the candidate is led forward, caused to stretch out on her face on the rug while the old woman performs some kind of incantation over her. Then the girl stands erect, steps successively in each of the footprints, runs to the feather, circles it, picks it up and brings it back to the starting point. Meanwhile all the crowd watches closely.

At the conclusion of this part of the ceremony the parents of the girl and the woman who is in charge of the ceremony exchange valuable gifts such as horses, saddles, or other worthwhile property.

The second part of the ceremony is a great feast which lasts four days and nights. The food consists of barbecued cattle as well as wild fruit, berries, and roasted mescal plant. During this time you can hear the constant beat of the tom-tom making music for the fire dance. After the fire dance everyone joins in a circle facing the fire. The girl being honored takes a leading part all through these dances. On the last night of the feast and dance the men make presents to their dancing partners.

For the third phase of the ceremony a number of volunteers go out and cut four long poles each about eight inches in diameter and twenty feet or more in length. These are set in holes which have been dug at the corners of a square about five paces on the side. While the poles are being erected one of the elders of the tribe chants a song which keeps time for the men who are pulling the poles to an upright position. Now the poles are joined at the top with a number of limbs of trees, except that the east side of the square is left open. Thus a lodge is formed, in the center of which a small fire is built on the ground. Here the elder sings a special song meanwhile jingling a rattle made of the hoofs of a fawn. As he sings, the girl moves sideways, north and south, rising alternately on her toes and heels. At the same time she holds up her arms with her hands even with her shoulders. Of course during this time she is well decorated from head to foot. Her dress is the finest kind of buckskin, covered with many small tin jingles as well as much beadwork.

Early on the morning of the fourth day a brief ceremony is held before pulling down the lodge at the end of which the elder orders the four poles to be pulled down. They are dragged eastward about a hundred feet and laid side by side with their tops pointed eastward. The tom-toms then cease beating and the ceremony is ended.

On the occasion of our flight to Mexico the ceremony was very much shortened because the warriors were in a hurry to start the night march.

The Flight Is Resumed

About sunset the men who had been attacking the ranch came in with several more horses and mules. The leaders after talking among themselves announced that we would make a long night march, meeting at daylight at a certain spring or waterhole at the foot of Stein's Peak Mountains many miles to the south of us.

Night fell, dark and moonless. All through the night we rode close together, so that no one would stray away from the column. The warriors rode on all sides of us in order to keep us together but in spite of their watchfulness some members of the Warm Springs band managed to slip away and head north for the Navajo country.

My mother, my sister, and I were riding a big mule. Now and then we could hear the voices of the wild Indians on all sides of us as they called softly to each other in the darkness. Finally I dozed. It is a wonder I didn't fall off the mule but every now and then my mother punched me to wake me up. It surely was a tiresome journey, being the second night march we had made. It was not to be the last.

By morning we were completely worn out. Or so we thought. We were to change our minds about this a few hours later when fighting began. We rested at the spring at the foot of the mountains for a little while then continued on toward the southeast. During the night we had crossed the San Simon Valley, a wide rolling plain, and by noon had reached the tip of Stein's Peak a few miles northwest of the little railroad station of Stein on the Southern Pacific. The whole band moved half way up the mountainside while a dozen warriors were sent southeast on a scouting expedition.

The Fight At Stein's Peak

At this time a party of U. S. Indian Scouts moving ahead of some troops were looking for our band. Instead of finding us our reconnoitering party located them and at once attacked, killing one of the scouts. The latter though badly outnumbered put up a good fight. They set fire to the grass to tell their main body that they had met the hostile Indians.

Those of us who were watching the skirmishing from high up on the mountainside were getting restless. The real old men were hiding behind the rocks but some of us more adventurous young fellows climbed up where we could see. There was a clear view far to the north, east, and south. After about an hour we saw two troops of cavalry approaching from the vicinity of the railroad station. This was the first chance most of us had ever had to see a real battle and we were trembling with excitement.*

When the soldiers had reached a point about a mile from our hiding place our warriors stripped off their shirts and prepared for action. I heard the leaders calling all able-bodied men to assemble for battle. Of course the way Indians fought, this was all voluntary. The chiefs were not able to order any man to fight, as the officers could the soldiers. But the Indians would go into battle to keep from being shamed and to protect their families. I was still considered to be too young to fight, was without experience, and was not given a weapon. A few weeks later I was to be given more responsibility as an apprentice or helper to Geronimo.

Soon we saw our warriors moving down toward a deep U-shaped ravine. The soldiers were approaching up the canyon while our men were on the rim. The fighting began. Three of our men who were wounded were carried back up the mountainside. Maybe some were killed but I didn't see any. The firing grew very heavy, almost continuous. The soldiers fired ferocious volleys. Those of us who were watching were shivering with excitement as our men slowly withdrew under this fire. Finally toward sunset our whole band moved to the southwest side of the mountain and the firing died out. I don't think we ever found out how much damage we did to the troops.

As the wide valley to the west of us turned purple then black the Indians began getting their horses ready for another long night march. The chiefs told us to move very quietly down the mountain-

---

*The troops consisted of six, not two troops, being commanded by Lieut. Col. George A. Forsyth, 4th Cavalry. He calls this affair the Battle of Horseshoe Canyon. In detail the white and Indian accounts agree fairly well except as to casualties. The Indians do not remember any great loss on either side. Forsyth reports 3 soldiers and 4 scouts killed and 8 soldiers wounded. He states that the Indians later told him that they lost 13 killed and a number wounded. George A. Forsyth, *Thrilling Days in Army Life,* Harper and Bros., N.Y., 1900.

side, as they believed that the enemy might still be near. But we were undisturbed by anyone.

A person who has not traveled through these rough mountains at night cannot appreciate how dangerous and unpleasant such a flight can be. In addition to thorns, cactus, yucca, and other spear-like plants to scratch you, you must avoid knife-like rocks that you can't see, holes and crevices in the ground, and cliffs of all kinds. It's a wonder we made it safely but we did. When we came down on the plain we headed toward the Southern Pacific Railroad, intending to get into the Chiricahua Mountains south of old Fort Bowie. In the darkness some Indians who got confused strayed away from

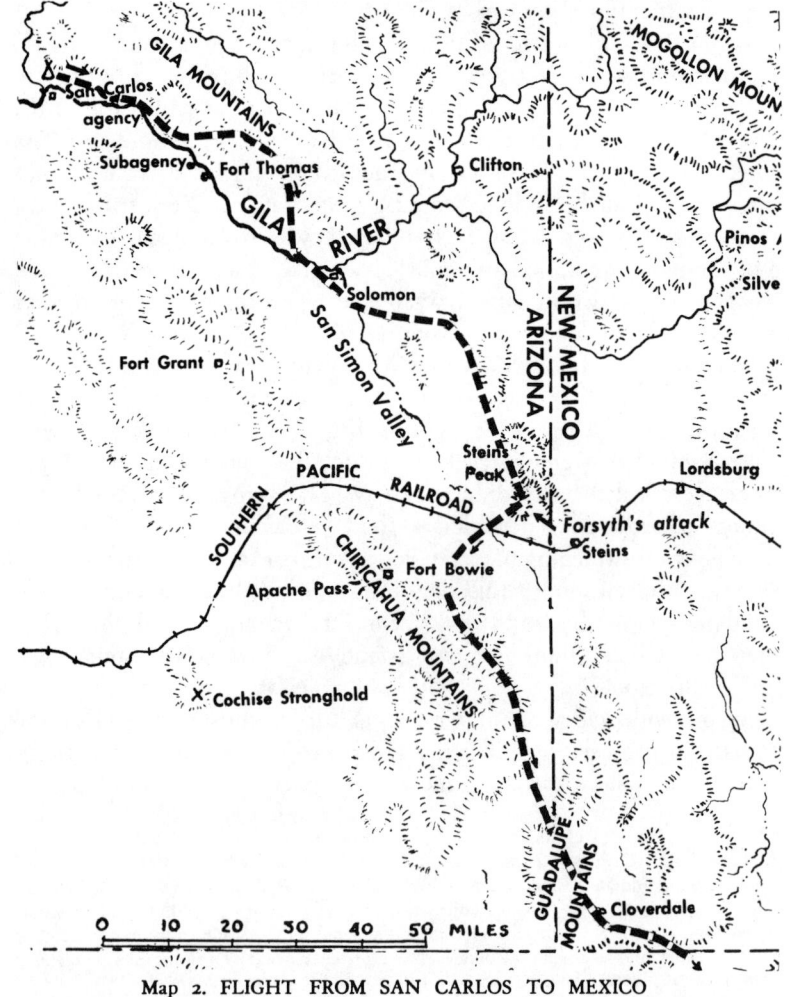

Map 2. FLIGHT FROM SAN CARLOS TO MEXICO

CAVALRY IN BOX CANYON TYPICAL OF SITE OF
FIGHT NEAR STEINS

the band. But by morning most of us had assembled at the designated rendezvous point and during the morning others rejoined us. By now no one dared to try for an escape or to make his way back to the San Carlos Reservation. It was too far and we were now too closely involved with the hostiles in the fight with the troops.

The Apaches when moving about like this always designate an assembly point for the end of a day's or night's journey. Such places are easily distinguishable landmarks that can be pointed out well ahead, or previously-used stopping places, such as springs, which are known to the tribe. If possible the assembly point is on high ground where we can get good observation and avoid suprise. So it was this time. We stopped on the side of a mountain southeast of Fort Bowie. Here we rested and slept during the day, getting in shape for another night trip. By thus moving mostly at night we escaped being seen and kept ahead of the troops, who usually marched only in the daytime. While we were on this peak some of the warriors did sentinel duty, observing especially toward Fort Bowie. We half expected to see troops come out toward us but none did. Maybe they stayed in

APACHE ROUTE TO MEXICO

the post to protect their own women and children or were looking for us somewhere else.

That night we headed southeast through the foothills of the Chiricahua Mountains, crossing and recrossing arroyos and hills. We stayed out of the main mountain range, whose peaks exceed 9,000 feet in elevation, but we had to go through several rough canyons. It was a terrible journey. During the following day we again rested in a hiding place while some of the warriors again did sentry duty. By now we reached the frontier of Old Mexico having marched at least 70 miles in the two nights since the fight on Stein's Peak. We were somewhere east of the present site of Douglas, Arizona, headed for mountains which stood in the wide plain south of the border. So far we hadn't seen a single enemy but rode along peacefully, some of us very tired and sore from the unaccustomed long rides. After we had crossed into Mexico we began to feel safe from attack by U. S. troops, not knowing that the troop commander, hot on our trail, intended to cross the border with or without permission of higher authorities.

Chapter 8

TRAGEDY IN MEXICO

A little before dark we heard the leaders calling for everyone to get ready for another night march. Since we were under the impression that we were out of danger there was much cheerful conversation as we packed our horses and mules and prepared to continue our journey.

This night march, in contrast to our past hasty and tiresome travel, was a delightful one especially for the young folks. The night atmosphere was cool and dry, the skies bright with stars. So we rode along across the plains, talking, laughing, and singing love songs in low voices—songs our people have long known and liked. Now and then some one would challenge a friend to a race which of course was only in fun and didn't last long. Here and there riders could be heard calling to companions in the darkness, with answers echoing from the hills and rocks on either side.

Several times we came to springs where we stopped to refresh ourselves then continued on until the sky began to lighten. Finally under a grove of cottonwood trees we came to a fine spring and stream where we pitched our camp and intended to remain for several days.

Sentries were sent out to the hills on all sides to watch for enemies. These men had a great responsibility for the safety of the whole group. They were supposed to remain awake and alert at all times, to let nothing escape their notice. Later on I volunteered repeatedly for this duty so I know how tense and tireless the sentries must be. In spite of its high importance the duty was sometimes poorly performed by some of the men who when they were discovered in a careless position, or not on the sharp lookout, were severely criticized by the others. Any criticism always led to much bad feeling.

Jealousy between different chiefs and bands was another cause of insecurity in Indian camps when bands were on the warpath or fleeing from a reservation. Sometimes a subchief would be trying to get control of the whole band against the opposition of the other leaders each of whom wanted the honor of being chief. All was not harmony at all times in the Apache tribe. Frequently in such disputes a chief or an influential man acted as a peacemaker, probably someone who had more common sense than the hot heads. A common subject of discussion among the Indians of those days was the fact that the Apaches were never able to form a strong confederation, on account of indifference and selfishness on the part of the different chiefs.

But on this occasion no such unpleasantness arose. Our leaders and the older people were so relieved at having escaped great damage from the scouts and cavalry that they relaxed completely that night, becoming careless in observance of safety precautions. Though we didn't know it U. S. troops were still on our trail, after having been delayed for a couple of days north of Stein. They had had trouble getting out of the canyon and finding our tracks down the rock-covered slopes of the mountain. Within a day or two their Indian scouts found our trail. Also another body of troops of which we were unaware were following us.

We were camped about twenty-five miles northwest of Janos near a little round, rocky butte that stood by itself west of some hills. Just west of our camp was a marshy place which Mexicans call a cienaga, where cattails grew, and where we could water our animals. To the west and south stretched a dry, treeless plain for as far as the eye could see.

For two days and nights we gave ourselves up to merriment and dancing. Our leaders had taken their usual precaution of selecting and announcing rendezvous points farther south in the mountains west of Casas Grandes, where we would assemble in case we were attacked and had to scatter. There was also chosen an alternate assembly point in case the first one proved to be unsafe or couldn't be reached.

Second Attack by U. S. Troops

Our two days of rest and relaxation gave the cavalry a chance to catch up with us.* On the third morning I was out at daylight looking for our mule, which had been turned loose to graze and was with the other animals a mile or so from camp. All at once I heard a gun fired from the foothills east of the camp. I opened my eyes wide in sudden excitement, for there in plain sight south of the horse herd was a troop of cavalry galloping my way. I guess they didn't notice me among the animals or they would have gotten me easily. I ran

---

*This was Captain Tupper, with two troops of the 6th Cavalry, who was one day ahead of Forsyth. Tupper was also accompanied by Indian scouts. Forsyth, *op. cit.,* pp 79-121.

just as fast as my legs would carry me toward camp. Arriving at the foot of the butte I looked back to see the soldiers driving away our horses.

All our people took cover in the broken ground at the butte, in some cases several trying to squeeze into the same crevice in the rocks. Our warriors were on the butte firing back at the troops while the rest of us were between the two firing lines. The soldiers were about a half mile away, so our men didn't waste too much ammunition trying to hit them at that range. This intermittent skirmishing lasted all morning, the soldiers apparently having little urge to make a real attack.

About noon we heard our leaders calling to the men to get ready to attack the soldiers, who now were in the plain southwest of the butte, near the marsh. The warriors stripped off their shirts ready for action. Then under shouted directions from the leaders the Apaches began sneaking down through the rocks toward the soldiers. In a few moments the firing began again. After this had gone on for awhile our men began withdrawing up the butte. The soldiers kept firing into the rocks in spite of the fact that no Indians were in sight. Therefore no damage was done, as far as I could see, except that Old Man Loco was wounded slightly in the leg while leaning against a rock right beside me.

Several hours passed, with occasional shots being fired from both sides. About noon an old Apache woman climbed up to the highest point of the butte where she stood in plain sight calling out to her son, Toclanny,* who was an Indian scout. She thought mistakenly that he was with these particular troops. In vain she called to him, telling him that we had been run off against our will by the hostiles from Mexico. But her son wasn't there; and she was shot and killed.

Early in the afternoon four young warriors slipped through to the southeast and circled around behind the Indian scouts. They attacked the scouts from the rear, driving them out into the plain where they joined the troops. The four warriors ducked behind some rocks and kept on firing. This diversion gave those of us who were between the lines a chance to escape. So while the soldiers and scouts were occupied with this party in their rear, we who were watching from the rocks on the butte ran for the foothills to the east leaving all our belongings behind. This was the worst thing that had happened to us since we left the agency at San Carlos. While it is true we hadn't been able to take much with us when we were forced to leave the

---

*Later known as Rogers Toclanny. He was a member of the Apache delegation to Washington in 1911. See Chapter 21.

agency, we did have a few blankets and utensils. Now we had nothing except our bare hands and the clothes on our backs.

While we were running toward the hills several women and children were hit. This added to our difficulties, for we had no way to help them to safety and no medicines of any kind to treat the wounded.

We were safe in the hills, the soldiers not pursuing us into that rough country. At dusk we assembled prior to resuming our flight south. Before we started we had a good drink of water at a spring and distributed what little food some of us had been able to grab up when we fled from the butte. We were now on foot again, the soldiers having captured all our horses and mules. No doubt they were rejoicing over this and laughing at us in our sorry condition. In counting up our losses we found that three women had been killed and four wounded but the warriors had suffered no injuries or losses. One wounded woman who had been shot in the ankle was carried for a ways on a stretcher made of reeds then on a recaptured horse. The animal bucked her off, so she asked her relatives to leave her there. They finally had to abandon her. I understand that she was later picked up by the troops, who gave her medical attention.*

About night, just as we were starting off, some of the warriors came in with a few horses which they had been able to recapture. We were very proud of these brave young men, who were some of the best fighters in the Apache tribe.

During the night we crossed a wide valley and continued on toward the north end of the Sierra Madre Mountain range.† While we were still far from the foothills we had to stop to rest because many of our band were completely worn out. We rested and slept for an hour or so, then early in the morning continued the march. We were now traveling very slowly on account of being mostly on foot and nearly exhausted. Those who were mounted did not stop but went right on to the foothills. Early in the morning they saw some Mexican soldiers, but were afraid to go back and let us know. Some of the men who took part in this disgraceful abandonment of their mission as a security detachment were subchiefs Chatto and Naiche and one of Nanay's warriors, a man named Kaahtenny. I will have more to say about him later.

The rest of us in the main party were unaware that we were be-

---

*Forsyth states that the wounded woman informed them that the Indians lost 6 braves in this fight.
†This portion of the Sierra Madres is called the Sierra Huachinera.

tween two hostile groups, the U. S. troops who were following us, and the Mexican troops who were ahead, preparing to ambush us.

Massacred By Mexicans

We took up the march in daylight, since we were now within a few miles of our next assembly point in the foothills where we expected to stay during the day. A few warriors were out in front leading the way but most of them were coming along perhaps two miles to our rear. Our route ran south, parallel to the Rio de Janos, which was a dry stream bed in a small arroyo. On our right were some low hills, ahead were the Sierra Huachinera Mountains. When we were within a mile and a half of the foothills, probably due west of Ramos, the warriors who were our "advance guard" stopped to

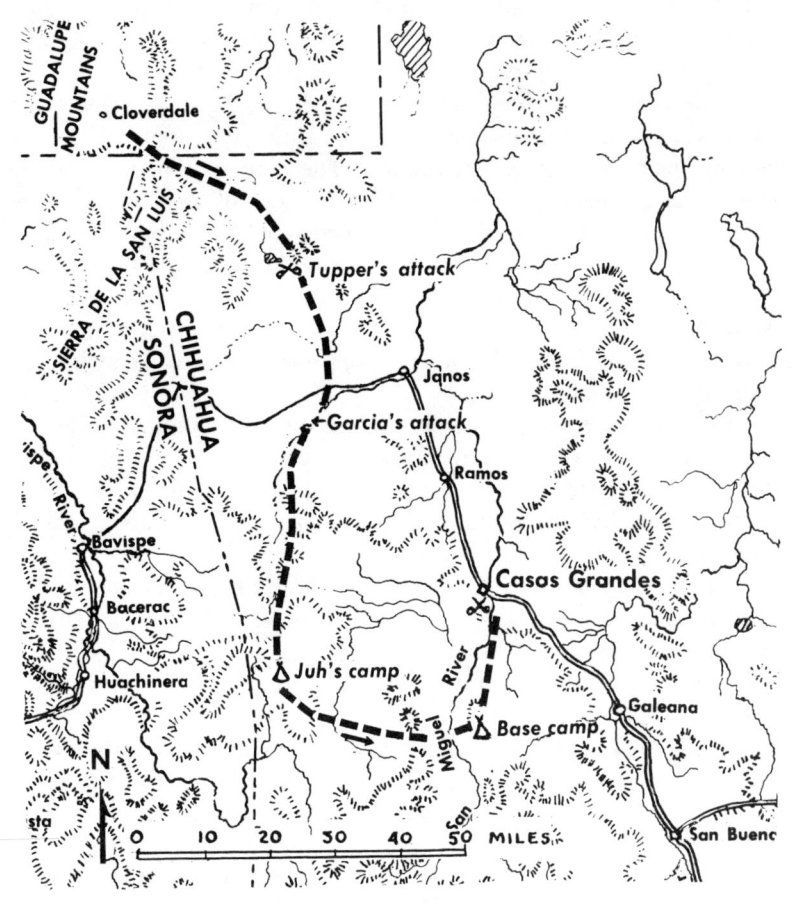

Map 3. GERONIMO'S ROUTE SOUTH OF THE BORDER

rest and have a smoke. We passed them and kept right on going, strung out in a long, irregular column.

When we had gone a few hundred yards we were suddenly attacked by Mexican soldiers who came at us out of the ravine where they had been concealed. The first thing I saw was Mexicans firing at the Apache women who were about a quarter of a mile ahead of where my mother, sister, and I were. Almost immediately Mexicans were right among us all, shooting down women and children right and left. Here and there a few Indian warriors were trying to protect us while the rest of the band were running in all directions. It was a dreadful, pitiful sight, one that I will never forget. People were falling and bleeding, and dying, on all sides of us. Whole families were slaughtered on the spot, wholly unable to defend themselves. These were people who had never before been off the reservation, had never given any trouble, and were from the most peaceloving band of the Apaches—the Warm Springs band.

Those who could run the fastest and the farthest managed to escape. There weren't many such but my mother and sister and I were among them, being excellent runners. The hard training my mother had given us again paid off. I had no weapons of any kind, not yet having been made a warrior. We headed rapidly for the mountains. As we ran, my mother and I heard Geronimo behind us, calling to the men to gather around him and make a stand to protect the women and children. We learned later that thirty-two warriors responded to Geronimo, around whom some women and children assembled for protection.

Mother and I continued to flee. While we were running in among the confused crowds of women and children I lost sight of mother but had no chance to search for her as we were all under very close pursuit. Ahead of me was another young Apache running up hill. I soon passed him, for he didn't have my speed and wind. As we came out in the open the Mexicans wasted a lot of ammunition on us but neither of us was hit and in a few moments we were over a little hill and safe at least for the moment.

Here we found about fifteen Apache warriors sitting under a tree smoking. These were the men who had ridden ahead that morning and had failed to warn us of the danger they saw. Thus they were partly to blame for our Warm Springs Indians being slaughtered. Here they were sitting well armed and with plenty of ammunition, yet doing nothing. I felt dreadfully ashamed of them. They never fired a shot, while a half mile away beyond the hill their fellow tribesmen and the women and children were being butchered.

About this time another man came running up. He had been fighting to protect the women and children. His ammunition was all used up but his own party had been saved. He pointed southwest saying, "Your mother went toward the mountains."

Looking in the direction in which he was pointing I saw a woman running nearly a mile away. She seemed to be out of danger but I hadn't seen my sister since we had started across the valley. Later I found out that she had been picked up, along with another girl, by a mounted Apache who had been wounded in the leg. I hurried to where I had seen the woman running. Soon I found mother squatting on the ground by a small fire roasting a young century plant. This mescal, which is found nearly everywhere in the desert, furnished emergency food for the Apaches. So mother and I had something to eat, which gave us renewed strength to continue the flight if that became necessary.

While mother was cooking the mescal I went to the top of a nearby hill and called loudly. Some one answered from the dense pine forest. It was an old White Mountain Apache woman, whom I led to where mother was, then I went back on the hill to shout again. Finally some other refugees heard me so that we gradually assembled quite a few of the survivors around us. We then moved on toward the rendezvous point, on the way finding tracks of others who had escaped the massacre. In the canyon we soon heard more Indians calling to one another. Moving up the steep mountain we found part of the band in camp. The night air was very cold at that altitude, we had lost all our blankets, and it was unsafe to build fires. Nevertheless by gathering grass and covering ourselves with it we managed to sleep with a fair degree of comfort.

Meantime what had happened back at the site of the fight with the Mexicans? We learned all the details when our men rejoined us. As I said, thirty-two warriors had rallied around Geronimo and Chihuahua. They stood off the Mexicans while the few women with them dug a big hole in the dry creek bed. Here they made their stand in this rifle pit in the center of which a little water, mixed with blood from the wounded, seeped in so that they could quench their thirst. The women also dug holes for other warriors in the bank of the little arroyo, around the center strong point. This made a good defensive position from which the men began shooting down the Mexican soldiers as fast as they appeared. The Mexicans quickly learned that the Apaches were skilled marksmen.

Right in the thick of the fighting one old Apache woman volunteered to go out for a sack of 500 cartridges which some exhausted runner had dropped while fleeing. The old woman successfully brought in that bag of ammunition just as the men were running short. Not all heroes are warriors!

The Mexicans made several determined charges against the Indian stronghold, shouting as they advanced, "Geronimo, this is your last day!" One of our men who understood Spanish interpreted this for Geronimo and Chihuahua, who directed the warriors, "Now get ready! Steady, men! Here they come. Let them get close then shoot them down!"

The fighting kept up violently all morning.

At noon the soldiers disappeared. It was quiet for some time but Geronimo suspected a trick. Presently a young Indian woman a little way off, who was up in a mesquite tree, called to our men that the soldiers had all gone home. Geronimo didn't recognize her voice. He and the other men discussed this development, deciding that perhaps she was someone whom the Mexicans had sent up a tree to fool us. One of our warriors said that he had a good notion to shoot her. But he didn't, and we never discovered who it was that had tried to induce our men to leave their stronghold.

Shortly after this it became clear that the Mexican soldiers had indeed tried a ruse, for they now came back attacking our men more fiercely than ever. But the Apaches were still too good shots for them and had plenty of ammunition. The Mexicans tried all afternoon to dislodge the Indians. After dark they set fire to the grass hoping to burn the Indians out. The latter were now in a serious condition. They were surrounded by the prairie fire, the circle of it drawing closer. The warriors asked the consent of the few women who were there to let them choke the small children so that they wouldn't give away their movements by crying. Then they all crawled through the fire and got away without being seen.

All during the night in our camp on the cold mountainside we could hear people mourning and wailing for their relatives who had been killed or captured. There was no help for the wounded, no food, no chance of getting reinforcements. When morning came we looked down far off into the valley where we saw United States troops and the Mexicans come together. We expected a fight to occur but nothing like that happened. I have since learned that the Mexican leader revealed that a battle had been fought. He showed the U. S. commander the bodies of the slain Indians and told him that the results of their combined expeditions had been accomplished, so that the Americans should return north across the border.

We lost nearly half our families in this tragedy.*

The Flight Continues

Our leaders gave orders to move eastward. Half way down the mountainside whom should we meet unexpectedly but Geronimo and his warriors! We learned of the stand they had made and the great fight they had put up to protect the families. Our sorrow over our great losses was partly offset by our pride and happiness in hearing the story of those who had fought so well for us. During this recital those warriors who had stayed in the hills without firing a shot stood silent having nothing to say for themselves.

After quite a bit of excited conversation Geronimo gave the order for the march to be resumed. On account of the many wounded who had to be helped or carried we had to move slowly, painfully crossing successive ranges of hills. Geronimo sent some men out to distant ranches to steal some cattle, with orders for them to meet us at the next rendezvous, which was a spring not too far ahead. The foragers were successful in driving in some beeves so we had a good meal for the first time since we had had supper at the little butte the night before the troops had attacked us.

We rested for two days then moved south along the foothills. Three wounded Indians, unable to travel, decided to remain at the old camp where there were the picked-over carcasses of the beeves we had feasted upon. To show how tough the Indians were in those days, and how well they recovered from injuries without medical care, these Indians rejoined us a month later, well and strong. One of them was a man named Kay-i-tah, who with his friend Martine was to act as guide for Gen. George Crook in 1886. Another was Tso-ay (nicknamed Peaches), who also served Gen. Crook as a scout. The third was a woman whose name I have forgotten. The evening after we had gone off and left these three, Geronimo sent someone back to help them but this man returned to say that no one was at the deserted camp but the enemy. This report, which was later proved to have been completely false, and the result of laziness or fear, caused us to resume the march again in great anxiety—all unnecessary. Geronimo gave orders for the warriors to stay together

---

*The Mexican commander was Colonel Lorenzo Garcia, with 250 men of the 6th Mexican Infantry. They had seen the dust of the Indian column on April 27 on the western edge of the Janos plain, had followed the trail, then circled out ahead and laid the ambush in the canyon. In the fight Garcia suffered 37 casualties including 21 killed. The Indians lost 78 counted dead, mostly women and children, as well as 20 or 30 captured. See Geo. A. Forsyth, *op. cit.* Another report by Lieut. Bourke states that 85 were killed and 30 captured. Only 11 of the casualties were men.

in case we were attacked during the flight. Because of our wounded we moved slowly for the next few days.

The Camp of the Wild Indians

After one more day's march and one more camp we came to the main camp of Juh's Netdahe. These were the outlaw Indians from whom had come the party who had driven us from the San Carlos reservation. They lived deep in the almost inaccessible Sierra Madres, from where they would make forays on the Mexican settlements or even into the southern part of Arizona and New Mexico. As I said before, when they couldn't find anyone else to mistreat they fought among themselves. They were hard to deal with on friendly terms.

Though most of the faces we saw in this camp were those of strangers we did encounter some old friends and relatives from different Apache bands, people who had left their hated reservation at San Carlos or had followed their menfolks during the outbreaks of about 1877 or 1878. There were some happy reunions. These people attempted to make up for our recent sorrow. They gave us food and blankets and by talking to us cheerfully tried to take our minds off our losses.

GERONIMO IN MEXICO

Remarkable photo by C. S. Fly made before Geronimo
surrendered to Gen. Crook

Several hundred people were now assembled in this one camp, seventy-five of them being first-line warriors. This was the largest number of Apaches that had come together in many years. Many of the young boys and old men could also have been used as fighters if guns and ammunition had been available but there were none for them. The older warriors were using single-shot Springfields of the Civil War pattern while the younger ones were armed with repeating rifles—Winchesters and Marlins. In addition many of the men had pistols and other miscellaneous firearms which had been taken in raids on the settlements or attacks on travelers on the lonely roads in Arizona and New Mexico.

Our camp was high in the mountains some thirty miles southwest of Casas Grandes. These Indians never stayed long in one place, so after a few days the camp was moved eastward near the San Miguel River. Here for the first time in my life I witnessed some returning Netdahe raiders perform what they called the Triumph Dance, which old-time Indians used to stage after they had come in from a successful foray. The men who had been on the raid got together in the center with the women in a circle around them. Then they sang at the top of their voices some kind of a chant of triumph and rejoicing. Afterwards they all danced for enjoyment.

For the next few days everything in camp was quiet. There was nothing to do all day long but play games and gamble. Both men and women were devoted to gambling.

Several days later it was time to move again, still farther east to a place where there was plenty of good spring water. Our camp was then pitched between a range of mountains on the east and another on the west, with a wide open prairie between. We continued to enjoy peace, with no enemy to fear so far.

Our group contained Chiricahua, Warm Springs, Mescalero, San Carlos, White Mountain, and other Apaches, as well as a few Navajoes and even some Mexican and white boys who had grown up to young manhood among the Indians. Some of them had married Indian women and had families. Mostly they were fully Indianized and made good, brave warriors.

We had two principal leaders, Geronimo and Juh.

Treachery At Casas Grandes

In a big council the leaders decided to make a peace with the Mexicans at Casas Grandes. I think that Geronimo was largely responsible for this, his motive being to get whisky,* that great curse

---
*That is, mescal or aguardiente.

of the Indians. Accordingly about a third of the whole band went with him toward Casas Grandes, stopping to camp about three miles east of the town. They sent in to the town a woman who could speak Spanish with a request for the town officials to meet the Apaches at an appointed place between the camp and the town, for the purpose of making a peace. The alcalde came out accompanied by a few soldiers and held a peace council with Geronimo and Juh. The smiling Mexicans told the Apaches that all past troubles were forgotten, there were no hard feelings, and that from now on they would be on friendly terms. They assured our leaders that it would be safe for all Indians to come into town to trade and to get acquainted. The town was wide open to them. So most of our Indians went into Casas Grandes where the men got to drinking and having an uproarious time. The first day everything was fine. The Mexicans were courteous and hospitable. The next day was the same. The Indians were now completely off guard, satisfied that all was peace and friendliness.

Mother and another woman went back to camp the second day but I stayed in town because I had been asked to help an old woman, who wanted to sell a horse, look after her other two horses. That night most of the Indians slept just outside the village walls along the river, but a few of us bedded down several hundred yards farther south. During the night I could hear the drunken Indians in their camp, howling and dancing. This was what the Indians, and some other races, regard as having a good time.

Early next morning while it was still dark our "true friends" the Mexicans stole into the camp where the Indians were lying around in a stupor and commenced killing them, just as at Ramos many years before. Not many got away.* I did hear of one man, wounded in the leg and unable to run far, who jumped in the river and hid under some driftwood and thus escaped being found. Geronimo, of course, was one of those who got away. So was Juh.

We who were camped farther out had a better chance to escape. I almost didn't make it because the old woman I was helping was unable to get on her horse. Finally I lifted her up and she rode away. By this time it was broad daylight. I was the last one to leave camp. Again I was fortunate in being a fast runner, always a good accomplishment when you tangle with your true, everlasting friends, the Mexicans.

---

*Lieut. John G. Bourke states that ten or twelve warriors were killed and 25-30 women captured. *An Apache Campaign in the Sierra Madre,* p. 6. New York: Chas. Scribner's Sons, 1886.

NEAR CASAS GRANDES

As I ran towards the hills the bullets were cutting my flying shirttails to ribbons. That was the closest I ever came, in all my experiences as an Indian on the warpath, to being hit. I never was wounded, even.

A Mexican soldier was also running toward the hill trying to cut me off. So I dived into some tall Johnson grass. I had a hard time crawling through the thicket but presently came to a wagon trail which I followed to the river. Here I crossed to the west bank, found a few tracks leading away from the water, and followed them upstream until I finally overtook some other fleeing Apaches. I didn't remain with this party but continued straight on south to our main camp in order to check up on what had happened to mother. About 10 miles from our main camp I came upon a place where some of the band had started a fire and roasted some beef. I filled up on meat then went on, running most of the way. Arriving at the main camp I found that the camp had been moved. Apparently I had gotten there before any others fleeing from Casas Grandes. I followed the tracks of the camp movers until I found our main camp, now located on the side of the mountains. I was the first one in from the disaster at Casas Grandes.

As I walked up the mountainside, those in camp wondered who was approaching. Mother and sister recognized me and came running to meet me. They were exceedingly glad to find that I had escaped without harm, because from the sound of the yelling and firing at Casas Grandes that morning they were afraid that no one had gotten away.

The other survivors of the everlasting peace began coming in one by one during the several days during which we camped at this place. The old woman whose horses I had been caring for showed up four days after the attack. Some of those who straggled in were wounded. All were tired and hungry. Finally it was thought that all those who were still living were in.

In this treacherous attack by the Mexicans quite a few warriors were killed and a larger number of women and children captured. One of Geronimo's wives was made prisoner and taken to Chihuahua, never to be seen again by us. From having been an eyewitness to the Casas Grandes massacre I could understand why the Apaches thought of Mexico as being a land of treachery. Once again the Indians had fallen victim of their own weakness, the love of strong drink, which has been their ruin. They never seemed to learn from tragic experience.

Chapter 9

ON THE WARPATH WITH GERONIMO

For four days after the slaughter at Casas Grandes we waited for more of our missing people to come in. Then the leaders decided that it was time to move. Game in the vicinity was getting scarce and many of the weaker members of the band were beginning to show the effects of continued shortage of food. So we moved southwest to the brink of a great canyon through which ran a stream which with others was to form the Yaqui River. Here we found much game, both deer and wild horses. The men organized a hunt, from which they returned with plenty of venison and wild horse meat. Others went off and drove in some cattle.

Our camp was on the eastern edge of this deep gorge, which with its vertical cliffs seemed to be impassable for some distance north and southwest of us. Nevertheless a small portion of the canyon could be crossed, the men said, but with great difficulty and danger especially to our livestock. The wild Indians, and our experienced leaders, who knew where to find paths down the cliff, seemed to be confident of getting across whenever it was necessary.

Bound For The Yaqui River

We camped on the brink of this canyon for quite a time, far from our enemies and in no danger. Our leaders were not satisfied, however. Soon they began to get restless and anxious to move deeper into the mountains. They were like true creatures of the wild, always sensing or anticipating danger. We got busy packing up our few possessions then started down the precipitous walls of the gorge. We were cautioned especially about not dislodging loose rocks, always a danger to those who were ahead on the trail. The descent was made slowly and in a zig-zag course. It took us nearly a whole day to cross the canyon but I doubt if many people, especially with women and children, could have made it at all.

That night we camped on the opposite ridge, getting a good rest after our difficult and dangerous journey. In the morning we moved westward toward the Yaqui River. It was a rough route through canyon after canyon. Finally we came to another tributary of the Yaqui and at length to the river itself. Here we pitched our camp on the east bank while the men spent several days looking for a place to ford the stream. Eventually we got across and again camped on a ridge. We enjoyed this move in spite of the great difficulty in crossing the river because now we felt absolutely safe from further pursuit by our treacherous friends the Mexicans.

As usual we kept on moving from place to place. We now were headed west into less mountainous country. Eventually we camped near a little town or hacienda near the Yaqui River satisfied that we were well out of danger.

Our peaceful days were not to last long. Already our leaders were planning a raid on a town some 15 miles away from our camp. Geronimo asked me to go with him as his assistant. I decided to do so. I was now old enough to learn to be a warrior, and the way to learn was to go on several raids with an experienced man, taking care of his horses and equipment, standing guard, and cooking his

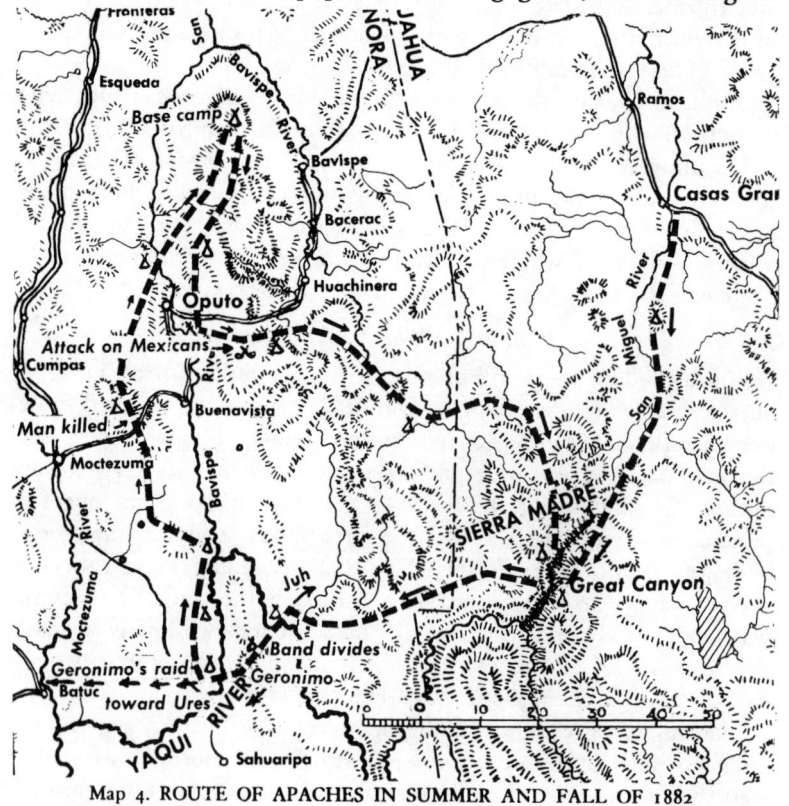

Map 4. ROUTE OF APACHES IN SUMMER AND FALL OF 1882

meat for him. That was the Apache custom. No young man was to be trusted with weapons until he had served a long apprenticeship and was judged to be fully qualified. As a result of this system our warriors, though never numerous, were extremely capable and resourceful. They had been fully trained and tested. Now I was to get my chance.

Several other young beginners went along on this raid. Arriving near the ranch our warriors sent a small party to scout out the situation and find out if there were any soldiers at the hacienda. They came back to report that there were a great number of soldiers there. So it was decided to let this ranch alone.

Just as this decision was made we saw a whole company of soldiers behind us on a high hill. We scattered like quail and hid among the briars and rocks. The soldiers marched behind a little knob whereupon we ran to the other side of it. Before we disappeared the soldiers saw us and opened fire. Though no harm resulted I was filled with great fear and trembling. It made me wonder how many times in the future I would have to run like this with the bullets zipping past.

To the wild Indians this was a small incident, just the beginning of a campaign. But I wasn't sure that I was going to enjoy going on the warpath!

Somewhat uneasy over the fact that there were so many soldiers in the town our leaders kept scouts on the high hills watching for threatening movements by the enemy. This was one of my jobs. We younger Indians were usually required to stand close guard over the camp during the night. Early in the mornings and in the daytime we were on lookout duty a mile or so from camp.

The Band Divides

About this time a difference of opinion arose among the leaders. There was no hard feeling about it. Chief Juh and some of his people wanted to retreat back into the heart of the Sierra Madres where there was good shelter and refuge. Our enemies could scarcely follow us into such almost impassable regions. Chief Juh knew more about those mountains than any other man. A highly capable leader, he was particularly liked by his own band. Therefore he thought that he ought to lead his group, as well as other Indians who had no one to look after them, into that hideout. Everyone agreed that this was a sensible plan.

But Geronimo, Chihuahua, Kaahtenny, and others wanted to go west and north on a rough and dangerous expedition. It was ad-

APACHE CAMP PACKED READY TO MOVE

mitted that this would be no journey for the weak. The men who sided with Geronimo were mostly our kinsmen, so mother and I decided to go with them. Geronimo asked us not to go but we insisted, stating that we preferred hardship to safety.

There were about eighty of us—men, women, and children—who chose to go with Geronimo. There were also three or four white boys and Mexicans who had been captured during Victorio's campaign of a few years before and who already had been adopted into the tribe. In my judgment the warriors who made up our party were the pick of the fighting men of the whole Apache tribe. All of them had seen much action in battle.

When we were ready to move west, farewells were said to those who were going with Juh. As we pulled out, they were still in camp.

The first day we made good time in spite of traversing very rough country. A few miles out we crossed a road which ran to a ranch but soon afterwards a heavy rain fell, washing out our tracks. After making 10 miles or so we came again to the Yaqui River. Our leaders were anxious to get across and camp on the other side before the river crested from the recent rain. It is a good thing that we did cross that evening because during the night the river rose to a mighty flood. We spent an uncomfortable night on account of our wet clothes and blankets.

When we camped that night we drove our horses and mules two

miles farther down the river and tethered them there. The reason for this was that if an enemy should be following he would spot the trail of the animals and would not notice our camp. Then we packed everything on our backs, climbed up the mountainside to the summit, and made camp there. By such measures we usually escaped surprise in our camps.

We stayed in this camp on the mountaintop for several days. The men talked over plans for invading the southwestern part of the State of Sonora. Geronimo, who never forgot what the people of that state had done to his family, carried that bitterness in his heart all his life.

A Raid Into Sonora

Preparations for the raid deep into Sonora consisted of making extra pairs of moccasins, cleaning our hair, sharpening knives, and cleaning and greasing guns. We had no tomahawks, arrows, or spears. The Apaches never did have tomahawks and by 1882 arrows and spears were rarely used.

We established most of the young boys, women, and children on top of the mountain where they could keep a good lookout and take care of themselves. Mother and I went with the men at least part of the way. Our job was to bring back stolen beeves to our camp so that the women and children would have plenty to eat while the men were away.

After crossing a mountain range we bivouacked for the night. The next morning our leaders told us to travel close together because of the dense timber, briars, and cactus. The trip was to be dangerous and difficult; it would be almost impossible to travel at night. We were nearly among the enemy now but kept on going to the vicinity of the nearest town. Then our men began scouting around for horses and mules while mother and I, together with five young boys, waited on a hill top where we could see the surrounding country and watch out for signs of the enemy.

After a long and anxious wait, toward evening we were relieved to see our men coming, driving some horses. It had been a risky adventure for us. Even one Mexican cowboy spotting us would have meant serious trouble, we being without weapons.

The next day the men killed several head of cattle, which we cut up and loaded on horses. Late in the afternoon mother and I, together with five boys, started back toward the rest of our band. We traveled part of the night through the thick timber. In the morning we resumed our journey, our horses heavily laden with meat, arriving late in the afternoon within sight of camp. Some of the women came out to help us carry in the beef. As we climbed up the mountainside we were very careful not to leave tracks that would show. After we got to camp and unloaded the animals some of the boys drove the horses down to the river away from camp. We now had enough dried beef to last us for at least a month.

Meantime our men went on west to where a main road passed between several towns, south toward Ures, the then capital of Sonora. Where the road ran along the river through the timber was the locality in which the Apaches were accustomed to lie in wait for travelers especially pack trains laden with drygoods.

Our men were gone about fifteen days. Meanwhile we lived very quietly at camp. One day a woman standing in front of her tepee saw a white object approaching us in the distance. The women and children immediately became very excited and fearful, thinking that the enemy were coming. Two of us boys going out to investigate found that it was our warriors coming home with great quantites of dry goods, bolts of cloth and wearing apparel. When they arrived at the foot of the mountain they called up to us whereupon all the people in camp hurried down to meet them. We surely were glad to see them and they to see us. One thing we *didn't* see was scalps. The Apaches did not practice the custom of scalping a fallen enemy. There may have been exceptions to this but they were very, very rare. Concerning Geronimo I never knew him to bring in a scalp. Much nonsense has been written about this.

After our warriors returned, we hiked farther up the Yaqui River, camped for awhile, then again moved upstream. Here we had plenty of food and nothing to worry about. Nevertheless we were very careful not to disclose our presence because we were quite near a number of Mexican towns. Every day our men stationed lookouts on the hills. Our camp at this time was at the junction of the Bavispe and Yaqui Rivers.

The leaders decided to raid toward the northwest. This time we started off on foot leaving all the animals in the valley near the Bavispe River where there was plenty of good grass. We concealed in caves our saddles and the loot which the men had brought back from the earlier raid, as well as all our camp gear which we could not carry on our backs. We took only one mule, my big mule, on which Geronimo's wife and baby rode.

Our band moved straight west toward a Mexican town. Just when it appeared that we were going right on into the village the leaders stopped a few miles to the east. The plan was to avoid stealing any horses or mules while we were sneaking around in between these towns, two of which lay to the west and one to the east of our route.

From the last campsite the band turned northwest toward the mountains. Since we were about to cross the main road we were especially careful not to be seen or leave any sign that would put the soldiers on our trail. Our men knew that each town contained a garrison of troops. So we carefully covered our tracks.

We camped at the foot of a mountain a few miles from the road running between Buenavista and Moctezuma. Early next morning Geronimo told the men that they could now go out to look for horses and mules. They should drive in all that they could find, as we needed them for the expected move north into the mountains. About noon our men drove in quite a number of animals stolen from the Mexicans. We had a great time roping them and breaking them for the women and children to ride. My cousin roped a mule but it broke away from him. I chased it out into the prairie for nearly two miles. I nearly went too far. Suddenly I saw Mexican soldiers only a short distance away.

As I galloped back to the group of Apaches I heard my cousin shouting to me to hurry up, the enemy were coming along behind me. Meanwhile the Indians were taking up a position from which to attack the soldiers. As I sped over a low ridge I heard the shooting start. The Indians charged so fast toward the enemy that they failed to notice one soldier who was hiding in the bushes. This man shot and killed the last Apache to ride by him. The warriors, hearing the shot, came dashing back just in time to shoot the Mexican.

The band felt dreadfully sad over losing a warrior. He was a Warm Springs Apache who had no near relatives in the band with us.

Late that afternoon we started off to the west then camped at the foot of the mountains for supper. While we were thus engaged, a sentinel ran in to report that the enemy were at the skirmish ground of that afternoon, not far behind us. We moved out hastily into the foothills where we remained in concealment during the night. In the morning we saw the soldiers following our tracks and approaching our hill. At once the warriors took up positions ready for a fight. But the Mexicans didn't attempt to follow our trail up the mountainside.

Finally our men got tired of waiting, so we moved on, traveling very fast right on into the night. We came to a short steep canyon where we made camp and enjoyed a good night's rest.

In the morning we set a course across the wide valley of the Bavispe. Although our horses and mules were in good shape we traveled slowly, enjoying the trip and the pleasant surroundings. That night we camped beside the Bavispe River. The chiefs told the men not to shoot any deer because the Mexicans might hear the firing.

This country looked as though it belonged to us. For some days owing to the wise leadership of Geronimo we had not been disturbed by an enemy. We crossed the river and moved through the woods discussing the fact that the country seemed to be full of deer and other game. In fact the deer just stood and watched us pass. It seemed that they had never been disturbed by anyone hunting them. A person living in this favored spot would never have to go hungry. There were plenty of wild animals and other food, easily obtainable. But at this time the men all obeyed Geronimo and didn't fire a shot. Besides, we still had plenty of dried beef.

Arriving at our next objective we again settled down for an indefinite stay. It was just like peacetime. We had plenty to eat, good clothing taken from the stolen stocks, and no enemies nearby. We were about thirty miles southeast of Fronteras.

During this period the women, assisted by some of the boys, were gathering and drying the fruit of the yucca, preparing for a winter to be spent in the Sierras. It was in the late summer or early fall of 1882.

Only one incident disturbed our quiet. One day hearing an uproar in camp I saw a man and a woman running away. The man was a San Carlos Apache whose wife was a Chiricahua. They had decided to return to the safety of the San Carlos agency. The girl's father was so enraged that he told the men to hunt them down and shoot them both. An unsuccessful search was made for the couple but they succeeded in getting clear away, eventually making their way back to San Carlos.

A Raid Into The United States

At a council the men planned an invasion of southern Arizona. The reason for this was that all the guns used by the warriors were of U. S. manufacture, fairly modern. No ammunition for these was obtainable in Mexico, so it was necessary to make a raid into the United States to get some cartridges.

All able-bodied men participated in this raid. I wanted very badly to go along but the men refused to take any inexperienced young men or boys. It was to be a hard and dangerous trip, the group moving long distances at great speed and in constant danger from the troops. My cousin told me that I would have to stay in camp to look after my mother and sister. Besides, there was a lot of sentry duty and other work to be performed.

After the men had departed in a northwesterly direction we moved camp to a new location at the foot of the mountain where there was plenty of water and abundant supplies of wild fruit to be put up for the winter. We lived here quite contentedly, when one morning I heard a shot fired down the creek about a mile west of camp. At once the women and children were thrown into a panic. We had no protection and thought the enemy might be coming. Everyone ran from the camp and hid in the hills. From here we could see two men approaching our camp. Soon we learned that they were some of our own warriors returning from the raid. They had started back before the main body in order to bring a young man who had been wounded. He had died on the way. One of these men now took charge of our camp greatly relieving our anxiety.

After a long time we moved further south to a place which had been designated as the rendezvous where we were to meet the returning war party. We arrived in good order and camped for several days when a messenger came in and told us to move down nearer the Bavispe River. Next day about noon, as we had just completed this move, we saw our warriors approaching. They had had a very successful raid, securing great quantities of ammunition also many articles useful for camp life.

That same night our leaders planned a big victory dance, which was customary when warriors returned with spoils from a successful foray. Soon we heard the beating of tom-toms and saw the women and girls gathering on the outer circle. The men were singing at the top of their voices rejoicing over their victories. Then the women began choosing their partners for the all-night dance. In the morning the men made valuable presents to their partners, things such as horses, saddles, bridles, blankets, or other useful articles.

We camped here for several days giving the men a chance to get a good rest before moving back into the Sierra Madres. Then we started southward along the Bavispe River, camping here and there for several days until we came near to the town of Oputo. Here we divided into two groups, one going eastward into the Sierra Madres the other continuing on toward Oputo. Most of the older Indians went due east while we younger ones under Geronimo marched south along the foot of the mountains until we passed Oputo. Here we stopped for the night. The next morning the men went out looking for horses, driving in several head. Then we hiked over the mountains, stopping for the night on the east side of the range.

In the morning we moved on again, very cautiously because we were crossing the main road between Bavispe and Oputo. We com-

NEAR OPUTO

pleted this stage of the journey unobserved by Mexicans and went right on into the mountains where we came upon the trail of the other group of Indians. About sunset we met some men who were returning from the raid after horses. We then moved for about a mile south, where we camped for the night.

That night Geronimo told us that Mexican soldiers were on our trail. He prophesied as to the exact moment they would appear. The next morning the women and children were, as usual, on the mountain top while the men were watching the back trail. Sure enough just as Geronimo had predicted Mexican soldiers appeared in the very place and at the exact time that Geronimo had foretold. The Mexicans went on to the creek then retraced their steps toward Oputo. Our warriors followed and attacked them at about sunset. Our men captured all the enemy's horses and did considerable other damage. Some of this group went on down the river near its junction with the Yaqui to bring back the articles we had hidden in the cave.

While our main band was camped on the hillside our sentinels sighted our warriors returning with the booty obtained in the fight with the Mexicans. Soon we heard the beating of tom-toms and a great triumphal dance commenced. One of the most comical acts in this pageant was put on by a young Mexican member of our band and an Apache woman who dressed like a Mexican. They paraded around, the man with a gun over his shoulder like a Mexican soldier, the woman acting like a señorita. It was a gay and jolly occasion.

A few days later we followed the group that had been ahead of us. Our way led through a forest where the pines were so thick on the canyon floor that we couldn't see the trail ahead. Finally we crossed a clearing about two miles long then plunged again into the dense pine woods. It was a tiresome day for us all especially for the horses in forcing their way through the thickets.

Next morning when we were ready to start again we were pleased over the arrival of our warriors who had gone down to the cave to recover our cache of horses and drygoods. We remained in camp all that day to give them a chance to rest.

Next day we all started out through the pines until we again reached the brink of the great canyon, where we pitched our camp.

The Two Bands Reunite

The band who under Juh had gone into the heart of the Sierra Madres now arrived and camped on the opposite side of the canyon. Some of our group made their way across while some of them came over to see us. It was a very happy time for us all, exchanging presents and reminiscences. We could hear their tom-toms at night across the canyon and I expect they could hear ours. The bands were celebrating the safe return and reunion.

We learned that Chief Juh and his band had had at least one encounter with the Mexicans. On this occasion the warriors had been skirmishing with Mexican troops for two days. Finally their ammunition was almost exhausted. The soldiers still followed them, so the Indians made a plain zig-zag trail up a steep mountain to a point just below the summit where the trail ran parallel to the ridge line. Here is what that wily old chief, Juh, devised against the enemy: He had the men roll a line of big rocks into place along the trail, ready to be dislodged down the mountainside. The warriors took their positions as the enemy appeared on a ridge across the ravine. The Indians were well concealed with brush, grass, and leaves. They lay there motionless but impatient for the Mexicans to get within the danger zone. The latter confidently marched up the zig-zag trail. When they reached the summit the Apache warriors sprang out and attacked them. The Mexicans started to withdraw down the mountainside whereupon at Juh's command the Indians began rolling the great boulders down upon them. Some of these rocks were so big that they knocked down pine trees. Many soldiers were crushed by the tumbling boulders and falling trees. Not many escaped.

After the rocks had stopped rolling and all was silence except for a few groans the Indians went down and gathered up the Mexicans' guns and ammunition. As a consequence the survivors among the troops marched home without weapons. But the Indians didn't bother them further.

Not one of Chief Juh's warriors was lost in this battle. Geronimo and our band had lost two during the summer.

We decided to cross the canyon to join Juh's people. As before the trip took all day and again it was very difficult and dangerous. In many places the cliffs were several hundred feet high, and as always there was the danger from falling rocks. Although Apaches had been killed and injured a number of times during trips such as this, we didn't have any accidents this time. We made our camp on the eastern edge of the great canyon where we remained all winter. The only unusual happening was when one of our Apaches, a man named She-neah, suddenly decided to shoot the lone Navajo who had been with Geronimo all this time. The Navajo while previously serving as a U. S. scout had killed one of She-neah's relatives. As usual the Apache never forgot nor forgave, so without warning She-neah killed the Navajo. We were all sorry that this happened but no one did anything about it.

Chapter 10

EXPEDITION AGAINST GALEANA

After spending several weeks beside the great canyon in the Sierras our chiefs held a council at which they decided to move against Galeana. After camp was broken we started to move by easy stages toward our objective. When within about thirty miles southwest of Galeana we stopped for four days to celebrate a Fire Dance. We hadn't had one of these tribal affairs since leaving San Carlos. It was fascinating to watch and to participate in. Sometimes the Fire Dance had been held when there was an epidemic in the tribe, in order to drive out the contagion.

After a gay time at the dance the tribe again moved nearer Galeana. We camped in a valley some twenty miles southwest of the town, and here the tom-toms started up again. The chiefs were staging a war dance which was quite similar to the one I described in Chapter 1.

Young Indian boys who wanted to become warriors had to practice this dance as if it were a real battle. In this way they gained much skill. Of course the other way to learn to fight was to go with the warriors on an expedition and watch closely how the experienced men behaved in action against an enemy. But the war dance was considered to be an excellent preparation.

When the dance was over we moved to the north side of the mountain range where we camped for the night. A council met that night to make plans for the next day. The leaders decided to send a few men toward Galeana as decoys. They were to be well armed and mounted on fast horses. Their object was to steal horses right outside the town and thus draw out the soldiers. Meantime the main band would be waiting in a concealed position to attack the enemy.

Fight Near Galeana

The next day everything went according to plan. Warriors were assigned in groups to take post concealed at intervals all along the ravine that paralleled the road. The main body was in ambush in a

GALEANA

depression, as shown on my accompanying sketch, while the women and children watched from the mountainside.

The volunteers who were acting as decoys rode up close to Galeana and started driving several Mexican horses along the road leading northwest toward Casas Grandes. In a few minutes a small troop of Mexican soldiers came riding out of Galeana in hot pursuit. The decoys kept ahead of them just out of range. As the Mexicans swept past the ravine our detachments hidden there came out and began attacking the enemy from the rear. Then when the Mexicans were within range of our main body they were heavily fired upon from their front whereupon they swerved off the road toward a little rocky hill north of the highway. Their commander saw that they were nearly surrounded and had been decoyed too far, maybe eight miles from the safety of Galeana. He dismounted his men on the hill where they hastily began piling up loose rocks to form a breastwork.

Meantime the Indians rode behind another knoll four hundred yards west of where the Mexicans were fortifying their position. Here they dismounted and turned their horses over to a few apprentices. I was one of the latter. We horseholders were able to peer over the hill and watch the whole attack from short range.

The Indians sneaked among the rocks to the foot of the enemy's hill, near which stood a single cedar tree. They started crawling up the slope firing at the Mexicans, who returned the fire. For protection against the Mexican bullets each Indian rolled ahead of himself a round rock about the size of his head.

At the same time a group of eight young men who always fought together as a group volunteered to circle to the north so as to attack the enemy in rear. They slipped unobserved around to the opposite side of the hill from the main group of attackers.

The older men, like Geronimo and Juh, together with the best marksmen, stayed near the cedar tree during this encircling maneuver. Some of them fired rapidly on the enemy to keep the latter from taking notice of the fact that other Indians were getting around the north flank. On the whole, however, the Indians were saving their ammunition at this time while the Mexicans did most of the firing.

Both Apache groups continued to work their way up the hill, pushing rocks ahead of themselves. Finally when the attackers were within a few feet of the crest of the hill the man who was leading the attack of the encircling group looked back to see how his men were coming. Just at that moment he saw his cousin She-neah raise up to fire through an opening between two rocks. As he did so a Mexican bullet struck She-neah on top of the head making a furrow from front to rear in his scalp and skull. He was not killed outright but died later. At that, the leader was so enraged that he screamed the order for the final attack. The men jumped up and went right in on the Mexicans. When the main group on the south side of the hill saw this they rushed in too. In the brief hand-to-hand fight that followed, all Mexicans but one were killed. This one managed to flee toward Galeana.

Geronimo shouted, "Let him go! He will tell the rest of the soldiers in the town what has happened whereupon more Mexicans will come out to the rescue. In that way we can destroy other soldiers."

We lost two men in this fight. One was a well-loved Warm Springs Apache named She-sauson, a very promising young warrior of whom we were very proud. The other was the old-time brave, She-neah. He was the one who had killed the Navajo in camp, when we were staying on the brink of the great canyon.

The Mexican dead included their commander, a major, and twenty-one men. We were all the more pleased later when we heard a report that this officer had been in immediate command of the enemy who killed Victorio and his band in 1881.

It was now late in the afternoon. Soon we saw coming from the

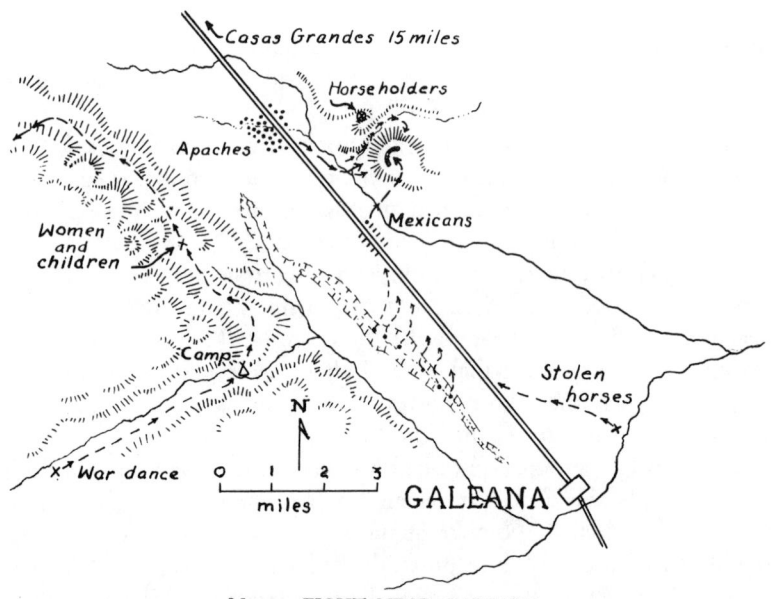

Map 5. FIGHT NEAR GALEANA

direction of Galeana another company of soldiers. They stopped about a mile away. We mounted up and rode toward the Mexicans until we noticed that the enemy had stopped and were digging holes for defense. As it was now nearly sunset and the enemy position seemed to be strong, Geronimo decided not to attack. The day's fight had been a hard one, but we had been completely victorious, so the leaders said, "Let's go back to see how the women and children are getting along." We stayed on a hill until about dark watching the soldiers digging their trench, then rode to where the women and children were camped on the mountainside. It was a great victory for us but there was no triumphal dance on account of the fact that two of our men had been killed. Indians frequently omit the victory celebration if they have suffered any losses.

That evening while our leaders were planning to move southwest along the foot of the mountain, word came in from some of our scouts that Mexican soldiers were coming toward us from Casas Grandes. At once we got so excited and confused that we took off at a fast rate toward the main range of mountains. It was nearly midnight before we stopped to rest. The next morning we crossed the range when, feeling safe once more, we pitched our camp for a longer stay.

Chapter 11

WE INVADE SONORA

After several days of peaceful camping, the chiefs and other prominent fighting men began to get restless once more. Chief Juh and his followers were anxious to get back into the heart of the Sierra Madres. Geronimo's group preferred the less mountainous country. More than half the entire Apache band, including the older people and those who depended on others for help, went with Juh.

We who had more confidence in Geronimo went with him and subchief Chihuahua toward the southwest where the country was not so rugged. For several months we camped near the headwaters of the Bavispe River. No enemy bothered us, and we were very comfortable with plenty of good water, firewood, and game in the vicinity. During our pleasant stay in this area the men were discussing plans for making raids into the southwest.

Raiding Toward Ures

Full preparations were made for an extremely hard journey. Some of the young boys had never experienced such fast traveling through rough country as was now planned for us. A few old men were to remain in camp as a guard for the women and children. I was one of those who was going on the expedition. My cousin, an experienced older man named Beneactiney, was going too and I knew that he would look after me.

Leaving our families we marched straight west, taking again the old war trail which we ourselves had made during the previous fall of 1882. (See Map 6) The first day we made thirty miles, stopping for a night's rest at a point near the end of the Sierra Madre range. The following day we marched nearly to the Bavispe River south of Oputo. Early the next morning we waded the river and moved close to the mountains, where we located some cattle. We chased these on foot, catching several and killing them with butcher knives. In this way we saved ammunition, which Apaches always conserved carefully. But it took some fast running.

We continued moving in rapid stages in a southwesterly direction

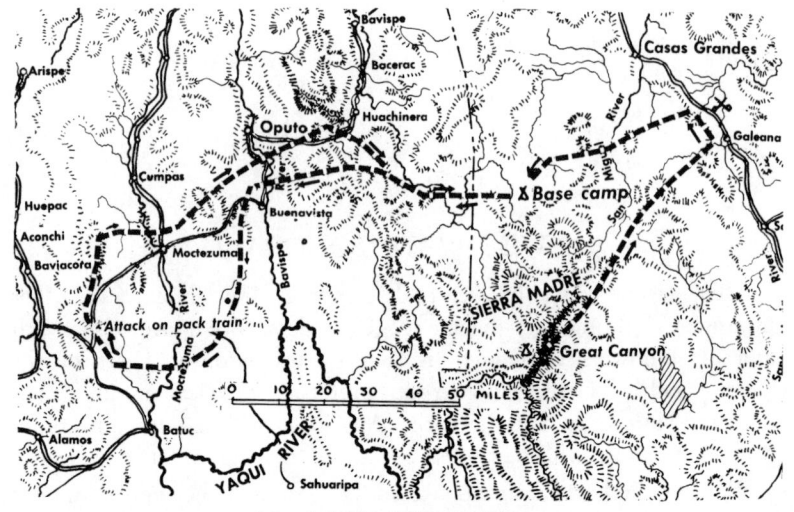

Map 6. RAID INTO SONORA

until we had crossed the road which ran between Buenavista and Moctezuma.

After a good night's sleep a few miles east of the road Geronimo took the lead early the following morning. He started to trot, maintaining this pace for miles. Every man had to be in good shape to keep up this kind of travel. A little after noon Geronimo stopped for a breather while others of us kept on going until we came to a little hill where a year ago mother and I had waited for the raiding group to come back with horses. After a very short rest we started toward another river. Eight or ten of the younger warriors were running as if they were in a race but I was right up with them. When we came to the brink of the canyon through which the river was flowing we saw other members of the band down below us chasing cattle. They were still able to do this even after having run most of the day! So we had beef to eat again that night.

Geronimo with a few men didn't reach camp until late in the night. Chihuahua and his party didn't come until morning; and some others, for whom the running was too much, didn't show up at all.

The next morning after crossing some mountains we came to the road which ran between several Mexican towns northeast of Ures. This was the area in which our men usually laid in wait for pack trains. We saw several small parties of Mexicans moving on the road but no pack trains. After much patient waiting we saw coming out

[98]

of the woods two heavily laden burros. This appeared to be the head of a column. Our men prepared to attack.

I was about a hundred yards to the rear. As soon as I heard the firing I hurried forward to the highway where I found that our men had just captured a whole pack train.

We drove the burros across the river where we unloaded them and helped ourselves to the drygoods and other articles which were needed by our band in the main camp.

The same night we started rapidly back toward the base camp, our object in the raid having been accomplished. This journey would require several days, as we were now mounted. In that rough country the Apaches actually made better time on foot than when mounted. The first night we passed east of Baviacora, where we knew that a large number of Mexican soldiers were stationed. So we kept on going the rest of the night eventually arriving on top of the mountains where we stopped for a day of rest and sleep.

We saw no enemy, although we suspected that they might be aware of our presence in the neighborhood. Having dodged between the inhabited areas at night, however, we weren't too greatly worried about being observed.

Just before sunset we started east down the mountainside then took the whole night to cross a wide valley in which several towns were situated. We knew that there was a garrison in each town. This kind of traveling in pitch darkness was difficult for a young fellow like me occupied as I was with driving eight or ten captured horses. I had no help and for a time was lost but kept right on driving the animals as fast as I could. Just before we came to the Moctezuma River I caught up with the main party. Was I glad to see them!

I could hardly believe we could get across this river. It appeared to run through walls of solid rock. Also we were not far from Moctezuma. Nevertheless we made it safely. We had been going due east, but now Geronimo and Chihuahua, after consulting among themselves, agreed that we had better turn northeast toward the mountains once more. At about daylight we arrived at the foot of the ridge and climbed up a very steep slope. At the summit we stopped to rest and sleep during that day. From here we could look back over our route for many miles. No enemy seemed to be following us.

Late in the afternoon we packed up again and started down toward the Bavispe River, which we crossed between the towns of Buenavista and Oputo. In a few days we would be home. How happy we would be to see our families!

The rest of the trip was a hard one for me, driving the animals, but one day I was thrilled to have Chief Chihuahua compliment me for my good work. Some of the men began teasing me at this, especially because one of the animals in my herd was carrying two 50-pound cakes of sugar. They claimed that I was getting into the sweets.

Finally we had just one more road to cross, the one that ran between Bavispe and Oputo. This was particularly dangerous because each of these towns had a large military garrison. Since there was some fear that these troops might block our path we used especial caution in moving in this area.

In the morning while we were packing our horses and getting ready to move out, our leaders sent scouts to the north and south. When we had traveled some distance we stopped to wait for them to catch up. They came in to report that we were not being followed. Leaving two men behind as a rear guard and sending four ahead as an advance party we moved rapidly to the southeast until we came to the west end of the Sierra Madres. Now we were in the thick timber. After several miles we came to our own outgoing trail, which led toward our base camp. That night was the last bivouac before we reached the main band.

Early in the morning Chihuahua and another man were sent ahead to get in touch with the women and children, whom they found camping in groups in different localities. Chihuahua said that he had no trouble in locating them, as when he rode up on top of a hill and shouted loudly they all came running to him and guided him to camp. The women and children, eager to see their menfolk, began preparing a big welcoming feast.

As the rest of us were getting to start that last day's march Geronimo called out, "Are you all ready? Keep in line, close together, as we move on." Crossing several low ridges we arrived at camp amid great rejoicing on the part of all.

About sunset we heard a man in camp call, "Tie up!" This meant for the musicians to tie on the heads of their tom-toms. Soon we heard the beat of the drums and a man calling to everyone to come to the dance. This triumph dance gave the Apaches their greatest excitement and pleasure in those days, because it was a reward for and a recognition of their bravery and the hardships and danger they had gone through successfully while on a raid. As a member of the raiding party I was invited to assemble with the warriors in the center of the circle. The musicians sang the triumph song to honor those of us who were on the raid. I always was full of rejoicing on these occasions not only because I had come through without harm

SOME OF THE ENEMY WERE KILLED

but also because of my tremendous pride in being allowed to accompany the warriors and share their dangers. Although I was still considered to be only a boy, I was strong, in good health, and as a fast runner was well able to keep up with the men on their hazardous trips. So why should I have stayed hiding in camp with the women and children during those exciting days?

This raid was the first experience I had had in being separated from my mother and sister for a long time, so we were especially happy to see each other.

Again I must tell you that, although some of the enemy were killed on this raid, we brought back no scalps, for scalping was not an Apache custom.

What Happened To Chief Juh's Band

Our group continued to live in this part of Mexico for several months, moving occasionally, and finally going back to that favorite spot on the brink of the big canyon. Meantime we had heard nothing of Chief Juh and his band. One day we heard that they had been attacked by Mexicans early one morning, losing quite a few women and children captured and a number killed and wounded. Chief Juh's wife had been killed and his only daughter seriously wounded. This was hard on the chief though he still had three sons.

As the Mexicans were leaving the scene with their prisoners the Apaches attacked them, in the course of which fight two more Apaches, considered to be among the best warriors, were killed.

Now Chief Juh's people were in bad circumstances owing to the heavy loss of women and children as well as much of their belongings. This incident led to much dissatisfaction in the band, who began to quarrel among themselves. Some of the men worked up so much bad feeling against Juh that they refused to do sentry duty. This continual quarreling brought much sadness to the band.

Meanwhile our own band under Geronimo were enjoying excellent health, quiet, and good feeling among the various families.

One day Juh's band arrived at the canyon edge where we were camped. Our hearts filled with sorrow over their plight. But we had the satisfaction of knowing that our warrior strength had now received reinforcements. We had upward of 80 fighting men not counting the young apprentices like myself who could be relied upon to assist the warriors in many ways.

Further Raids

Our warriors were not satisfied to live in peace. Already they were planning further raids against the Mexicans. Once more the war preparations were under way—cleaning and greasing rifles, making new moccasins and shirts, and plaiting good rawhide ropes.

Our party under Geronimo and Chihuahua again planned to go toward Ures and even farther south while Chatto and Benito proposed a raid north into Arizona and southwestern New Mexico.

Preparations being complete we were ready to move at a moment's notice, when we heard Geronimo giving the orders to march. He and Chihuahua took the lead, moving westward over our old war trail past the end of the Sierra Madres. After the first night's stop our two groups separated, Geronimo's and Chihuahua's continuing toward the Bavispe River while Chatto and Benito with their men headed north toward the United States.

Those of us under Geronimo made easy stages, stopping occasionally to kill cattle and to rest. As we passed a few miles southwest of Baviacora we thought that we had been observed by the people in a Mexican farm near where we had crossed the Sonora River. Therefore we picked up speed and went up the mountain. Stopping at noon for lunch and a little rest we looked back along our trail. Sure enough there were some Mexican soldiers following us. We sneaked down the mountain into the timber and headed in the direction of Ures. We succeeded in evading our pursuers by recrossing the river and taking an irregular route southward. Although some of this country was familiar owing to our previous expedition, much of it was unknown to us younger men and boys.

No pack trains, the principal objective of our raid, had been seen so far. The rapid traveling continued. But by now we all had very hard muscles and good wind, so we didn't mind it at all. Nevertheless our chiefs decided to steal some horses to ride. They got a few though not enough for everyone to be mounted. We were now getting into the more thickly settled part of Sonora. Soon more horses were stolen, after which we all were riding bareback.

After further difficult night marching we turned southwest down a valley until we came to a well where we watered our horses then continued a little farther to a ranch. Our warriors attacked here, killing a number of persons. From then on during the day we attacked every village we came to, capturing household articles and cloth but not killing very many people.

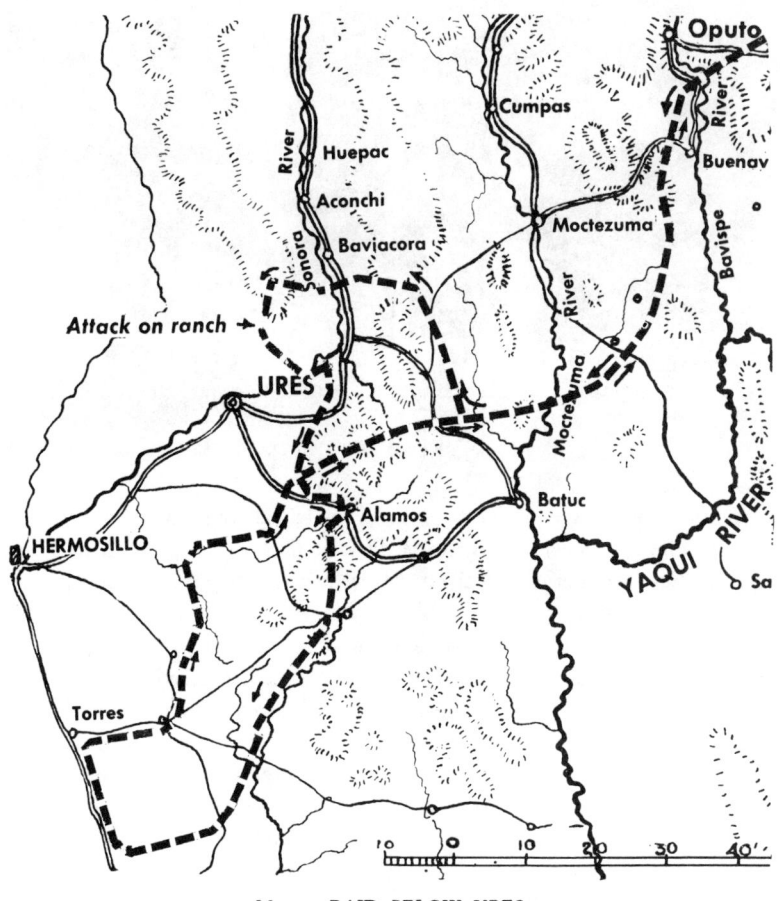

Map 7. RAID BELOW URES

East of the Moctezuma River Geronimo followed the Old Trail

[103]

NEAR URES

About sunset we arrived in good order at the day's rendezvous point. The night was going to be dark at first so we stopped to graze our horses and get some sleep while waiting for the moon to rise. However we were all famished for water as were the animals. One old man in the party, who had been all over this part of the country, said that there was a well about ten miles farther on. So as soon as the moon appeared we continued on toward this well. The route ran through thick briars and cactus. When we were a mile from the well two men went ahead to investigate while we waited anxiously. After nearly an hour we heard a mountain lion (one of the advance party) calling from the direction of the well. One of us answered with the same howl. Then, hardly able to wait for water, we hurried on to the well. As it was a very deep one, it took a long time to draw enough water for all of us and our horses. We also filled some skin sacks with water so that we wouldn't run short during the rest of the trip through this dry part of the country.

Early in the morning we arrived back on the road. Most of the men changed horses so as to be able to keep going at great speed. After following the road for three miles we approached a town, probably Alamos. We were riding in column of twos just like cavalry, with Geronimo and Chihuahua at the front. Two Mexicans appeared on a hill just ahead of us. They stopped for a moment to stare at us then seeing that we were hostile Indians they turned and galloped madly back toward town.

Now the fun began. We chased these Mexicans into the town, where all the inhabitants climbed up on the flat roofs of their houses. Geronimo ordered us to form a line outside the walls, facing the village. We stayed in this position for a few moments staring at the Mexicans cowering on their rooftops and jeering at them then turned off to the southwest. We could see them watching us fearfully while we watered our horses in the nearby creek. Then we went on beyond the trees lining the bank and stopped not far away to eat lunch.

Just as Geronimo was ordering us to resume the march, several Mexican soldiers were seen following our trail. Our warriors prepared an ambush for them, but the Mexicans changed their course and went in another direction.

We rode off to the mountains to the south where we found a former Indian camping ground littered with old cattle bones. We continued moving through some graveled country, thick with cactus and briars, until we came to a dry creek bed. There were several villages along this creek but we did not intend to bother them because we did not want to draw attention to the fact that we were headed for a canyon road where we hoped to encounter more pack trains.

Arriving at this road we stopped a ways off on a hill while some of the men went out to steal more horses. After a couple of moves one of our scouts came in to report that there was no chance of getting a pack train. This was discouraging news, for we had come upward of a hundred miles (by the route we had taken) southwest of Ures and were deep in enemy country. We continued to ride along into the darkness discussing what we should do. By now the moon wasn't due to rise until after midnight so we decided to bivouac in the darkness until there was enough moonlight to see better. And then there occurred a comical incident which helped lighten our spirits and which shows that everything was not hardship and grim adventure while on the warpath.

OUR WARRIORS PREPARED AN AMBUSH

Dead weary from almost continuous travel we stopped to get some rest. Chapo, Geronimo's son, unsaddled his horse and laid the saddle on a black rock. Then he lay down on the ground to get a little sleep. When the moon had come up and we were getting ready to move on, Chapo couldn't find his saddle. He couldn't even find the rock. We all stirred ourselves to help him hunt for it. Finally we found that the "rock" had walked off into the bushes carrying the saddle on its back. The rock was an armadillo! There was much hilarity in the band and Chapo came in for a lot of teasing.

By now Geronimo had decided that we might as well head back toward the Sierra Madres. So we started. Within a day or two we were backtracking generally along our outgoing trail. We passed near the point where we had had a fight with soldiers the preceding fall, taking care that the troops in this area did not pick up our trail. Soon we came to our familiar old war trail, crossed the road again between Moctezuma and Oputo where we rounded up some more cattle.

We came to the road between Oputo and Bavispe, followed it up the mountain about half way. Here we encountered a pack train. The Mexicans, opening fire on us, fled to the rocks and set up a red flag.

This red flag meant to us: "We are no friends! Come and fight us!" Now was the time for Geronimo and the other sharpshooters to show what good marksmen they were. They had long range guns, which they then used, but without effect on the Mexicans. Two Indians volunteered to slip around to the rear of the enemy and attack them from behind. In this manner we drove the Mexicans out of their stronghold and captured the pack train.

The pack animals carried loads of drygoods and whisky as well as blankets and other desired articles. My partner and I got one pack containing drygoods as our share of the loot. Everyone seemed to be satisfied with his portion. We loaded up and marched three miles to a place where we camped for the night. Many of the older men now proceeded to get drunk. As a result some of us young fellows had to go out and stand sentry duty during the night, for we felt that the older men in their drunkenness would leave our camp unguarded. Whenever the Apache can get whisky he loses all caution and restraint.

Next morning many of the men looked to be pretty tired and some of them were sick. We packed up and received orders to march. The leaders howled out, "Head for the Sierra Madres." Geronimo and Chihuahua, again in the lead, remembered to send out scouts. Soon we were following our old familiar trail. When we reached the top of the mountains we were met by a couple of men from base camp who gave us the sad news that my cousin Beneactiney, who had gone with Chatto and Benito, had been killed.

My cousin was one of the bravest men of our band, the son-in-law of subchief Chihuahua. After we had learned of his death, Chihuahua came over and laid a hand on my shoulder saying, "Young man, don't grieve too much over the loss of this beloved relative of ours. He was a very brave warrior."

At this time some of our party couldn't wait to get back to camp. They hurried ahead, so that when we arrived at camp the women were waiting for us. A guide met me to show me the way to my mother's lodge where I received an affectionate greeting from my mother and sister. We felt sad because we had lost the man who was the leader of our little family group. I was now the only one left to take care of us. I was not yet a full warrior, being armed only with a revolver which wouldn't be much use in a real fight with an enemy.

Several days after our return Chatto's and Benito's party came in from their raid into the United States. In addition to guns and ammunition they brought in a little white boy whom Benito had cap-

CHATTO

tured near Lordsburg. This boy, named Charlie McComas,* quickly learned to speak Apache, and was well liked and kindly treated by the Indians. The family who took him in charge behaved toward him as if he were their own boy. Charlie would have probably become a full member of the tribe had not a sad thing happened, as I will tell later.

---

*Son of Federal Judge H. C. and Mrs. McComas, both of whom were killed on the main road, now US 70, near Lordsburg.

Chapter 12

PROPHECIES OF DISASTER

After a time the leaders moved our camp a few miles northeast of the mountains to a fine pine forest. Since we were beginning to suffer a food shortage again, volunteers were sought for a raid toward Oputo to obtain cattle. Fifteen of the hardier men who responded to this call were gone several days, returning with a hundred head of cattle. These were killed and butchered the day they were driven in. We had another big feast and triumphal dance.

Our camp was on the eastern edge of a high and steep mountain in a thick grove of young oaks and tall grass, now dry and brown. A half mile from camp was a spring where we obtained water. I had just returned from having hobbled my horse in the vicinity of the spring, where there was good grazing, and was about to go to a nearby butte on sentry duty, when I heard mother calling me. She said that a grass fire had started east of the spring and was spreading.

I ran rapidly down the slope to where my horse was standing directly in the path of the fire. The flames were roaring now, seemingly thirty or forty feet high and rushing toward us behind a strong wind. By this time the smoke and heat were so intense that I wet my bandana kerchief in the spring and tied it over my mouth and nose. Then I caught hold of the horse's tail and drove him at a fast clip up the hill out of the way of the fire.

A number of young Indians in the vicinity were fleeing. By the time I got past the line of the blaze I could see people around the camp fighting the fire in an effort to save their tents. This was the most dangerous and exciting fire I ever saw.

After the fire died down we went to the spring where several tethered horses had burned to death. A great cloud of smoke was billowing high above the Sierra Madres, visible for a hundred miles in all directions especially from the southwest where our men had been on the recent raid. Therefore the base camp was moved to the mountains west of Huachinera. We greatly feared that soldiers would be coming our way, so Geronimo and Juh sent sentinels back on the trail. Early in the morning one of them reported that Mexican soldiers were coming. They were having no trouble following the broad path made by the cattle which our men had driven in to our camp.

Hastily and with great excitement we all got ready to move eastward. With the older chiefs in the lead and the rest of the warriors following behind us we scurried down the steep slope into the canyon and up the other side of the gorge. We stopped for the night, some distance beyond, while the fighting men sent back a detachment to keep a watch at the brink of the canyon.

Battle of the Canyon

Early next day a sentinel was again sent out. About noon he reported that soldiers were just starting down the steep trail on the opposite side of the canyon. Warriors rushed back to our edge of the chasm, well armed and with plenty of ammunition. The chiefs stationed them at easily defended points along the ridge. All the best fighting men were deployed astride the trail. Others were sent to a steep slope at the head of the canyon nearby with orders to prepare to roll rocks down on the enemy. This was to prevent the Mexicans from geting out of the gorge in that direction.

The Mexicans were slow to leave the stream at the bottom of the canyon and to start up the trail, which made our men restless and impatient.

Finally the head of the military column appeared. Our men let it pass our lower line of warriors who were concealed waiting for them. When the leading enemy soldiers arrived at the top of the canyon our men sprang out and opened fire. The Mexicans turned and ran back. Our men were close on their heels. Then we heard the rocks commencing to roll down into the canyon. Meanwhile our warriors were rushing right among the enemy on the trail, shooting right and left. In the confusion they even shot one of their own men.

The din in the canyon was tremendous what with the shooting, the yelling, and the crashing of huge boulders. The sound echoed and reverberated through the canyon and its side gorges. Although the soldiers outnumbered our side they lost heavily in their initial headlong retreat. Soon they turned and fought bravely, making several successive efforts to take our position by storm. Our sharpshooters from their excellent positions on the edge of the canyon were just a little too much for them.

After several hours the shooting stopped. Our men withdrew from the brink leaving a small rear guard in observation. The main party went back a couple of miles to where the women and children were camped. The soldiers did not again appear. Our rear guard reported that they had gone the way they had come. Though we were greatly

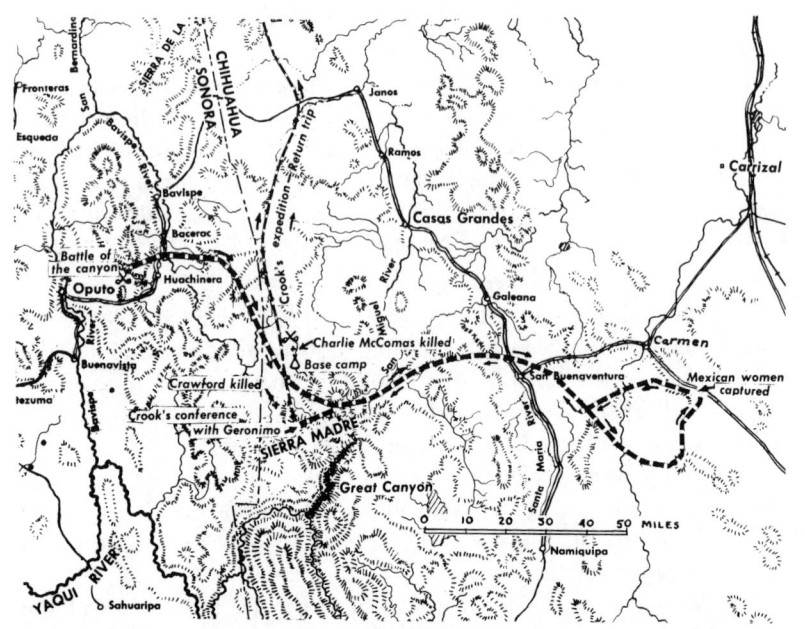

Map 8. BATTLE OF THE CANYON AND RAID TOWARD CHIHUAHUA

relieved, our leaders took no chances. They sent out parties in different directions to see if the soldiers were coming against us by some other route. Our chiefs always took good safety measures like this. That is the reason they were usually successful in evading troops.

Our band moved eastward, crossed the Bavispe River, then marched up a very steep mountain where we pitched camp under the pines.

Several days later the tom-toms beat out the invitation to another victory dance.

We enjoyed excellent health in this high mountain camp among the pine forests. We still had plenty of meat, and no enemies were near. Though we took it easy for a time the warlike spirit of the Apaches couldn't stay quiet for very long. Soon a war dance was begun to stimulate interest in a raid toward the city of Chihuahua. Many volunteers responded after which the chiefs held a big council to lay plans.

Raiding Toward Chihuahua

It was decided that the object of the raid was not to destroy people but to take prisoners who could be used as hostages and for exchanging them for the Apaches whom the Mexicans had taken from us at Casas Grandes and in the attack on Juh's band. Afterwards another peace could be made with the officials at Casas Grandes.

After the usual preparations the expedition took their families southeast over the mountains for about thirty-five miles where we left them camped in two or three groups among the hills. The able-bodied men and we young boys acting as helpers then continued on into the plains where we stopped in a large grove of oaks. Here we had a lot of fun chasing a big flock of wild turkeys. We watched where they flew into the trees then after dark easily shot several thus providing a good feast.

The second day we crossed the main road south of Galeana. It was comical seeing us walk on our heels here, just leaving little round holes in the dust which didn't look like human tracks. We traveled rapidly that day towards the mountains to the south stopping before dark to kill a few cattle. During our journey through the mountains we saw indications that some tribe of Indians whom we believed to have been Lipans had been there some years before. These people are very much like the Mescalero Apaches.

Early next morning we marched due east for many miles to our objective for the day. During this march some of the men made a high-pitched, bird-like singing which seemed to say, "Here they come, on horseback." This keyed us up considerably.

Soon we turned north again over a range of hills where we stopped to reconnoiter. We boys held the horses while the men went to the road just over the hill to watch for travelers. But at sunset they came back without having seen anyone.

Early the next morning the warriors again went out to ambush traffic on the road. About noon they captured six women, wives of soldiers stationed at Casas Grandes. Geronimo told the prisoners not to be afraid, that we weren't going to harm them. He sent one old woman to Casas Grandes to inform the Mexican authorities that we had captives whom we would like to exchange.

The men went to the road a third time but were disappointed to see no one. When they returned we boys roasted some beef for them and for the captives. But the latter refused to eat.

We were sitting there eating. Geronimo was sitting next to me with a knife in one hand and a chunk of beef which I had cooked for him in the other. All at once he dropped the knife, saying, "Men, our people whom we left at our base camp are now in the hands of U.S. troops! What shall we do?"

This was a startling example of Geronimo's mysterious ability to tell what was happening at a distance. I cannot explain it to this day. But I was there and saw it. No, he didn't get the word by some messenger. And no smoke signals had been made.

SOME OF THE MEN DROVE IN SOME CATTLE

Every one of us replied to Geronimo that we wanted to go back right away. We believed what he told us.

At that time we were at least a hundred and twenty miles from our base camp and completely out of touch with it. We started out that very evening and traveled all through the night. Our journey was slow because of the Mexican women captives. In the morning we arrived on the south side of a mountain range where we stopped to breakfast on more roast beef. Once again the captives wouldn't eat. Geronimo urged them to eat, so that they would have strength for the journey. He explained that we were in a hurry. But they remained stubborn. Then to our amazement, a slight, short Apache strode up, pretending that he was a chief. He spoke to the women something like this, "Now, women, if you want to live, you must eat." He walked back and forth talking loud and threateningly. Becoming frightened they called for roast beef, which they ate with good appetite. The pretended chief walked away smiling.

From here the journey continued slowly. We tried to help the women and get them to go faster but we really didn't expect Mexican women to walk as far and as fast as Apache women.

Before we crossed the road again south of Galeana some of the men drove in a big herd of cattle to take back to our base camp. Though the herd stampeded and many of them got away, we still had a few.

We realized now that we were within two days' journey of where the women and children were to meet us. On the first day we crossed the mountain range. On the next we marched for many miles through an open plain where we had to take care not to be observed by an enemy. As is customary with Apaches we sent out an advance detachment far ahead. The last night before we arrived in the vicinity of where we were to meet the women and children of our particular group (not the main band) we noticed that our Mexican captives did not seem to have been bothered much by the tiresome journey.

Early in the morning another man and I went ahead as messengers to the camp. Being most anxious to see our families we ran practically the entire distance. We found the women and children already on their way to the rendezvous of the main band.

During the council that evening Geronimo made another prophecy: "Tomorrow afternoon as we march along the north side of the mountains we will see a man standing on a hill to our left. He will howl to us and tell us that the troops have captured our base camp."

We marched quite early the next morning, straight west through a wide forest of oaks and pines. About the middle of the afternoon we heard a howl from the hilltop to our left. There stood an Apache calling to us. He came down through the rocks to tell us that the main camp, now some fifteen miles distant, was in the hands of U.S. troops. General Crook with some cavalry and Indian scouts had taken all the rest of the Apaches into custody.

Thus the event which Geronimo had foretold when we were still several days' journey away, and had repeated last night, came to pass as true as steel. I still cannot explain it.

Chapter 13

SURRENDER

We continued climbing up the ridge until we came to a little spring where we camped for the night. At the evening council our leaders decided that on the following day we would investigate the situation at the main camp.

After going across some steep canyons and continuing to ascend a high mountain we reached the summit where we could look down on the place where the troops were camped with the Indians. Geronimo, who determined to find out just what was going on before he took us all down, detailed some men to take up firing positions in the crags overlooking the camp. Then he sent two of the older men to find out what General Crook had come for. If they did not return within a certain time we were to attack.

Instead of returning to where Geronimo stood the two men came back halfway up the mountain and called for us all to come down. They wanted us to meet General George Crook, who was commanding the Department of Arizona, and as such was in charge of all Indians in the southwest.

Surrender of the Hostiles

Our warriors descended the mountain side, went up to General Crook's tent where, after a lengthy conference between the leaders, we all surrendered to the General. I am sure that this was one of the happiest days of the year for General Crook, who had thus successfully completed the purpose of his expedition into Mexico. We Apaches felt the same way about it. It was a great relief to give up to superior authority, to have some one take charge. No more worries, no more sleepless nights, fearing attacks by an enemy.

General Crook had been led to our mountain hideout or stronghold by one of our own warriors, a San Carlos Apache named Tso-ay,* or as he was nicknamed by the soldiers, "Peaches." This man and my cousin had been partners on the warpath. They had made the raid

---
*Also spelled *Tzoe*. Although he was said to be a full-blooded Indian, Peaches had light, pink complexion and smooth skin. Hence the nickname.

with Chatto and Benito into Arizona and New Mexico several months before, during which my cousin had been killed by a prospector or miner.

Shortly afterwards the war party had stopped on a high mountain. Peaches stood there looking toward his homeland, crying. At length he said to the others, "Friends, you know I have been with you all

APACHE HIDEOUT IN THE HEART OF THE SIERRA MADRES

Photo by Captain Henry W. Lawton taken near head
of Bavispe River

through this hard and dangerous raid. I have suffered when you suffered. I have been hungry when you were without food. Now I have lost my best friend. I cannot go on. I'm going to leave you and return to my old home country."

The other Indians did not argue with Peaches. They gave him some things which would be useful to him when traveling alone. Then they said goodbye.

Peaches was filled with happiness to be able to go back to San Carlos and be welcomed by friends and relatives who were still there.

Peaches Enlists As A Guide To General Crook

Peaches told us that General Crook's expedition had been formed at San Carlos and Fort Apache. The General had collected a large pack train, numerous troops, and had organized a strong detachment of Indian scouts including some Apaches. He had selected the best Indians he could find at San Carlos and Fort Apache, all strong men, in good health, and noted for their endurance and ability to stand hardship. Peaches was chosen as guide because he had the reputation of being dependable and besides was perfectly acquainted with the area in Mexico where the expedition was to operate.

After entering Mexico, the troops marched for several days into the Sierra Madres, where they found our old Apache war trail. This was familiar to Peaches, he having been over it a number of times while he was with us.

They passed by the battle ground in the canyon where our warriors had fought with Mexican soldiers a short time before then turned southeast up the canyon of the Bavispe River. They came to the summit of a mountain near our old base camp, where they saw one Indian coming toward them from across a canyon. General Crook wanted to catch this man without hurting him but the scouts, owing to a misunderstanding, fired on the Indian who then disappeared into the thick timber. The scouts made this mistake because they didn't understand the orders which had been given by the commander.

When they found this particular Indian camp, the scouts, still not aware of what the General wanted, attacked. In this affair one old woman was killed. She was the mother of an Apache named Speedy. Speedy was so enraged by this that he turned, and using rocks, brutally killed the small white captive Charlie McComas. The Apaches of this group later told the soldiers that the little boy had run off into the brush and was never found. I was not there, being still with Geronimo many miles to the east. But I later was told the true story by an eyewitness, Ramona Chihuahua, daughter of the chief, when

TSO-AY (PEACHES), GUIDE TO GENERAL CROOK

we were students together at Carlisle. This settles the "mystery" of what happened to Charlie McComas. At that time the Indians were protecting one of their own band from possible punishment, so they lied about what had happened to the poor little boy even though they disapproved of the murder. Everyone connected with this tragedy is now dead. So the truth can at last be told.

In spite of this attack made on the camp by the scouts, Peaches went after the fleeing Indians and persuaded them to make peace with General Crook. From then on General Crook was a true friend of ours. He was a hard fighter, a strong enemy when we were hostile.

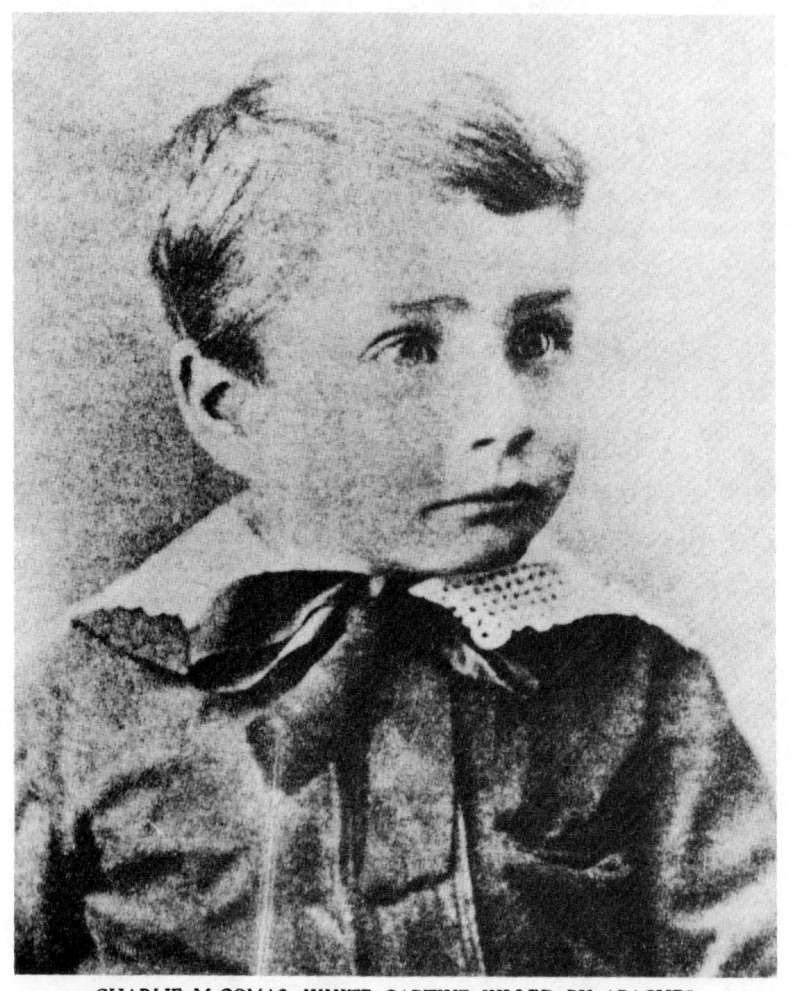

CHARLIE McCOMAS, WHITE CAPTIVE KILLED BY APACHES

But he played fair with us afterwards and did what he could to protect the Indians. We actually loved General Crook, and even today think of him, and talk about him, with genuine affection. He probably never knew that.

Soon all arrangements were made for us to return with the troops to San Carlos. Geronimo, Juh, and a few others asked General Crook if they could have permission to come in later. General Crook said that it would be all right for them to do so but he expected them to keep their promise.

At this time General Crook sent the Mexican women who had been captured by Geronimo back to their homes.

Return To The United States

Having said farewell and good luck to the few who under Geronimo and Juh were remaining for a time in the wilderness, we started northward. Peaches and General Crook were at the head of the procession. On the way we were well treated by the troops and the scouts. The first night we stopped at a place where there was plenty of water for the stock. One of the leading Indian scouts from Fort Apache, who had known my mother, asked us to camp near him while we were on the trip. He would look after us, he said.

The next day General Crook was anxious to get an early start; he wanted to get out of this mountainous country. Leaving the north end of the Sierra Madres we went through the plains west of Janos where, a year before, our women and children had been slaughtered by the Mexicans. Their skeletons were still visible, the bodies having been eaten by buzzards. Again we felt deep sadness over the loss of so many friends and kinsfolk; the memory of that terrible day was still fresh in our minds.

From here we turned west and followed for a distance the road which ran between Casas Grandes and Fronteras. Our people and the scouts now feared that we might be attacked in camp by Mexican soldiers. Ten of the scouts wanted us all to camp near them for protection. Fortunately nothing happened.

Early the following morning we marched on, our General and Peaches again at the head of the column. Ahead of us lay the last range of mountains to be crossed before we passed the border. On the way to the mountains our ex-warriors and the scouts went on an antelope hunt during the course of which they killed many antelope. We camped that night on the western side of the mountains due north of the famous spot where three years later Geronimo was to surrender for the last time.

There being one more day's march to the international boundary we hurried to get across before something unpleasant should happen. North of the border we were met by more troops and U.S. scouts who were camped in that area. We rested for a few days then proceeded toward San Carlos. This stage of the journey was a slow one because of the necessity to stop at infrequent waterholes to water our animals. After the second day we were joined by a wagon train from an Army post, which loaded up the women and children and our camp gear. We now moved by road through Fort Grant and Fort Thomas.

Better Days

All our arrangements for living on the San Carlos reservation were made for us by Army officers. From then on we had no further dealings with Indian agents from the Department of the Interior. This pleased us, because it was one of the latter who had been responsible for moving us from our old Warm Springs reservation in the first place.

The San Carlos Indians showed us no friendliness nor even courtesy. We felt that we were not welcome here, that they wanted us to be removed from their reservation. Probably this was because their Chief of Scouts, Mr. Sterling, and one of his Indian policemen had been killed when we were run off the reservation in 1882.

During that summer (1883) Geronimo and his little band came in, fulfilling the promise which he had made to General Crook. Unfortunately Geronimo made the mistake of driving along with him a large herd of cattle which he had stolen from the Mexicans. This seemed quite proper to Geronimo, who felt that he was only providing a good supply of food for his people. The authorities, taking a different view, pried these cattle loose from the Chief.

Chief Juh's people also came in. But Juh wasn't with them. He had suffered a sad mishap while on the way back from Mexico. As the band passed near Casas Grandes Juh sent a woman into town to get him some whisky. She being successful, Juh got good and drunk. While in this condition he rode his horse along the rim of a bluff, fell over the edge, and was killed. Juh had been a good leader but whisky brought him down just as it did many other Apaches.

To Fort Apache

In the spring of 1884 we heard that we were to be moved north to the Fort Apache reservation. That area, having a higher elevation than San Carlos, and consisting of pine-covered mountains and upland meadows traversed by clear, cold streams, was much more healthful and pleasant than the hot, desert wastes of San Carlos. We were thankful, too, at the opportunity to get away from the unfriendly San Carlos Indians, who had never invited us to share in their privileges or take part in tribal councils and business affairs. At the new reservation we would be with the somewhat friendlier White Mountain Apaches.

The first morning we marched east on the road to Fort Thomas. We were escorted by a troop of cavalry. They had a pack train and several wagons in which they carried food for themselves and us. At Fort Thomas we turned north up the slopes of the Gila Mountains, following the narrow wagon track which we had taken two years before when the Netdahe drove us from San Carlos. That night we camped on the north side of the first ridge. All relations between ourselves and the troops were peaceful and harmonious.

On the following day we ascended an even higher range of mountains to the north. The road was so steep that we Indians had to push the wagons but by sunset we had the satisfaction of reaching the summit and looking off into the green valleys beyond. We camped that night on the brink of the divide.

The journey on the next morning took us down the slopes toward the Black River, still moving on a poor and winding road. We reached the river shortly after midday but could not cross. The river was over its banks, too deep to ford. A nearby ferry was so waterlogged we couldn't use it, consequently we camped on the south bank for two days while waiting for the water to subside. The men and older boys could have swum across but that method was not possible for the women and children.

Finally our officer in charge, Lieutenant Britton Davis, borrowed some heavy canvas from the troops, which he soaked in water then lashed around the wagon bodies to form pontoons. The women and children climbed into these, whereupon four or five good swimmers shoved each wagon like a boat through the water. In this way we ferried the whole party safely across. Afterwards the men brought over our belongings in the same manner. Four of us boys drove all the horses and mules down the river about a mile where we found a good place to get them into the water. Then we had some fun making the animals swim across. After they had made it safely we tied our clothing in bundles on top of our heads and swam to the opposite shore. That was the custom of the Indians in crossing deep rivers.

We camped near the crossing for another two days. Here our beloved General Crook caught up with us. We were truly glad to see him, the first time since he had brought us to San Carlos a year

MAJOR GENERAL GEORGE CROOK

Photo in Mrs. Crook's Scrapbook

before. He called for a conference with the Indians. There was no smoking of a peace pipe. The Apaches never knew that custom. General Crook gave us some good fatherly advice, mainly to settle down and go to work. I took this to heart and have followed General Crook's word ever since.

JASON PLANTS SOME BARLEY

The next day we moved out to our designated location near the head of Turkey Creek about fifteen miles from Fort Apache.

New Surroundings At Fort Apache

We were camped in a pine forest while waiting for orders from the authorities as to where to settle permanently. The different bands and small groups were to be settled along the various creeks, each with a plot of land which they could irrigate and plant to crops.

Some of us, perhaps most of us, didn't realize that this meant the virtual end of our old nomadic life, that from now on we would have to work hard and earn a living for ourselves and our families. A few of us thought that it was an opportunity to learn farming, with a really worthwhile future.

Geronimo, another family, and myself were neighbors. My plot of land adjoined an irrigation ditch, which meant extra maintenance work. But I didn't mind that. Those of us who settled along the head of Turkey Creek did real well with our crops. The first year, 1884, we raised corn and potatoes. Spring came early the second year. Geronimo, another man, and I sowed barley. But during corn planting time when I was going home one evening, tired and hungry, I was met by my sister's husband who gave me the discouraging news that the Indians along Turkey Creek again had gone on the warpath.

Chapter 14

THE LAST OUTBREAK

After settling on the Fort Apache reservation Geronimo and many others made a beginning in the effort to change from warriors to farmers. Nevertheless turbulent days still lay ahead. A trouble-maker named Kaahtenny was partly to blame. This Apache, who had fought under Victorio and had been with the Netdahe, was regarded by his people as being a great fighter. I never thought too highly of him because I could not forget that on that tragic day when our women and children were being slaughtered by the Mexicans west of Janos he sat at ease in the shade of a tree with a dozen others, calmly smoking and not firing a shot in defense of our people.

On one occasion, probably in 1881, he with a few followers were raiding in Arizona. They came upon some White Mountain Apaches who were out hunting. Kaahtenny and his party killed several of these innocent people. So when, at an Indian dance on the Fort Apache reservation in 1884, he boasted of this and other exploits and hinted at future raids to come, the White Mountain Apaches complained to our agent Lieutenant Davis. Davis had Kaahtenny brought to trial. He was convicted of homicide and sentenced to three years in the Federal penitentiary at Alcatraz, California. This alarmed and angered Geronimo, Naiche, and others who had been associated with Kaahtenny on the warpath.

The White Mountain Apaches had a bad man of their own. This fellow, Nah-de-ga-ah, caused a lot of trouble in those days and even made the newspapers. Today he is forgotten, but at that time we thought he was something awful.

Nah-de-ga-ah was a good-looking young man, strong and quick in his actions but with a jealous disposition and a violent temper. One day seeing another Apache riding by on a fine horse, he ambushed and shot the man, took his horse and rode it home. He bragged about this feat, which turned his people against him. He ran off into the mountains. The Indian scouts pursued, overtook him, and returned him to San Carlos where he was thrown into the guard house. After several months of confinement, in the spring of 1882

NAH-DE-GA-AH, APACHE DESPERADO KILLED NEAR
FORT APACHE

he participated in a prison outbreak in which several prisoners were shot but he escaped. This story is remembered clearly because in escaping Nah-de-ga-ah ran along a line of telegraph poles for nearly a mile, dodging behind the poles to avoid being hit. Two scouts went after him, one being his kinsman. After a chase of some twenty miles the scouts overtook the fleeing prisoner but he ambushed them. In the ensuing fight Nah-de-ga-ah though slightly wounded succeeded in killing the scout who was his kinsman. This gave him arms and ammunition.

From that time on Nah-de-ga-ah was more dangerous than ever. He lived in the White Mountains for several years as an outlaw, preying on other Indians and white and Mexican inhabitants. The Indians greatly feared him while the authorities made repeated efforts to recapture him. Finally in the spring of 1885 the military authorities asked the Chiricahuas to hold a big dance. It was hoped that the desperado might show up at this affair. Lieutenant Britton Davis engaged three Chiricahua scouts to catch Nah-de-ga-ah if he appeared. A company of scouts stationed themselves in the scrub oak near the dancing grounds while an Army police wagon was held in the vicinity and the three special scouts secretly mingled with the dancers.

I was standing with the other spectators by the bonfire enjoying the dance when suddenly I saw Nah-de-ga-ah in the crowd by the fire. At the same moment one of the scouts grabbed him and threw him to the ground. This was done so quickly that hardly anyone saw it. There was no disorder in the crowd. The dancing went on without interruption. The prisoner was hauled off to the guard house at Fort Apache, where they fastened shackles on him.

The guard house sentries were White Mountain Apaches, who permitted the prisoner's mother to visit him frequently. On one of these occasions she must have told him that she had hidden a loaded gun in the bushes outside the guard house. One night Nah-de-ga-ah asked to be let out for a few minutes. This request was granted, one of the sentries walking behind him. In a few moments the desperado squatted, reached into the bushes for his gun and quickly shot and killed the scout who was guarding him. Then he made his way back to the steepest part of the mountains where he resumed his career of bloodshed and robbery.

One night while some of the Apaches had gotten together for a session of story telling, Nah-de-ga-ah came into the camp. A middle-aged woman recognized him, seized and held him while her husband got his gun and shot the outlaw.

This brave couple then had to flee to the protection of Fort Apache to escape the inevitable revenge of Nah-de-ga-ah's relatives.*

Some Chiricahuas Leave The Reservation

Nah-de-ga-ah's activity had little or no bearing on the next Apache outbreak. This came from dissatisfaction because Lieutenant Davis tried to stop some of the men, like Kaahtenny, from beating and otherwise mistreating their wives, from too much drinking, and from a suspicion on the part of Geronimo and others that they were to be sent to Alcatraz as Kaahtenny had been. A lot of the unrest undoubtedly was caused by complaining and indignant talking among themselves. They really hadn't been mistreated at Fort Apache but weren't ready yet to settle down. Geronimo also resented the violent criticism of him that was appearing in Arizona newspapers, stories that interpreter Mickey Free passed on to him.

In the spring of 1885 Geronimo, Chihuahua, Mangas (son of the old chief Mangas Colorado), and a number of others got to making and drinking Indian beer in violation of orders from the authorities. This homebrew made the Indians drunk and quarrelsome. They were brought before Lieutenant Davis who threatened to report them to General Crook. At this the Indians got the idea that they might be sent off to prison as Kaatenny had been. Geronimo later claimed that Mickey Free either didn't interpret accurately for him or had made untrue statements to Lieutenant Davis. Having been placed in irons once before when the band was shipped to San Carlos, some of the leaders determined not to undergo such treatment again. They plotted to leave the reservation, taking their immediate families as well as some other Apaches whom they induced to go with them. Chatto, Benito, Loco, and about three-fourths of the band refused to go.

As told you, I learned of all this as I was coming home from planting the barley field which Geronimo and I had been farming together. My brother-in-law having met me on the road, we discussed the whole situation. It appeared to us that we would have to go with our family group leader, Geronimo. Some of the young men who were our close friends and blood relatives had already joined him that very afternoon. Late that night I started off southward accompanied by my mother and sister. Then I told them to go on ahead, I wanted to return for my brother-in-law, who had not come with us. We would catch up with them later.

---

*Britton Davis, in *The Truth About Geronimo* (New Haven: Yale University Press, 1929) refers to this incident on pages 133-134, calling the Indian "Gar." The version given here, however, is Jason's.

Unable to find my brother-in-law, I hastened to overtake my own family. As I hurried along the main road through the dark moonless night, my thoughts were very troubled. I came to the conclusion that it would be foolish to throw away what I was just beginning to learn of a better way of life. So when I came up with my mother and sister I informed them of this decision and told them to return to our camp.

We were now off the reservation, having reached the point where the road starts up the mountain. If troops were following the runaways my location would identify me as being one of the hostiles. Furthermore it would compromise my womenfolk if they were seen with me. So for their safety I directed them to return to the reservation without me. I would spend the night in the canyon like a wild Indian and endeavor to return without being seen, after it was light enough to move through the timber.

In the morning I reached the agency sub-issue station without incident, where I was relieved to find that my mother and sister had also arrived safely. Quite a crowd were assembled. Looking around I saw not one of my several cousins or the other young men with whom I had grown up. They had all gone with the hostiles. I stood there thinking what good times we had had together and how much I would miss them. All at once big tears started running down my cheeks.

Mother said, "Son, be brave. There are many other young men here with whom you can associate." She went to to tell me that it was better that we had not gone with Geronimo even though he was the leader of our band. My mother's advice was a great comfort and relief to me.

Returning to our camps I found that some greedy Indians had already appropriated the horses which Geronimo's party had left behind, to which they had no right whatsoever. Furthermore sub-chief Chatto had arbitrarily claimed the field of barley which Geronimo and I had planted. He went to see Lieutenant Britton Davis to confirm his title to this field, but the lieutenant said no, the field belonged to Batsinas (then my name) because he had worked it.

Geronimo's War Party

To return to the account of what happened to those who had left the reservation on the afternoon of the preceding day: They had, according to what we learned later, crossed the Black River, climbed the mountains to the south, and camped on the summit where they could observe any pursuit. After resting there the remainder of the night they took off straight south toward the border, not stopping to camp again until they had covered 120 miles. After reaching Mexico they separated into several small groups each under its own chief.

Two troops of the 4th Cavalry together with some Indian scouts under Lieutenants Gatewood and Davis promptly followed but were unable to catch the runaways. People who have been in this rugged country can well understand how easily the Apaches, with their superior speed and endurance, and their willingness to take to the rocks and the mountain tops, were able to evade their pursuers.

Another habit of the Apaches contributed largely to their success in keeping out of reach. During Captain Crawford's subsequent expedition deep into Mexico Geronimo and his warriors used this method more than once. It was a mysterious manner of vanishing completely when the soldiers and scouts had just caught up with them or were about to attack their camp. Each day the chief designated an assembly point, as I have previously described. Then when the troops would find them or were about to launch an attack the Indians would scatter, keeping their minds firmly fixed on the assembly point far away. The scouts, who were experienced warriors themselves, had a hard time tracking down the hostiles, as they were forced to follow the many diverging trails, most of which disappeared in the rocks anyway.

The hostiles would converge on their predetermined rendezvous point but instead of camping there would make an imitation camp. They would build several small camp fires and tie an old worn-out horse to a tree to make it look as though the camp was occupied. Then they would move on for several miles and establish their real camp elsewhere. The scouts knowing that their fellow tribesmen, the hostiles, would assemble at nightfall, would lie in wait all through the night ready to attack at daybreak. The attack would land upon a fake camp. The scouts were of course disgusted and disappointed but presently they would laugh, saying, "Oh my! We were fooled!" They took it as a great joke on themselves.

Crawford's Expedition

Early in the fall of 1885 a carefully prepared expedition was organized to hunt down Geronimo. Indian scouts were enlisted at Fort Apache and San Carlos. Captain Emmett Crawford was selected to lead the expedition, which included troops as well as Indian scouts. Crawford, an unusually tall man, was known to the Apaches as "Tall Chief." Some of the other tribes called him "Captain Coffee." He was a very efficient officer with a great deal of experience in Indian war-

GERONIMO ON THE LAST WARPATH

To Geronimo's Left is his Son, Chapo; to his
Right is Naiche

fare. The Department Commander had confidence in him and he was highly respected by the Indians. Captain Crawford placed great reliance on his Indian scouts, who were especially chosen for their amazing endurance and physical strength and who were perfectly acquainted with the desolate country which they were going to penetrate.

Crawford's command located the trail of the hostiles below the border. After following it for many miles over successive mountain ranges they came upon the Indians. In the following attack several women were wounded and others captured. But as usual the main band scattered and disappeared. This occurred again further south. Finally when Geronimo apparently was considering surrendering once more, and was just on the point of communicating with the troops, a Mexican column attacked Crawford's command. Geronimo and his band were a short distance away on a rocky ridge where they could see what took place.

The Mexicans had also been on Geronimo's trail. When they unexpectedly encountered Crawford's column they attacked without investigating. Captain Crawford jumped up on a high rock and waved his white handkerchief to show that his troops were friendly. But the Mexicans shot him. As he fell he struck his head on a rock and was injured further. When the Warm Springs scouts saw this they were so mad that they rushed at the Mexicans and shot the Mexican commander. That stopped the fight. A short conference took place between the two expeditions. Then, carrying their wounded commander, the U.S. troops began to move north toward the border. On the way Crawford died. He was well liked by the Indians, who accordingly were quite downcast during the journey.

In the meantime Lieutenant Marion P. Maus, who had succeeded to command when Captain Crawford was shot, met with Geronimo. A time and place was set for a conference between the runaway Indians and General Crook, who would come south for the purpose. At this time old Nanay turned himself in, returning to the U.S., together with a few others including the wives of Chihuahua and Geronimo.

Geronimo Sends A Message To The Mexicans

Prior to this time Geronimo had sent two women to one of the Mexican garrison towns in the northern part of Sonora to try to arrange for a council at which peace terms could be drawn up. Geronimo and the warriors hid in the mountains for a number of days waiting for the women to return from their mission. As time went on and the women failed to return Geronimo and his men began to fear that the messengers had become victims of the familiar Mexican treachery. They imagined that the Mexican authorities might be forcing the women to lead the enemy to where the Indians were concealed.

Apaches were always alert to signs of Mexican trickery, having experienced it many times in the past. So now all their caution was aroused. After the women were considerably overdue, the men decided to move further north. Shortly after they had gone the two women arrived at the hideout, worn out and hungry, but with a favorable reply from the Mexican authorities. Surprised that the men had pulled out, the women followed their trail. At the same time the U.S. Indian scouts and troops were also on Geronimo's tracks and had pretty well closed up with the outlaws. Nevertheless the two women, outwalking both parties, rejoined Geronimo's band a little south of the U.S. border. They told Geronimo that they had delivered his message to the Mexican authorities, who had agreed to the council and were coming along behind to take part in it.

Meantime General Crook made contact with Geronimo.

General Crook's Conference

General Crook met with Geronimo, Naiche, Chihuahua, and others near San Bernardino Springs for a series of conferences during the period March 25-27, 1886. General Crook, who only brought a few soldiers, was accompanied by a photographer* who got some good pictures of the council as well as of the hostile leaders. The general told the Indians that the only terms he could offer them was complete surrender. If they didn't accept these terms he would allow three days to elapse after which he would send soldiers and scouts to hunt them down. On the other hand if they did surrender, their lives would be spared, though they would have to suffer imprisonment in the East for two years before being returned to their people.

Geronimo, after talking at length about his reasons for running

---

*C. S. Fly, of Tombstone, Arizona. He actually photographed Geronimo before the surrender was arranged.

SURRENDER CONFERENCE BETWEEN GEN. CROOK AND GERONIMO, MARCH 25, 1886

Seated in the inner circle, from left to right: Lieut. Faison, Capt. Roberts, Geronimo, Nanay, Noche, Lieut. Maus, 3 Mexican guide-interpreters, Capt. John Bourke, Gen. Crook, and Charlie Roberts, age 13. The latter, now Brig. Gen. Charles D. Roberts, USA-Ret., lives today in Chevy Chase, Md.

away, including the fact that he was disturbed over the many lies which had been told and printed about him, abruptly agreed to General Crook's terms. He said that he needed time to gather up his people after which he would follow the troops in to Fort Bowie.

The Mexicans arrived while Geronimo was still camped near the place where the meeting with General Crook had taken place. Geronimo told the Mexican general that he was too late. The Indians had already arranged to surrender to General Crook. At this the Mexican officer got very angry, saying that Geronimo had broken his word. Geronimo replied by pointing to the military pack train standing nearby, and saying, "You can see all those goods over there? They are for me and my people. These U.S. soldiers and scouts are good to my people. From the Mexicans we have received nothing but harm. So there is no use your talking peace terms. We are going back with the U.S. soldiers and scouts."

That night Geronimo and his men, fearing that the Mexicans would attack them, moved out secretly. They marched north toward Fort Bowie, soon overtaking the military expedition. The soldiers and scouts were rejoicing that Geronimo had surrendered to them and were on their way in. Unfortunately the next night when they were in the vicinity of Fort Bowie a renegade white trader sold the Indians some whisky. As usual they couldn't resist it. Naiche and a few of his men got wild drunk. Naiche fired his gun in the air a number of times. Geronimo thought that fighting had broken out with the troops. He and Naiche stampeded, taking with them some thirty followers. They headed back into the Sierra Madres. Chihuahua, however, remained with General Crook. Preferring imprisonment to further warfare he continued north with the troops.

General Crook Succeeded by General Miles

Geronimo's defection was the cause of General Crook, our good friend, being relieved and sent away. The higher authorities, not understanding how General Crook could have let Geronimo get away again, disapproved the terms of surrender. The General, feeling that his policy was not being supported by his superiors, asked to be relieved. He was replaced by General Nelson A. Miles.

General Miles came to Fort Apache in the summer of 1886 to plan a campaign for running down the Apaches who still remained out. He held a meeting at the agency at which I was present. He explained that he wanted to form a large expedition to corral Geronimo's band and thus bring all the Apache troubles to an end. Though most of the Indians present were Chiricahuas and Warm Springs Apaches,

SOME OF GERONIMO'S BAND AT TIME OF FINAL SURRENDER
Front row, left to right, 4 female members of Naiche's family; Naiche; La-zi-yah; Harold Dick, later a fake medicine man, see Chap. 19; Hustinney; Kactlhaya. 3d from left, middle row, is Martine; back row, 2d from left, is Perico.

many of them related to Geronimo and his men, great enthusiasm was shown. The Indians were excited and happy over the prospect of going out on another campaign. Hardship and danger meant nothing, adventure was what they wanted and it didn't seem to matter that they were going to fight their own people.

Then General Miles said that he hoped to be able to make contact without fighting and that he wanted volunteers to take a message to Geronimo.

At this point in the meeting the Indians were sitting around quietly but shivering with excitement. For awhile there was no response. Finally Kay-i-tah held up his hand.

"I will take the message from you to Geronimo," he said. "But one man is not enough. It would be very risky for a lone man to go up to Geronimo. Two men would be better. Let me take a companion."

General Miles agreed. Kay-i-tah then asked his close friend, Martine, to go with him. Martine accepted too. General Miles gave them the message which they were to carry in their minds. The Indians had wonderful memories. In this case they were elated over the great responsibility and trust which had been placed upon them.

They were proud, too, of their own bravery, for they knew they were risking quick death to go near renegades who might shoot first and ask questions afterwards.

Word was sent out to the different bands, including the Chiricahuas, White Mountain Apaches, and Warm Springs band, that two companies of scouts were to be enlisted for the campaign. Only the best physical specimens were to be selected, men who were rugged and healthy. A few volunteers were rejected at the physical examination or, like myself, for other reasons. I passed the physical examination but was turned down because I was too closely related by blood to Geronimo.

General Miles chose Captain Henry W. Lawton to lead this final expedition. His assistant in command of the scouts was Lieutenant Charles Gatewood. Since Gatewood was a tall man who wore very large shoes, the Indians named him Chief Long Foot. In addition to the troops and scouts the expedition contained a large train of pack mules which carried the food, ammunition, medical, and other supplies.

After the scouts were well organized they asked permission to hold a war dance in which they amused themselves for two nights before leaving for San Carlos where they were to be joined by other scouts. While waiting to get going the scouts could hardly contain themselves for impatience. Finally the orders came whereupon they started out joyfully, straight down toward the border of Sonora. It was a difficult and tiresome journey, but not for the scouts, who bounded along ahead of and on the flanks of the troops, looking for the trail of the hostiles. It was especially dangerous for Kay-i-tah and Martine, well out in the lead, for they probably would make the initial contact. Martine and Kay-i-tah didn't want to carry arms, feeling that there was less likelihood of the hostiles shooting them if they were unarmed. But Captain Lawton said that everyone, soldier and scout alike, had to carry a rifle. They might be attacked by Mexicans. So they did. Furthermore they carried a white flag as a sign that they wanted to make a truce. Apaches had been accustomed for years to carrying a piece of white buckskin when going on a mission of this kind.

Upon entering one Mexican town Kay-i-tah and Martine found evidence that two women of the renegades had been there a short time before. They thought that they had a good chance to catch up with these women but for some reason were unable to do so. Therefore they went back to the camp of the expedition.

Contact Is Made

Meantime Geronimo and his warriors were moving slowly toward the U.S. border. It was August 1886. They had not been suffering but were driving some stolen cattle.

One day the scouts told Captain Lawton it would be a good idea to camp along the creek while Lieutenant Gatewood, Mr. George Wratten, Kay-i-tah and Martine, and ten soldiers should go out to find the hostiles. From the tracks and signs of old camps Kay-i-tah thought that Geronimo was in the mountains to the east of this camp.

So this small party moved toward a long peak which the Apaches called Mountain Tall. At one point the ridge rose in a steep bluff. The keen eyes of the two Indians spotted something on top of the escarpment. Soon they realized that it was Geronimo's band. Motioning to Lieutenant Gatewood to stop his advance, the two Apaches moved up to the foot of the bluff. Kay-i-tah shouted in a loud but quavering voice, "I am Kay-i-tah. Let me come up. I have a message for you."

Geronimo called down, "All right. Come on. We'll listen."

Leaving the other men behind, the two scouts climbed up the steep mountain. Arriving at the summit, on legs trembling with fear, they saw Geronimo and his men there with ready guns. Up to that moment Kay-i-tah and Martine didn't know whether they would be permitted to live. But the outlaws greeted them warmly. They really were glad to see each other, as close associates among the Apaches always were after a considerable separation. After much friendly chatter and a recounting of what had occurred since Geronimo had left, Kay-i-tah delivered General Miles' message. The General wanted them to give themselves up without any guarantees.

For a few moments there was silence. The Indians seemed stunned. Finally Geronimo's half-brother White Horse (Leon Perico) spoke out. "I am going to surrender. My wife and children have been captured. I love them, and want to be with them."

Then another brother said that if White Horse was going, he would go too. In a moment the third and youngest brother made a similar statement.

Geronimo stood for a few moments without speaking. At length he said slowly, "I don't know what to do. I have been depending heavily on you three men. You have been great fighters in battle. If you are going to surrender, there is no use my going without you. I will give up with you."

[138]

LEAVING FORT BOWIE ON WAY TO CAPTIVITY

Geronimo's band, under troop escort, departing from Fort Bowie to take train to Florida.

Geronimo Surrenders

Kay-i-tah was a happy man, for his dangerous mission had been accomplished. He hurried down the mountainside to the little group of soldiers where he told Lieutenant Gatewood that Geronimo and his men would surrender. Later the hostile Indians, led by Martine, came down to turn themselves in. They surrendered first to Lieutenant Gatewood, who accepted in the name of General Miles.

Gatewood took the Indians to Captain Lawton at the camp along the creek. Lawton sent a message to General Miles to meet them on the way to Fort Bowie. On receipt of this good news General Miles hastened south with his bodyguards. Meeting the expedition he received the final surrender of Geronimo. After this the whole party continued to Fort Bowie.

Thus ended Geronimo's war campaigns. Peace could now prevail throughout Arizona, New Mexico, and northern Mexico. People could at long last enjoy peace, prosperity, and the pursuit of money. We Indians said to ourselves: "You white people can now go about your business without fear of attack by the Apaches. But you are still subject to being preyed upon. Beware of your own race, who are seeking an easy path to wealth at your expense!"

Chapter 15

PRISONERS OF WAR

Chihuahua and some seventy-five members of his band had come in as a result of the conference with General Crook in March. They were shipped off as prisoners to St. Augustine, Florida. They were confined there in a former Spanish fort, Fort Marion, which had been used by the United States as a seacoast defense but more recently had been in the hands of a caretaking detachment.

Chatto, a number of other leading men in the tribe, and many of the best warriors, all of whom had remained peacefully on the Fort Apache reservation when Geronimo and the disaffected had broken out, had volunteered their services as scouts to aid the troops in hunting down their own people. Officers who were engaged on these campaigns have testified that without the excellent assistance of these Apaches the campaigns could not have been concluded successfully. They were to be rewarded in a peculiar way.

In June of 1886, Chatto and a number of other leading Apaches who had served in the recent campaigns against Geronimo were sent as a delegation to Washington, D. C. The purpose of this mission was never known to the Indians but after they were in the east they were told that they had the choice of working against the Apaches or of being thrown into prison. Refusing to betray their own people they were sent to St. Augustine where they were confined with Chihuahua and the others.

Although those of us who were still on the reservation at Fort Apache didn't know it, plans were under way to seize us too and send us to Fort Marion as the third increment in the wholesale, indiscriminating prisoner-of-war operation.

While the recent campaigns in Mexico were in progress we had continued our efforts to become a civilized people. Under the instruction of Army officers we planted crops and tried to raise some livestock. Personally I was convinced that a man must go to work to earn a living for himself and his family. I still had my mother and my sister to support, hence had been unable to get married. My sister was married but her husband had left her. We had no teams of domesticated horses, no plows, wagons, or farming implements other than salvaged shovels and hoes. But, as I have said, I managed to raise a good crop of potatoes and corn the first year, which encouraged me to plant even more the second year. I sowed some barley as well as corn. That summer I made hay and cut firewood, all of which I sold at Fort Apache. It was a deep satisfaction to receive this, the first money that I had earned by myself. I began to realize that work is good for all mankind, Indians as well as whites.

This change in our lives had hardly started when it came to an abrupt ending. One day in the late summer of 1886 we were called in to Fort Apache. All men, women, and children were lined up and surrounded by soldiers. The commander ordered the men and boys into a building where he informed us that we were now prisoners of war. We were separated from our women and children, who were assembled in other camps, while we were placed under guard in tents. Some time in September they loaded us all into wagons and started us off under armed guard for Holbrook, Arizona. Our group of prisoners now included many Apaches who had served as scouts, some of them never having been on raids of any kind. These men couldn't understand why they were thus being rewarded for their hard and faithful service by being hauled away in disgrace. It seemed a bit unjust. But I will not dwell on this, as it has been commented on quite pointedly by General Crook, Lieutenant Bourke, and by more recent writers.

We were all the more unhappy because we felt that the Government itself had at least contributed to, if not being largely responsible for, starting the Apache troubles by moving us from our own reservation in 1876 to San Carlos. At the latter place, sickness in the tribe, hatred of us by the San Carlos Indians, and the general desolate condition of the country had caused our chiefs to break away and go to Mexico.

Despite these gloomy thoughts we Apaches were, especially for a somewhat primitive people, accustomed to misfortune. As far back as I could remember we had never had a permanent home or a place we could call our own. Some of us were beginning to prefer quiet and security to the ever present worry and fear of being hounded from place to place and in constant danger of attack. I think that we realized dimly, as we jolted along in those wagons, that even as prisoners our worst troubles might be coming to an end. At any rate we actually took pleasure in the long wagon trip to Holbrook, especially those of us who had never ridden in a conveyance on wheels.

We arrived on the railroad at a point some distance from Holbrook, the troops probably not caring to expose us to the enmity of the local

THE TRAIN TRIP

Geronimo's party are allowed to stretch their legs while en route to captivity. Front row, left to right, are two of Geronimo's half brothers, Fatty and Perico; Naiche; Geronimo; Chapo; Chapo's wife. Geronimo and Naiche are wearing new cowboy boots which they bought at the canteen in Fort Bowie.

population. So, out in the country, we were loaded on a train and shipped east.

We stopped at many stations along the way where hundreds of white people gathered to stare at us to see what kind of wild creatures had made so much trouble in Arizona and New Mexico. Our first stop was at Gallup, New Mexico, where in addition to many whites and Mexicans we saw some Navajoes. During the night the train crossed the Rio Grande, passed through Albuquerque, and plunging through a tunnel, left the mountains behind. We saw the last of the Rockies at noon when we stopped for lunch.

I rather enjoyed this, my first train ride. As we got deeper and deeper into Kansas we were greatly surprised to see one farm after another, towns at more frequent intervals, and many more people. We had had no idea that there were so many whites. Larger and larger crowds gathered at the depots to see our train go through. Their curiosity was equaled by ours for we had never imagined so many strange things and queer-looking people. You may be surprised to learn that the Apache has a strong feeling of racial superiority and regards others as being lesser creatures.

Some time during the night our train passed through Kansas City, Kansas, then Kansas City, Missouri. In the afternoon of that next day, before we reached St. Louis, there occurred an incident which illustrates strikingly the superior endurance and resourcefulness of the Apache warrior. I refer to the escape of Massai, so remarkable—yet in a way so typical—that it deserves more than passing notice.

Massai

Massai, a member of the Warm Springs band, had enlisted as a U.S. Scout during the 1880 campaigns against Victorio. Two years later while returning by train to Arizona in company with other scouts he learned that the Warm Springs band had been forced from the San Carlos agency and was on the way to Mexico. Massai jumped from the train and, eluding capture in a country infested with troops who were following the runaways, headed south for the Sierra Madres. He succeeded in finding our band while we were camped on the brink of the great canyon where he was happy to be reunited with his family.

But Massai was one of those restless individuals who could not remain long in one place. Furthermore he seemed to have a distaste for the rest of us, possibly because we were at that time outlaws. So with his family he stole my horse, slipped away secretly, and headed back toward San Carlos. We didn't know he was gone until I missed my horse.

In 1885 when we all were together at Fort Apache Geronimo and others broke out again, as I have related. Massai was one of those who went with Geronimo, leaving his family behind. After several months on the warpath he seems to have tired of the ever-constant dodging from pursuers. He deserted the war party, returning to Fort Apache by himself. This long and rough journey gave him further experience in traveling alone through relatively unknown and difficult country. After crossing the U.S. border he continued north, forded the Gila River, climbed up into the Gila Mountains, then down across the Black River. At length he reached the summit of the last range, looking beyond to the Fort Apache reservation. After resting here for a time he went on down until he came to the creek where our camps lay just northeast of Fort Apache. Seeing him coming our Indians were thrown into fear and confusion, thinking that the hostiles were coming to drive us off the reservation as they had done in 1882. He calmed us by calling out that he was alone. Once more he was reunited with his family.

The authorities at Fort Apache did not arrest Massai but treated him just like the other Indians there. He stayed with his family until we were all seized in the summer of 1886 to be sent east to prison.

I remember well that while we were prisoners in one of the old post buildings prior to being hauled off to Holbrook, Massai tried to stir us up to revolt. When he found that no one was paying any attention to him and that nobody would join him in an effort to escape, he quieted down and remained peaceably with the rest of us during the subsequent journey as far as Kansas. After the train left Kansas City Massai became restless again. He tried to borrow a butcher knife from several of us. I understand that he did get one. Late that afternoon, before we reached St. Louis, and I suppose while the train was moving slowly at some point, he jumped from the car.

From then on for weeks no human being ever saw Massai. Traveling on foot at night, stealing food and water, and hiding by day, he succeeded in getting back to his native country in the Black Mountains of western New Mexico south of the old Warm Springs reservation. To appreciate this amazing feat you should remember that this Indian could not read printed road signs, did not dare ask questions, had no map, and had never been in this country before except while on the train. Like a coyote or a wolf he lived off the country, remaining completely out of sight even while passing through a thickly settled part of the country in Missouri and Kansas.

After Massai had been in the Black Mountains for some time he began to yearn for human companionship. He went secretly to the Mescalero reservation where he stole a young Indian woman and took her back with him into the mountains. They remained there for years, having four children born to them. From time to time Massai would sally down from his remote fastness to steal cattle or waylay a trader or traveler. After Massai had been in hiding for some twenty-five years he disappeared, probably being killed. His wife told me the story in 1911 when I visited Mescalero and shortly after she and her children had returned to the reservation. One day about sunset Massai and his eldest son were chasing a horse north of the former Warm Springs agency. Massai, having outdistanced the boy, was approaching the horse when a shot was fired from that direction. The young Indian hastily retreated, later telling his mother that he didn't know whether Massai had been killed or wounded. They never saw him again so supposed that he was dead.

Thus Massai was the last Warm Springs Apache to be on the warpath. I had known him for many years, as we were members of the same band while on the reservation, and he was with us for a time in Mexico. We never considered him to be outstanding as a fighter. He was just an average Apache. Yet he had demonstrated, in his long journey and his subsequent years as an outlaw, the almost superhuman power of the Apache to find his way through unknown country and to survive great hardships.

A few other last-ditch hostiles remained in the mountains of Old Mexico. These were Chiricahuas, less than ten in number originally, who refused to surrender with Geronimo in 1886 and were joined by several San Carlos Apaches. They must have lived a dreadful life filled with sleepless nights, always in fear of pursuit or attack, and subsisting on seeds, wild fruits and nuts, and the flesh of such animals as they could steal or kill. I understand that these outlaws or their descendants are still hiding out in Old Mexico.

Our Arrival In Florida

At St. Louis (to resume the story of our ride east) we changed from old tourist sleeping cars to even older day coaches. From now on the trip was tiresome, since we were unable to lie down to get any sleep. In Illinois we were stared at by throngs of people at every station where the train stopped. Apparently they regarded us as some kind of wild animals.

Then we went down through Kentucky to Chattanooga, Tennessee. Here we crossed the Tennessee River over a higher bridge than any we had seen, then continued east through the mountains. Somewhere along the route the train stopped to give us a chance to get off and stretch. We walked around a bit, feeling stiff from the long ride in the day coaches. We arrived at Jacksonville, Florida, from where we were taken that same night to St. Augustine. At the station we were met by some of our tribesmen of Chihuahua's group who had been there since earlier in the year. Picking up our little bundles of belongings we followed them through town to old Fort Marion where we filed across a draw bridge and through a large gate into the compound on the interior of the fortress. Here a sergeant of Coast Artillery who was in charge of the caretaking detachment told us to climb up the stairs leading to the top of the embankment where we could select our own tents which had been erected there for us.

I went to the east end and picked out a big conical tent near the east sentry tower, which was one of the four towers at each corner of the fort. I made my bed as best I could and tumbled in, falling asleep immediately. We were all very tired from our long ride from Arizona in the old tourist cars.

Early next morning I awoke, yawned, and looked out to the east. I was amazed to see there what appeared to be a limitless field of waving grass. As my eyes cleared I was still more surprised to see that it was the ocean with its continually moving waves. Never before had we seen such a great body of water. As it had been dark the night before when we arrived, we didn't realize that the fort was right beside the sea.

Life At Fort Marion

I felt that we were honored to be living in the oldest Spanish fort in the United States, even as prisoners of war. As a young man the life of a prisoner didn't make much difference to me, for I was able to find pleasure and interest there just as I had in less favorable circumstances. But even more important to me, I was able to put into effect my recent conviction that a man's future lay in being able and willing to *work*. In this we had some assistance at Fort Marion. The War Department bought lumber and carpenters' tools. They appointed instructors to teach us the trade of a carpenter, at least all who wanted to learn. I'll admit that many of the Indians preferred to loaf but for myself it was a very welcome opportunity. Later in life I was able to look back on my period at Fort Marion as having been useful to me, especially when I became a farmer and had to build things around my home.

You might think that the prisoners of war were confined in the old dungeons at the fort. Actually we were kept in only at night when the great gate was shut. During the day we were allowed to wander around at will, go down town, or any place we chose, without getting permission from the caretaker sergeant. He only required that we be in by dark. On Saturdays and Sundays there were organized for us numerous excursions to near and distant cities and other points of interest. Also we had many visitors at the fort. Our women sold beadwork and other handicraft to these sightseers while the men and boys sold souvenir bows and arrows which they had made.

For my own part I had a flair for drawing and painting. So in the evenings I made pictures of various wild animals and other scenes from the west, which I sold to the tourists and other visitors.

On several occasions the Indians were given permission to hold a dance. These were embarrassing events for me. None of the Indian girls wanted to dance with me, as my shirt wasn't bright red or my face painted. I spent too much time trying to learn a useful trade or drawing pictures at night, hence wasn't very romantic to the girls.

OLD WARRIOR'S CLUB

Some of Geronimo's fighters "in retirement" at Mt. Vernon Barracks, Alabama. Left to right, seated: Olzonne, Chatto, Nanay, George Wratten (interpreter), Loco, two whose names are forgotten. Back row, left to right: Connie, Binday, Fawn, Chichil, Naiche, Geronimo, unknown, Perico, Yanozha.

The majority of the men had no occupation and didn't learn a trade. The most any of them accomplished was to whittle a few bows and arrows or serve on a detail to clean up around the fort.

I have been asked as to whether I was ever homesick while at Fort Marion or whether I missed "my country." How could I be homesick, when I had never had a home? Or pine for a country I never had—a country where I was only considered to be an enemy? No, I was never homesick, my home being where my mother and sister were. I now began to regard the whole United States as being my country where some day I could enjoy freedom and security under the great flag.

As a matter of fact I doubt if any of the Apaches were homesick. They had always been wanderers, never becoming attached to any one locality. Most of the land where they had roamed for the last century they now remembered for its inhospitable features, both natural and human. We had all been dodging behind rocks and through the cactus for a long time and I think that many of us left that life without regrets.

Other Groups of Apache Prisoners

The fourth batch of prisoners to be sent to Fort Marion consisted of a small party belonging to Mangas, mostly women and children. They had strayed from Geronimo's band when the latter was under pursuit.

A fifth and final group consisted of the women and children of Geronimo's own party, some of whom had come in with Chihuahua and the others who surrendered with Geronimo himself.

Geronimo and his warriors were sent via San Antonio to Fort Pickens, at Pensacola, Florida. They were accompanied by their longtime interpreter, Mr. George Wratten, who voluntarily went with the band into exile and remained with them most of his life. After several months these men were transferred to Mt. Vernon Barracks, Alabama where, nearly two years later, they were joined by all the other Apache prisoners of war. Thus Geronimo and his men finally were reunited with their families.

These Indians never did well in Alabama. Their death rate while there was tragically high, most of the sickness supposedly being caused by the low, swampy country and its "fevers," and the humid climate, which did not agree with a people accustomed to the western mountains. Seven years later, as I will describe, all the Apache prisoners were moved to Oklahoma, then called Indian Territory.

Chapter 16

GOLDEN DAYS

In April 1887, when I had been at Fort Marion for less than a year, Captain Richard H. Pratt, Superintendent of the Carlisle Indian Industrial School, paid us a visit. He was looking for candidates for his school. He brought with him, as a testimony of the value to the Indians in attending this school, a Carlisle student, an Apache boy who happened to be my favorite second cousin. This had no effect on me nor on the other prisoners. No one volunteered.

They lined us all up in front of Captain Pratt, who went down the line choosing forty-nine boys and girls to return with him to Carlisle. He also selected thirteen young men including me. The other twelve were married and some of them had children, but it was explained that families could accompany the married students. I well remember that when Captain Pratt came to me he stopped, looked me up and down, and smiled. Then he seized my hand, held it up to show that I volunteered. I only scowled; I didn't want to go at all. I was twenty-seven, too old to be a school boy. I had never been to any school, didn't know a word of English. This made no difference to Captain Pratt. He must have seen something in my face, sensed some future possibility in me, that I didn't know was there. At any rate this turned out to be one of the biggest events in my life.

A Great Humanitarian

Richard Henry Pratt was a lieutenant in the 10th Cavalry during the Indian wars against the Kiowas and Comanches in Indian Territory. In 1870 during the construction of the frontier post of Fort Sill, he was detailed to take charge of some Negro troopers who were cutting timbers along Medicine Bluff Creek. For this reason the local Indians called him "Lieutenant Timbers." These pickets were used to construct the first post headquarters, which stood near the creek just north of the present Academic Area officers' quarters.*

In 1876 the plains tribes in that part of the southwest were sub-

---

*Jason gained his knowledge of the early history of Fort Sill from a former 10th Cavalry soldier who worked for Mr. William H. Quinette, the Post Trader.

jugated, the leaders being sent as prisoners to Fort Marion, in St. Augustine where ten years later the Apaches were confined. Pratt went with them as officer in charge. During the next few months the lieutenant became so interested in trying to improve the lot of the Indians that he obtained permission from the War Department to establish an Indian Industrial School at Carlisle, Pennsylvania.

Carlisle Barracks, which was turned over to Pratt, was a former cavalry post which had been established long before the Revolutionary War but which after the Civil War had fallen into disuse. It required almost superhuman effort on Pratt's part to get it back in shape to be used as a school. The barracks, quarters, shops, and warehouses had to be rebuilt and refitted to serve as dormitories, classrooms, shops, hospital, bakery, laundry, chapel, Y. M. C. A., printing shop, central heating plant, dining hall, and homes for the superintendent and teachers. But when the work was completed and the school ready to open, there were no students. So Pratt, now a captain, went to the Dakotas where he secured some eighty young Sioux whom he brought back to Carlisle to form the first student body. This was in October, 1879. In subsequent years Captain Pratt was able to get students from other Indian tribes in various parts of the United States. Not all of them were wild Indians by any means. Some had been civilized for some time.

Pratt had the wisdom to select teachers who were mature, experienced, and possessed of firm religious convictions. Although he intended for disciplinary and other reasons to make the school military in its outward appearance, at the core it was to be strongly religious in character. Pratt believed that discipline, kindness, and religion were the three foremost elements in rehabilitating these primitive children.

Since I was one of Captain Pratt's rather more pitiful charges for nine years I can testify to the excellence of the foundations on which he built his school as well as to the greatness of his character. Students who obeyed him and behaved themselves were always met with a kind word and a ready smile. One could go to him in his office at any time and be greeted with a "Son, what can I do for you?" But if anyone should make unpleasant remarks about his school, then there was a quite different expression on his face. A cell in the guard house was kept ready, too, for those who caused serious trouble. I myself was on guard duty on many occasions and had the job of guarding some of my fellow Indians who had gotten drunk or committed offenses of a more serious nature.

Captain Pratt made a fine appearance, especially when we passed in review before him during parades. He was over six feet tall, had

ARRIVAL AT CARLISLE
Some of the young Apaches photographed at the Indian Industrial School at Carlisle Barracks on their arrival. Contrast this with the appearance of a similar group after they had been at Carlisle for a year or so (next illustration).

broad shoulders, and stood erect. We greatly admired his military bearing.

Mrs. Pratt was a great help to her husband. She was of the motherly type who always had a sweet smile for us when we would meet her on the campus. This contributed no small part to our content to be at the school. The girls who volunteered to help her in her home always considered it a privilege to be chosen for this task.

We Go To Carlisle

But to return to the story of our departure from Florida in the spring of 1887. Our group of sixty-two Apache "volunteers" left Fort Marion on a Saturday afternoon, traveling by train to the seaport town of Fernandina. After a weekend there we embarked for Charleston, South Carolina. Of course this was the first ocean voyage for any of us, not pleasant for everyone, but a new and thrilling experience. At Charleston, where the steamer docked for a day, Captain Pratt took us into the city to see a parade. Then we loaded aboard the steamer again for the voyage to New York. After we had sailed from Charleston the sea became rough. Quite a few of our party were sick. I got disgusted in hearing them crying in their cabins so I went up on deck where I lay down with a blanket and enjoyed the fresh air. After all I was a grown man who shouldn't exhibit weakness like some of the younger Indians.

Our ship docked at the foot of Brooklyn Bridge but as it was during the night we weren't able to see the sights. We at once loaded into horse-drawn cabs in which we crossed Manhattan and thence by ferry across the Hudson River to Jersey City.

We traveled by train from Jersey City through Philadelphia to Carlisle, Pennsylvania, arriving a little before noon exactly one week after we had left St. Augustine. Our train stopped on a siding just outside the post of Carlisle Barracks, where we were met by a delegation of faculty and students. Then we marched through the gate near the present hospital, past the historic guard house which had been built by Hessian soldiers. After we had been assembled on the steps of the mess hall for a photograph the boys were separated from the girls and each group was led to its respective dormitory. The boys

CIVILIZING INFLUENCE OF THE SCHOOL

Some of the Indian students after a year or so at Carlisle. Jason Betzinez is fourth from the right in the back row. The girl with glasses is his first "flame." In front of Jason is Ramona Chihuahua (daughter of Chief Chihuahua), who witnessed the killing of Charlie McComas.

were quartered in the converted old cavalry stables, back of the present classrooms of the Army War College. Here we were each given a haircut and a bath but not as yet issued new clothing.

About that time a bell rang. We looked out the windows to see the other students forming in ranks and being marched to dinner. Soon we were motioned to fall out and follow them. In the dining hall the other students looked us over with great curiosity for we were still wearing blankets like any camp Indians. As I look today at our first photographs I realize what unkempt and wild-looking creatures we were.

But this was soon to change. The school tailor shop turned out blue Army-type uniforms for the boys while the dress shop made neat dresses for the girls. We wore these uniforms proudly. Never before had I owned such fine-looking clothing.

We soon learned that the school was run on military lines. There were rules to be observed as well as a schedule. I suppose that some of the young Indians, who had had little discipline, fretted under this just as do children of other races who have not had the benefit of firm control. But we conformed. I am happy to say that for my own part I took to this regulated life quite naturally. From the outset I made up my mind to be a true young man, to obey the rules, and try to please the warmhearted man who had brought us there. This was my great good fortune, to have determined to take full advantage of this opportunity to make something of myself, to lift myself to a more useful life than the old pitiful existence to which I had been born.

Our rising bell in the morning was at six o'clock, breakfast at six-thirty, cleaning up our quarters and other work at eight, school at nine, dinner at twelve, supper at six, study period from eight to ten, then lights out. During the evening study period we were not allowed to visit back and forth between rooms, sing Indian songs, or make any noise. For those who could speak English there was a rule against speaking Indian. We were not allowed to use tobacco nor profanity. Each Saturday night we were expected to report ourselves for any violation of these rules. I recall one summer when I had been out working on a farm in the country for several months and had been using tobacco during that time, I got back to school just in time for the Saturday report. We were lined up as usual and those who had violated any of the rules during the past week were asked to step one pace to the front. Without thinking I stepped out all by myself, in front of the company. This got a big laugh, for the other students knew that I hadn't been at school during the past week but must be reporting myself for having smoked tobacco while on the farm.

Learning My ABC's

Our first teacher was a nice little lady, Miss Flora F. Low, who gave us names and taught us to write them on the blackboard. My childhood name of Nah-delthy, which means Going-to-Run, had been changed in 1878 to Batsinas. Batsinas was an old Indian at San Carlos, a great friend of my mother who had given me his name. Miss Low now changed the spelling of this to Betzinez. I suppose she thought it was a Spanish or Mexican word though actually I think "Batsinas" was Apache. It was also the custom at the school to give those Indians (most of us), who had only one name, another name—to be our first name. Miss Low selected for me the name of Jason. She said that Jason was some man who hunted the golden fleece but never found it. I thought that was too bad but it didn't mean anything to me at that time so I accepted the name. In the intervening years I believe that the story of Jason and his search for the Golden Fleece has set a pattern for my life.

It was extremely difficult for me to learn to speak English. At first I was unable to make many of the sounds. I even had trouble pronouncing the letters of the alphabet. I couldn't tell the difference between the strange sounds as readily as the younger people in the class. As a result I progressed very slowly, so slowly, in fact, that for the first three years it didn't seem that I would ever learn. Luckily I wasn't ashamed of myself or discouraged, saying simply that I would have to work extra hard to catch up with the others. In this I was helped by my teachers, who patiently went over with me again and again the words and phrases I was trying to say. Finally I was pleased to have my teacher, a Miss F. G. Paull, of Blairsville, Pennsylvania, compliment me by saying, "Jason, you have made quite an advance. You are beginning to show improvement in your English." Thus encouraged I began to make better progress not only in English but in my other subjects.

Learning A Trade

One day Mr. W. P. Campbell, a Chippewa Indian who was our first disciplinarian, called me out and took me to the old blacksmith shop where he assigned me as an apprentice. I had previously asked him to put me in the carpentry shop, in which type of work I had become interested, but for some reason he wouldn't do it. So I remained in the blacksmith shop for a short time as helper to Frank Lock, another young Indian, until Frank graduated from the school.

Now I had a better chance to learn, for I was right under the boss himself. One day he said to me, "Jason, we have received an order to make several hacks (carriages) for service out west. I want you to get started on it."

I said, "Mr. Harris, I have not had any instruction in welding axles. Will you weld them for me?"

"No," he replied. "I used to have to do that work for Frank Lock, who had never learned. Now I'm not going through that all over again with you. So you will have to learn how to weld. Here. Watch me and pay attention to this instruction."

I did what Mr. Harris told me and soon learned how to weld. My welding of steel carriage axles turned out fine; in fact after thirty-two years of blacksmithing I was never able to do a better job of welding than I did right there at Carlisle.

The School used the first hack that I made. Afterwards I made several more, one of which won a prize in the annual school exhibit. Then it was sent to the World's Fair in Chicago where it was seen and purchased by a missionary from South Africa who took it back to that country with him.

Other Influences At Carlisle

During my ten years in Pennsylvania I became well acquainted with the country, and very fond of it, too. In addition to the Saturday night sociables and other entertainment which was provided for us at the post, I used to go down to Carlisle on Saturday evenings to loaf on the street corners just like the young white farmers. One of my most pleasant memories is that of eating oysters at a little stand back of the market square. I must remind you that this is a bit unusual for a western Indian, whose tribe had a taboo against eating anything that lived under the water. But I made strenuous efforts to shed the Indian superstitions. In so doing I suppose I picked up a few of the white man's like carrying a rabbit foot for good luck. I understand that the whites in turn got this from the Negroes.

Another memory of Carlisle was Kronenberg's clothing store on Hanover Street, founded by a very nice and friendly family of German Jews from whom I bought clothes from time to time. I was very pleased when visiting Carlisle in 1958 to find Kronenberg's still in business on Hanover Street and to buy another suit of clothes from them.

Some people have asked me if I knew Jim Thorpe, the famous Indian athlete who attended Carlisle. No, he was later than my time and besides was from another tribe in another part of the United States. Nevertheless like most of the boys at the school I played baseball, basketball, football, and many other sports and games. In the early days we used to indulge, too, in an old Indian game of shinny, a very rough sport something like hockey except that it is not played on ice.

The most powerful influence on my life at this or any other time was my introduction to the teachings of Christianity. While at the school we were required to go to church on Sunday mornings. I also got in the habit of attending Y.M.C.A. meetings on Sunday afternoons and prayer service in the evenings. This influence became stronger and stronger as I came to understand English better. It changed my whole life.

Summer Farmwork

During that first year at Carlisle I continued to attend school in the mornings and work in the blacksmith shop in the afternoons. In April I was sent out to work on a farm. Since I couldn't speak English and didn't know my way the school authorities tied a tag on my uniform addressing me, like an express package, to: Mr. Edward Cooper, Newtown, Bucks County, Pennsylvania. I went by rail to Philadelphia where the tag on my uniform got me safely transferred to another train. I arrived at Newtown about sunset. At the station a stranger came up to me, examined my tag, then motioned for me to follow him to a waiting buggy. This was my future employer Mr. Cooper. We drove to his farm where the family welcomed me and we all sat down to a good supper.

The Coopers were members of the Society of Friends (Quakers), who for some years had been interested in helping Indians learn the ways of the white man. They were warm-hearted people, who tried numerous methods to help me to improve myself. After supper that first night I had a chance to get acquainted with the children, there being one boy and three girls. The youngest was Mary, age three. At first when I held out my hand to her she ran to her mother crying, "Mama, Indian!" But we soon became great pals.

My work for Mr. Cooper continued for three months when, because of an injury, I had to return to Carlisle before the summer was over. I suppose that some people who have seen me in later years and have noticed that part of the index finger and the thumb on my right hand are missing, have come to the conclusion that I was wounded in the Indian wars in the wild west. My injury occurred in a much less romantic fashion—though for a wild Apache not less unique. My hand was caught in the gears of Mr. Cooper's corn shelling machine and partly crushed. I was taken to a doctor who wanted to give me an anesthetic while he amputated the injured members. I refused, saying that I could stand the pain and wanted to watch the operation. Which I did.

In the spring of 1889 I went back to work for Mr. Cooper and again the following year. As he had had wide experience in general farming I gained much valuable knowledge of agriculture from him which was useful to me in later years.

After these three long summers spent on a farm I realized that my education as well as my efforts to learn English were being retarded by being absent so long from the school. So the next year I remained

JASON BETZINEZ AT NEWTOWN, PENNSYLVANIA
Photo of Jason made while working for Quaker family on a farm

at Carlisle putting in more time in classwork and at the same time working in the blacksmith shop. I also had a chance to learn something of carpentry, plumbing, and general construction work, because we were detailed to assist in rebuilding some of the old buildings at the school and in erecting new ones. One of the most important of these latter projects was the construction of a new gymnasium. We Indians got up a purse of ten thousand dollars—a lot of money in those days—for the gymnasium, and besides we did a good deal of the work. Another five thousand was donated by friends of the school. The gymnasium was used for our Saturday night social gatherings, for indoor graduation exercises, as well as for athletics and games. When I revisited Carlisle Barracks in 1958 and was taken to the gymnasium, now being used by the Army War College, I felt considerable pride in the part I had played sixty years before in creating this fine structure.

The next year I again worked on Mr. Cooper's farm during the summer and in the fall went to a country school with his children. By this time I was practically an adopted member of the family. I was proud and pleased that the Coopers addressed me as "son."

However, the following year when I again put in my name as a volunteer for summer farmwork, I was sent to Mr. Chilyan Reeder, a cousin of Mr. Cooper who lived about two miles from the Cooper farm. From there I went to Penns Park, thence back, in the winter, to the school at Carlisle.

The following spring I was sent to Edgewood, New Jersey, fourteen miles northwest of Trenton and near the Delaware River. Here I worked for another Quaker.

During this period when many of us were working in Bucks County, the Indian girls were sent to the Philadelphia area to work in homes. I suppose that the school authorities felt that it was safer to keep the boys and girls separated. Because of this and the fact that I worked extra long hours at the school I was prevented from doing much courting. Also I was still shy when with the girls. I had had my eye for years on a young Apache girl whom I had known since we were children. But we were at the Carlisle school together for several years before I worked up my courage sufficiently to ask her to "go with me." (Captain Pratt had suggested that I get married.) But she turned me down, saying that my blacksmith work made me too dirty. Later she married a northern Indian and moved to Iowa. Though seventy years have elapsed I am still mad about this embarrassing outcome to my first effort to get a wife.

My last summer work on a farm was in 1892 when I was sent to

Pennington, New Jersey, eight miles from Trenton. I was met at the depot by an elderly German-American, a quiet, gentle fellow with a most pleasing disposition. This family, the Herman Fullers, were very fine people, devout Methodists. Unlike the other farmers who mostly raised corn and barley, Mr. Fuller ran a small dairy. He raised sugar beets for stock feed. When in the fall I told Mr. Fuller that I was returning to Carlisle, he expressed deep disappointment, saying that I was the most dependable and hard-working farm hand he had ever had. I greatly appreciated this compliment.

While working for Mr. Fuller I picked up a few words of German. Also I acquired a great respect and liking for Americans of German blood. They were hard workers, and good people. There are a few of them in my home town of Apache, Oklahoma. I have always enjoyed knowing these "donkey-shanes" as I call them.*

Work In The Steel Mill

After nine years attending the Carlisle Indian Industrial School I finally decided that I could not progress beyond the eighth grade. I was now over thirty years of age and it was high time that I began my life work. In my discouragement I went to Captain Pratt and told him that I wanted to leave school.

Pratt replied, "Jason, I want you to stay and graduate. After that you can leave school."

I left Captain Pratt's office feeling rather downcast, especially since I had been considering this important change in my life for some time and had made my decision only after much soul searching. But later that same day Captain Pratt sent for me to tell me that he had reconsidered. I had his permission to leave school and seek a job.

I knew that I would be sad at first to leave Carlisle and its happy memories. I would miss my many friends among the students and the faculty. Furthermore I would now be entirely on my own, a big change for one who had always had someone else to look to for advice. But I intended to seek work in a nearby community. Therefore I could easily return to Carlisle for visits if I became lonely or needed help. So I set forth with confidence and pleased anticipation to make my way in the world.

---

*From the German *danke schoen*, meaning "thank you very much." During Jason's 1958 visit to his old haunts in Pennsylvania he was taken out into the Pennsylvania "Dutch" (German) peach growing district. One of the farmers, having read of him in the newspaper, came up to the car and greeted Jason with "Wie gehts?" Jason instantly responded, "Siemlich gut," then roared with laughter at the surprised expression on the farmer's face.

Chapter 17

FOLLOWING A TRADE

After leaving Carlisle in 1897 I went to Steelton, where I applied for a job in the Pennsylvania Steel Company, now the Bethlehem Steel Works. Initially they employed me as a common laborer at a dollar a day, helping in the blacksmith shop. They said that so far as they knew I was the first Indian to work in a steel mill. Although a dollar a day seems like very small wages, in those days it wasn't too bad for unskilled labor, especially since I was able to get board and room with laundry for four dollars a week. Later I was advanced to a regular position as a blacksmith and tool dresser at thirty cents an hour. I also did much night work at forty-five cents an hour. Soon I was putting in eighteen hours a day. The steel workers were entirely satisfied with their modest wages, as the cost of living in those days was correspondingly low.

Many foreigners as well as native-born Americans worked in the Steelton plant. I associated with Germans, Swedes, Italians, English, Scotch, French, and others—all of us speaking what we thought was English in order to have a common tongue. Two of my best friends at this time were Harry and Abe Troup, whose brother founded the Troup Music Company on Market Square in Harrisburg. They were tall muscular young men who wore derby hats, even when at work, and handlebar mustaches. Once in a while they would challenge me to wrestling matches in which I always got them down. My old tough life in the west and my blacksmith work made me very strong. I used to spend much time at the Troup home where I was treated as a member of the family. The memory of those days is one of the most pleasant of my life.

I found time to play some baseball, too, and was fullback on the Steelton football team.

Shortly after I went to Steelton I was sent as a delegate to an international convention of the Christian Endeavor Society, which was held in Washington, D. C. The whole town was open to us so I took advantage of my first opportunity to see the sights of the world's most beautiful city. Being greatly interested in the eventual disposition of the Apache prisoners of war, I visited the office of the Commissioner of Indian Affairs, where we had a long talk concerning my people. While at Carlisle I had visited the Apaches in Alabama during one of my vacations and was saddened to see the pitiable condition into which they had fallen. As I told the Commissioner, truly they were the most helpless and hopeless of all the Indians at that time. I urged that something be done for them. In 1894 they had been moved to Fort Sill, Indian Territory. Apparently this was an improvement. But they still were prisoners, which was depressing to them, and they needed more help even though the War Department was giving them good care. Not having then been at Fort Sill I thought that the Apaches ought to be returned to their native country. Later I was to change my mind about this.

My affiliation with the Church in Steelton gained me many fine friends among some of the more influential people of the community. I had already been prepared for joining the church while at Carlisle. Now at Steelton, on January 10, 1897, I fully accepted the teachings of Christ, which I firmly believed then, as I still do, are straight from God. Accepting Christ as my savior I became a member of the First Presbyterian Church in Steelton. When I revisited Steelton in 1958 I was given the great privilege of preaching the Sunday morning sermon in my old church. I was honored, too, to have in the congregation Mr. Walter Lang, the head of the great steel plant where I formerly worked as a laborer.

After a year or more in Steelton some of my friends told me that the long, extra hours that I was putting in, and perhaps the conditions under which I was working, were ruining my health. Pointing out that I had developed a chronic cough, they predicted that I wouldn't live long unless I regained my normal good health. They felt that I ought to go out west. With this advice fresh in my mind, I happened to visit Carlisle one day. Captain Pratt, calling me into his office, told me that he had received a letter from Darlington, Indian Territory, stating that there was an opening there in the Indian service for a blacksmith. He urged me to apply for it, which I did and was accepted.

I Go To Oklahoma

I felt some uneasiness in leaving the plant at Steelton, where I had been working with and under the supervision of experienced men, to go to a new position where I would be on my own resources. I hoped that I was skilled enough in my work to make good.

The idea of going west wasn't altogether a happy one, either, even though I was headed for the land where my people now were

STEEL MILL FOOTBALL TEAM
Jason (on left) as a fullback on the Machine Shop football team at Steelton, Pa., in 1896

and where I would be employed in the Indian service. After all I wasn't "going back" to Oklahoma. I had never been there. Furthermore after ten years in the east I had come to regard Pennsylvania as being my home. Most of my friends were now in Pennsylvania. I also had established deep roots in the school at Carlisle, so that it was a real wrench to leave it. This was the first time that I had become attached to any one locality.

My first stop was at Washington, Missouri, where I was scheduled to change trains to the Rock Island for the last part of the trip. The ticket agent couldn't find Darlington on the map so I told him to sell me a ticket to El Reno. I knew that there was an Indian agency near there.

After leaving Wichita, Kansas, I began to experience a heavy sense of disappointment in the country. Remember I had been born and raised in the mountains. Then I had lived for years in a land of green grass, trees, blue hills, and deep rivers—Cumberland County, Pennsylvania. The treeless western prairies didn't look good to me. Already I began to regret leaving Pennsylvania.

Soon we began to see prairie dog villages, the first familiar sight. Though there were no prairie dogs in the Rocky Mountains, I remembered seeing them in the plains country which we passed through in 1886 as prisoners of war. I kept listening for the conductor to call out "El Reno" but he announced the next stop as being Darlington. I hastened to grab my valise and get off there. At the station I found a rural mail carrier who was going to the Indian agency and who offered me a ride. He assured me that I had gotten off the train at the right place. Darlington, not El Reno, was the site of the Cheyenne and Arapaho agency to which I was headed.

I had thought that I would find only strangers at the agency but was pleasantly surprised to be greeted by a number of my old schoolmates from Carlisle. They showed me the blacksmith shop and the carpenter shop then took me to the Arapaho school, where I was to board. I found other acquaintances there, good Christians and staunch friends whom I had known at Carlisle. They all helped me to get settled and acquainted.

The Indian agent wanted to test me for the position I was supposed to fill. Another young Indian who had preceded me there by ten days was trying out for the same job. There were two vacancies, one at Colony and the other at Red Moon. Colony was the more important of the two, so we both wanted that. After several days of work in the shop I was told by Mr. Smith, the head blacksmith, to gather up my tools and to pack some materials, as I had been accepted for the position at Colony, some fifty miles west of Darlington. I was to travel with two wagons loaded with supplies for the subagency.

One of the drivers was Wash Robertson, a Negro, the other a young Arapaho. Our first stop was at Powder Face Crossing on the South Canadian River. Because of quicksand this ford was greatly feared by travelers. Robertson decided to camp for the night and make the crossing in broad daylight the next day. It was nearly noon before we got across, even after putting four horses to each wagon, because of the deep, treacherous sand. We were now in the country of the Caddoes and Wichitas who since early Spanish times had been known for their beehive-shaped houses made of grass and who still built a few of these lodges though most of them now lived in frame houses furnished by the Government. By evening we had only made fifteen miles, camping for the night at the next stage stand. Next day we pulled out to the west along a sandy road. After going five miles we passed a landmark of the Plains tribes, called Ghost Mountain. It was merely a little hill.

Arriving at Colony about noon I was taken in charge by the agency clerk, Mr. Walcup. After dinner he took me to a baseball game near the Dutch Reformed Mission. I had played baseball at the Carlisle school and later at the steel works, so enjoyed this considerably.

On the following Monday I was shown the building in which were located both a sawmill and the blacksmith shop. There was scarcely room there for the shop but I made the best of it. My work consisted of general blacksmithing such as horseshoeing and repairing wagons and other implements. I was glad to be in this familiar type of work and to know that I gave satisfaction to my employers. I was able, too, to make many new friends among the white people as well as the Indians. There was a mission near the agency, under charge of Dr. Walter C. Roe and Dr. Frank H. Wright. The latter was a trained singer who had studied for grand opera and had been offered a place with the opera company in New York. But he declined because he wanted to return to his people as a missionary. Dr. Wright was an ideal man for this work, being an educated Choctaw. He was greatly admired not only because of his fine voice and musical ability but for his wonderful personality.

Transferred To Fort Sill

I was at Colony for eighteen months. During my vacations I visited my mother at Fort Sill, to which the Apaches had been moved from Alabama six years before. The officer in charge of them offered me a position in the blacksmith shop but I couldn't give him a definite answer at that time. On my return to Colony I was told that I was being transferred to Darlington as assistant carpenter and wheelwright. Although this pleased me greatly, in a short time I decided that I preferred to work for my own people. So in January 1900, I resigned at Darlington and went to Fort Sill.

On applying for employment in the post blacksmith shop I was told that this was impossible. The policy was that as long as the Apaches were at Fort Sill, special privileges were not to be granted to any individual Indians. I would have to live with the other Apaches and perform the same type of work even though I personally was no longer considered to be a prisoner of war. This was somewhat a disappointment since I had already been a Government employee at Colony and Darlington. But I accepted the conditions, hopeful that an opening would soon be found whereby I could ply my trade as a blacksmith.

Chapter 18

THE APACHES ARE MOVED TO FORT SILL

The Apache prisoners of war had been at Fort Sill for six years before I arrived. My mother and other members of the tribe gave me the story of that period, which I summarize here.

While they were at Mt. Vernon Barracks, Alabama, the Apache prisoners of war had suffered an increasingly high death rate. Finally it was decided to move them to a higher altitude and a drier climate. General Miles suggested that they go to Camp Supply, an old frontier post in Oklahoma which was scheduled for abandonment. But Captain Hugh L. Scott,* who had become known for his good work with the Indians, persuaded Miles that Fort Sill was a better location. Fort Sill, established in 1869 near the eastern end of the Wichita Mountains in the reservation of the Kiowas and Comanches, had also outlived its former role as a post for controlling the wild tribes. At this time it was a minor military station with a small garrison. But the reservation offered ample room for the Apaches, having good water, plenty of firewood, timber for constructing houses, and pasturage for a large herd of cattle. The soil was fertile enough to encourage the belief that the Apaches could make some headway in raising crops. The Kiowas and Comanches over the objections of a few of their chiefs were persuaded to make some of their land available to the Apaches, which land would be added to the military reservation.

On their arrival from Alabama in the fall of 1894 the Apaches detrained at Rush Springs, some thirty miles east of Fort Sill. No horses or wagons being provided them, they had to walk to the post carrying their few belongings. When they reached a point some two miles northeast of the fort, where they were to camp for the night, the Indians were met by a large crowd of curious people from Fort Sill together with several hundred Kiowas and Comanches. The newcomers, escorted by a company of the 12th Infantry under Lieutenant Allyn Capron, made a sorry appearance. They were dusty, tired, and bedraggled. They possessed almost nothing, not even a camp dog.

---
*Scott became Chief of Staff, U.S. Army, when the United States entered World War I.

[165]

None of the local Indians could speak the Apache language.* The Apaches didn't understand Comanche or the sign language, the common means of communication between the several plains tribes.

The prisoners of war hadn't seen any other Indians for eight years. Now, hungering for companionship with people of their own race, the first ones they saw were two tribes with whom they had usually been at war. There had never been much contact between the Apaches and the plains tribes, but occasionally the Kiowas and Comanches, in raids against the Navajoes, Utes, or Pueblo tribes, had collided with Apaches. Similarly the Apaches, while on their rare expeditions eastward after buffalo, had had fights with the prairie Indians. Now it was time to make peace. The Apaches on one hand and the Kiowas and Comanches on the other each shoved forward a Carlisle graduate who conversed in English. From this hesitant beginning the former hatred and distrust gradually were forgotten. The local Indians began to make friendly visits to the prisoners of war.†

Captain Hugh L. Scott had been selected as the first supervisor for the prisoners of war. He was assisted initially by Captain Marion P. Maus, whom many of us remembered as being the officer who succeeded Captain Emmett Crawford on the 1886 expedition into Mexico when Crawford was killed.

Villages Are Built

The Apaches arrived at Fort Sill too late in the season for them to attempt to build houses. Therefore they were assigned camp locations along Cache Creek and elsewhere north and northeast of the post, where they quickly erected their familiar tepees which they covered with salvaged canvas furnished by the Quartermaster.

In the spring Captain Scott planned to have the Indians build a number of small villages. In order to utilize the most suitable locations where water, wood, and grazing land were available, he divided the tribe into small groups each to live in a village. It was decided to retain so far as possible the normal family groupings, each with its own head man who would be enlisted as a U.S. Indian Scout and would act as supervisor of his own band. George Wratten, who had been with the Apaches for many years, and who was the only white man who was completely fluent in the language, was asked to choose

---

*In recent years, however, the Kiowa-Apaches, a small satellite tribe of Athabascan origin, long associated with the Kiowas, have stated that they understood a few words of the tongue spoken by the prisoners of war.

†Further data is given in *Carbine and Lance, The Story of Old Fort Sill*, by Col. W. S. Nye. Norman: University of Oklahoma Press.

these subchiefs. His recommendations wisely followed the leadership structure of the tribe. In the following table, which sets forth the chief of each village and the location, it will be noted that by now many familiar Indian names have been augmented by first names.

Geronimo, Scout	Village on east side of Cache Creek, near Geronimo Spring.
Charles Martine, Scout	Village a few hundred yards north of Geronimo's.
Leon Perico, Scout	Village a mile south of Geronimo's between Cache Creek and Beef Creek. The sawmill was also here.
Chihuahua, Scout	Village on a low ridge a little over a mile north of the Old Post, Fort Sill.
George Noche, Scout	Village near north boundary of reservation, a half mile west of the Frisco Railroad.
Jacob Kaahtenny, Scout	Village near twin lakes, northwest of Medicine Bluff.
Charles Mangas, Scout	Village near Wolf Creek.
Rogers Toclanny, Scout	Village west of Wolf Creek.
Chief Apache Loco, Scout	Village near Four Mile Crossing, north of Heyl's Hole.
Christian Naiche, Scout	Village south of Four Mile Crossing.
Alfred Chatto, Scout	Village a half mile west of Four Mile Crossing.
Tom Chiricahua, Scout	Village a mile west of Loco's village.

The type of house to be constructed for each family was the then familiar "two pens and a passage," or two rooms separated by a roofed passage which could be used for storage and could later be inclosed. Such buildings, which required relatively short ridge beams, had been in common use on the frontier since before the Civil War, being utilized even for officers' quarters in some of the early posts. They were constructed by cutting logs, sawing them into boards, then setting them upright to form a picket construction. Although this was a fairly simple method the Apaches, being unskilled in the use of carpenter tools, took several months to complete their villages. After the work was finished each of the various families was allowed to select a subchief or village supervisor under whom they wished to live and work. Then they moved from their temporary winter camps.

APACHE VILLAGE NEAR FOUR MILE CROSSING, FORT SILL

Indians Are Taught To Work

After the Indians were settled in their new homes the officer in charge started to teach them farming, the actual instruction being mostly given by Mr. Wratten. Each family was allotted ten acres on which the head of the house had to break the sod and prepare it for planting. Five acres of this had to be planted to kaffir corn, which Captain Scott had introduced as being more easily grown in that land of frequent drought. The other five acres could be planted to whatever crops the Indian selected, such as melons, beans, or yellow corn.

Initially the Government furnished mules, farm implements, and seed. However there were only sufficient mules to provide one to a family and these had to be used in turn. George Wratten was kept busy making the rounds to see to it that each Indian promptly used his mule then passsed it on to the next man who was awaiting his turn.

Having gotten the Indians housed and started farming the authorities purchased and issued cattle. Now the Apaches really had their hardest work, cutting fence posts, digging post holes, and stretching the fence wire. The entire military reservation of some seventy thousand acres had to be inclosed so that the cattle would not stray on to the adjoining land of the Kiowas and Comanches. This would have caused quarrels, stock stealing, and troubles with cattlemen from Texas who in many cases had leased parts of the Kiowa-Comanche reservation for grazing privileges. The fence erected at that time by

THE APACHES ARE TAUGHT TO WORK
Jason is on the right

the Apaches has lasted to this day, being repaired from time to time, of course.

Following this work the Apaches were given the task of constructing earthen reservoirs, or tanks as they are called in the west, for watering the cattle. These were built in places where the intermittent small streams could be dammed to form ponds, some of which were twenty acres or more in extent. Long years after the Apaches were gone these tanks provided a source of pleasure for fishermen and duck hunters from Fort Sill. Even where they were not stocked, fish and freshwater clams soon appeared, the eggs being deposited, it is thought, from the plumage and feet of migrating waterfowl.

Initially only a few of the Apaches had horses except for the Government mounts which were issued to the scouts who acted as supervisors. Consequently the men had to herd the cattle on foot. Probably this would have been impossible for anyone except the Apaches. In spite of their long years of relative inactivity the men soon got back in good physical condition and were hiking all over the reservation in pursuit of stray cattle or in repairing the fence. They actually enjoyed this work, all the more since they began to realize that the funds collected from the sale of cattle would mean money in their pockets.

The summer roundup was an especially strenuous time because even when they got a few horses, the men had to do most of the work on foot—cutting out calves, branding stock, and so on. The few horses that were available were untrained for cow punching.

In the summer when the prairie grass was in good height the tribe formed into small bands for haying. These groups camped in different parts of the military reservation where there was plenty of grass and water for the stock. Then everyone had to work rapidly and hard to cut and bale the hay while the weather stayed good. The men detailed for this work had to be strong and healthy, well behaved, and willing to work long hours. Many tons of fine hay were harvested in this manner. After sufficient hay was set aside to feed the cattle during the winter each family was given its prorata share for its own horses, mules, and cows. Then the surplus was sold on contract. Usually the Post Quartermaster bought many tons of hay from the Apaches, the proceeds being deposited in the Apache fund. Under Captain Sayre's careful management, and that of his successor, this fund grew rapidly so that we were soon able to pay off the indebtedness incurred for the purchase of implements and stock.

All these enterprises, well established by the time I went to Fort Sill, demonstrated that under proper instruction even wild Indians can be made self-supporting and kept contented. This all happened while the Indians were under the control of the War Department. I have always been convinced that our people did much better under this agency than under the Department of the Interior. Under the latter we were repeatedly deprived of our land and other rights, some think in order to satisfy the land—or mineral—greed of white immigrants, or to line the pockets of unscrupulous agents. We had been forcibly taken from our assigned reservation, which had been granted to us in perpetuity, and exiled to a barren land of hostile surroundings and unfriendly Indians and whites. Not until we were made "prisoners" and supervised by Army officers did we get fair treatment and an opportunity to make something of ourselves. I realize that this is a one-sided view and that many Indian agents may have been honest and dedicated to the welfare of their charges. I am only telling what I saw. But there is no need to dwell on this. I am not bitter. It is all long past and we have finally come to somewhat better times.

The Missionaries

Prior to 1899 the Apaches did not receive much religious guidance or teaching. In the summer of that year Dr. Walter C. Roe and Dr. Frank H. Wright came down from Colony to establish a mission of the Dutch Reformed Church for these Indians.

The two missionaries, both dedicated men, but both of them frail and Dr. Wright suffering from the beginning of the disease (tuberculosis) which was to carry him away, arrived at Fort Sill in good spirits, eager to bring the Gospel to the Apache prisoners. First they secured permission from the military authorities to conduct their work among the prisoners of war. Then they held a camp meeting for the Apaches just south of Geronimo's village. Here under a big elm tree it seemed that the Indians were responding well. Thus encouraged, the missionaries, with the financial backing of the Women's Board of Domestic Missions of the Dutch Reformed Church, built a combined school and chapel a mile north of Medicine Bluff. This was centrally located to all the Apache villages.

During the summer Dr. Wright found a young lady, Miss Maud Adkisson, who had been trained in Texas as a nurse, whom he persuaded to come to our people as our first permanent teacher-missionary. Miss Adkisson, who later married the Rev. L. L. Legters, stayed at first with a Comanche family until the school house was finished. Then she moved into a room provided for her in the new building. At first this was a lonely and desolate position for a woman, surrounded by half-wild Indians, all strangers. Then another school teacher arrived, who moved in with Miss Adkisson.

These two workers started out to teach the young Indians ABC's and Christianity. They were assisted to a certain degree by returning Carlisle students. A Christian Endeavor society and a Sunday School were also organized in spite of rather great difficulties. It appeared that a good start had been made in bringing The Light to the young Indians at least. Then during the winter a disturbing influence was

APACHE MISSION AT FORT SILL

CHRISTIAN ENDEAVOR SOCIETY

Back row, third from right, is James Kawaykla, present at Victorio's last battle. Jason is fourth from right. In center is Miss Maud Adkisson.

interposed by the start of a medicine dance along Medicine Bluff Creek.

An Indian whose English name was Harold Dick, seeing that money was to be made by playing on the fears of the Indians, especially since there was considerable sickness in the tribe, announced himself as setting up in business as a healer. He denounced the white man's religion, saying that it was good only for the white man. The Indians were urged to reject it and stick to the old ways and the old religion. This was a persuasive argument made all the stronger by Dick's claim to be able to cure ailments. He was clever enough to interest the Indians in staging a medicine dance, which had always appealed to them as a form of entertainment. This dance, which I will discuss more fully a little later, began to draw the Indians away from church and other religious instruction. During the winter of 1899-1900 attendance fell off to an alarming extent, only a few of the more faithful continuing to go to the services held by the missionaries.

Nevertheless as the springtime approached, the work of the two women began to bear fruit as more and more Indians began coming to church and Christian Endeavor meetings.

Some curiosity seekers from Fort Sill and the surrounding country, both Indian and white, came to see the wild Apaches in church. It was especially interesting when such a gifted missionary as Dr. Roe was there to preach the sermon, with Mrs. Roe at the little organ and the great evangelist-singer Dr. Wright rendering anthems and other stirring religious songs in his fine baritone. Our Apaches always enjoyed Dr. Wright's singing even when they didn't understand the rest of the service.

From then on it was an uphill fight on the part of the missionaries to win out over the evil influence of the medicine man and other temptations which I will describe later. There were many times in those days when it seemed that Christianity would never take hold in the Apache tribe. I recall days and nights, especially when the medicine dance was at its height, that I was the only Indian present at church services. At that time we sometimes almost despaired, I think, not realizing that the good seed which had been planted would grow —imperceptibly at first, but with an eventual full flowering.

There were other devoted workers who followed those first missionaries. I should mention some of them. Miss Mary E. Ewing, whose home was in New Albany, Indiana, had had long experience as a kindergarten teacher. She came to Fort Sill in November, 1900 to teach in the kindergarten at the Apache school. It was her first journey to the "wild west," everything being strange and, I suppose, a little frightening to her.

Miss Ewing had an especially difficult time teaching the small Apache children, for their minds did not seem to take hold as readily as those of white children, no doubt because of their imperfect understanding of English. Only a few had been taught English at home. Nevertheless Miss Ewing, realizing the importance of influencing these people when they were very young, worked hard to bring them the first glimpse of how to gain wider knowledge, as well as their first teachings of Christianity. She was a women small in body but big in heart. These little wild Indians soon began to respond to her cheerfulness, loving words, and soothing hands. They had found a real friend. Eventually Miss Ewing's work in the school as well as in Christian Endeavor Society and the church had made her much appreciated by most of the Apaches, old as well as young.

There were numerous changes among the primary school teachers but Miss Ewing remained there until the mission school was discontinued in 1913. At that time she returned to her home in Indiana, coming back to Apache later to help Miss Anna Heersma, the field matron. These two ladies worked together among the Apaches for eleven years, Miss Ewing having spent a total of seventeen years in the work.

Another missionary to whom the Apaches should always be grateful was Miss Anna Heersma. Miss Heersma, who was related by blood to the Royal House of Orange of the Netherlands, was living with her parents in a suburb of Chicago when she received the call to go to the Apache mission at Fort Sill. She at once left her host of friends and relatives and went to the mission in October, 1907. Everything there was strange to a young woman who had lived mostly in a great city. She had, however, been raised on a farm, which later proved to be a valuable background.

Miss Heersma worked principally among orphan children at a home established by the Dutch Reformed Church. Here these children were taught housekeeping, cooking, and other domestic arts and sciences. Like Miss Ewing, Anna Heersma was an affectionate mother to all these derelict Apache children.

She had to assume heavy responsibilities, especially when accidents or sickness occurred, to supervise the lives of these Indian children. They were difficult to teach in school, because the day students and their parents made endless trouble for her, undoing much of the good done by the workers in the orphanage. But today, when these orphans are grown, the former Miss Heersma often receives grateful recognition from them for the good she accomplished.

Colonel Pratt's Visit

Not long after I came to Fort Sill I heard that Colonel Pratt, our old school superintendent, was coming on a visit to Anadarko, some fifty miles northeast of the post. Several of us former Carlisle students went up to greet him. When our old friend got off the train his face lighted up to see us gathered there, most of us with tears in our eyes. We saw the pride in his face as he looked around him at the eager faces of his old students and he greeted each of us with hearty affection. This renewed our determination to live up to his wish to see us become good and useful citizens.

Chapter 19
WORKING FOR MY PEOPLE

On my arrival at Fort Sill, Indian Territory, in January of 1900 I went first to the post where, as I have related, I was initially unsuccessful in securing a position as a blacksmith. After being told that I would have to join the Apaches and work just like the rest of them, I went on north of Fort Sill to Geronimo's village where my immediate kinsfolk were living. But only my mother was there. The rest of the houses were deserted.

"Where are all the people?" I asked.

"I am alone here," mother replied. "Everyone has gone to Four Mile Crossing, where they are camped in tents, taking part continuously in the dance."

A few nights later I went to Four Mile Crossing to see this thing for myself. Being a Christian, and having pretty well rid myself of the old foolish notions, I wanted to see what was the cause of all the excitement. I was saddened to see that nearly all of my former schoolmates from Carlisle, who certainly knew better, and who had received the civilizing influence of the school and the Church, had slipped back into the old ways.

The Medicine Dance

The Indians have always enjoyed dancing, just as other races do. And, if you study dancing closely, and compare the styles practiced by various peoples, you will see that they have much in common. There is the excitement stirred up by the rythmic beating of the tom-toms, the monotonous, repetitious kind of singing, and the bouncing up and down and hopping around of the dancers, generally in unison. All of them wearing silly smiles or rapt expressions. It is primitive, no matter how you regard it. I suppose we are all primitive to some degree.

This Apache who claimed to be a great medicine man and who started the dance on the Fort Sill reservation, was playing on the fears as well as the pleasures of his people. The Indians for years had been deathly afraid of tuberculosis; and with good reason, for it had been a scourge ever since the white man had brought it to them. This medicine man claimed that he could cure anyone, even an Indian who was about to die, from the effects of tuberculosis. The main feature of the "cure" was taking part in the medicine dance.

The medicine dance with its religious overtones was supposed to produce a healing effect by driving away evil spirits. The dance form which was customary with the Apaches, and which our people found the most exciting, was called "The Fire Dance." It originated far back in our history, so long ago that no member of the tribe could remember a time when we didn't have it. The old Apaches said that the Spirit who gave them this dance appeared to them on a mountain. Since then the dance has never been changed, having been handed down from generation to generation.

Many preparations preceded the dance, such as the painting of the bodies of the dancers with special designs and the decoration of the weird headgear and other articles used in the dance. The patterns used in these decorations, and the form of the headgear, were the specific property and the right of the medicine man. Sacred to him alone, no other medicine man had a right to use them. In addition to all this costuming each dancer had to be put through some kind of ceremony or incantation prior to going to the dancing ground. Naturally this combination of mysticism, pageantry, and exhibitionism had a great appeal to these poor people, who had little other entertainment except gambling and drinking.

The dance started soon after dark each night. A bonfire was built, around which the spectators sat in a large circle. About twenty-five feet west of the fire sat the musicians, who beat a drum and a sheet of rawhide, making a great thumping noise. Meanwhile they sang at the top of their voices accompanied by the onlookers who howled as loud as they could. All this was designed to excite the dancers to the utmost exertion. In this it was quite successful, stimulating even the coyotes on the surrounding hilltops, who added their voices to those of their betters in the creek valley below. I doubt if modern night club entertainers can produce a more exhilarating effect.

My feeling was that, though the dance had been harmless enough in years past, at this time it was definitely dangerous. The weather that January was bitterly cold, with penetrating north winds. The onlookers were sitting on the frozen earth while the dancers were performing half naked—which was all right as long as they were moving, but risky when they stopped. Two features made the dance even more hazardous to health. It lasted all night after which many of the dancers fell to the ground in a stupor induced by prolonged exertion, self-hypnosis, bad liquor, or a combination. Here they lay for hours before waking. If pneumonia didn't result from this it was because the dancers were unusually rugged. Some weren't rugged enough. Then, too, the dancers changed headgear with other performers. The few available facial masks were thus passed from one group of dancers to another, spreading the deadly germs of tuberculosis. Since the dancing continued through the winter its over-all effects were that more deaths occurred as a result of this entertainment than from any other cause. In those two years when the dance was at its height there were more deaths than during the succeeding decade, in which it was controlled.

With a great deal of loathing I briefly watched the medicine dance. But the weather was too cold. I soon returned to my mother's house on Cache Creek. What I had seen had made me extremely apprehensive as well as discouraged. I had noted that most of the former Carlisle Apaches were present. I recalled the days when we were at school together, how most of the students had said that when they returned to our people they would try to help them. Instead of helping, this was what they did! Instead of showing the blanket Indians a better way of life, the old Apaches showed *them* how things had always been done. So the educated Indians joined the ignorant in order not to lose the good will of the tribe. The excuse which the Carlisle Indians made to themselves was that they could better teach the others if they associated with them in all the ancient ways, thus preparing them to accept the new ideas. It really took great strength of character to hold out against such arguments. If you did as the old Indians did you were a black sheep to your white teachers. If you minded your own business and tried to live in the white man's way then the Indians branded you as being some kind of an outcast who no longer loved his own people and who would not help them.

My friends from the Carlisle days knew full well that when we were at school I hadn't practiced making speeches as to what I was going to do for our people when we returned to them. Similarly at this time I was silent, studying ways and means to accomplish something. I was convinced that action was required, not words which, in any event, probably would be disregarded. It seemed to me that the only hope lay in working through the Army officers who were in charge of the Apaches. It turned out that I was right; many of us are grateful today for the wonderful work done by those kind officers in "rescuing the perishing" Apache race.

Captain Farrand Sayre

In the summer of 1900 Captain Farrand Sayre succeeded Captain Scott as officer in charge of the Apaches at Fort Sill. Taking a great

CAPT. FARRAND SAYRE AND HIS APACHE TROOP AT FORT SILL

Jason is second from right

interest in their money-making activities, especially the raising of cattle and harvesting of hay, he began building up the fund even more than before. As a result more farm implements, vehicles, and other equipment were purchased and more horses bought for use in drawing wagons and for riding the range and patrolling the fence. All this required a great amount of repair work for upkeep as well as other blacksmithing such as horseshoeing. Therefore I was permitted to enlist as a U.S. Scout and set up a blacksmith shop for the Apaches.

Prior to this time my work was that of an ordinary member of the tribe. I had been herding cattle and cutting fence posts, a form of exercise to which I had become accustomed while on the farm in Pennsylvania. Now I was able to devote my full time to my regular blacksmith trade, which made me happy, especially a year later when, as a result of the country being opened, I began to build up a large clientele of white customers.

As a U.S. Scout I drew pay, quarters, and rations and wore the Army blue uniform. I was rated as a sergeant. Since the period of my service overlapped that of the Spanish-American War I acquired a veteran's status, entitling me to wear the campaign medal and ribbon of that conflict. One day it was to secure for me a disabled serviceman's pension, because my vision is impaired as a result of a steel splinter in my eye suffered during my blacksmithing.

I entered upon my duties with confidence. I was young, strong, and healthy and fully qualified by training and experience. I am happy today in the knowledge that during the fourteen years in which I served as a blacksmith to the Apaches I gave full satisfaction to our officer in charge. I have strong testimony, too, that I pleased my white customers many of whom came a considerable distance for my services though they had blacksmith facilities closer at hand. The only people who failed to express gratitude were my own tribesmen, at least some of them. Jealous as usual and being chronic trouble-makers and fault-finders, a number of Apaches never appreciated the hard, careful work I did for them, all at no cost to themselves. I couldn't help but feel downhearted over this for I had given up a good job to come to Fort Sill and to try to help my own people. But, holding in mind the Golden Rule, I continued to work on the principle that every man should get along with those around him.

I Try To Stop The Medicine Dance

In October 1900 Captain Sayre visited my blacksmith shop. As usual at that time I was pondering over the problem of the medicine dance. There had been a number of deaths that summer, all caused, I was sure, by exposure resulting from the dance. The post authorities had built a little hospital for the Indians back of the military hospital but the Indians wouldn't take their sick to it. They called it "The Death House." I told Captain Sayre all this, explaining how destructive the dance was to the health of the Indians and how difficult it was to overcome their superstitious beliefs by persuasion. I asked him to take some positive action.

At first Captain Sayre didn't want to interfere. Like many officers who had sympathy for the Indians he was reluctant to stop any tribal customs or interpose in anything which pertained to the native religion. But after I had informed him of the recent funerals which could be traced directly to the dance he changed his mind. He told me that from that moment the dance would be forbidden during the cold weather, that in the winter time the Apaches would remain in their villages. Furthermore there was to be no more gambling. He made some other sensible and helpful rules for all the Indians who were under his charge. Since as a scout I had the rank of a noncommissioned officer, Captain Sayre sent me out to all the camps to tell the people about these rules.

As you can imagine, this did not increase my popularity among the Apaches. Many of them blamed me for having made the report to Captain Sayre which resulted in the curbing of their dancing and gambling. While I didn't like the resulting state of affairs, where many Apaches wouldn't speak to me, I was sure that I was doing right, so I stuck to it. Some of the worst hotheads began to threaten me, even hinting that I might get shot some dark night. For the most part I didn't take this seriously, considering it to be simply "talk."

There were a few incidents, however, which caused me some anxiety. One of these involved Kaahtenny. You will recall that this was the man who, while we were at Fort Apache in the eighties, had served a term in Alcatraz then was pardoned and served General Miles as a scout. His helpfulness and alleged reformation did not outlast his period of service as a scout, for as soon as he returned to our camps at Fort Apache in 1886 he began making trouble, getting

JASON IN HIS BLACKSMITH SHOP

drunk, and hitting women. Most of the young men, being afraid of him did not try to stop his cruelties to the women.

One night in 1886, while we were still in Arizona, Kaahtenny came to our tent, a strange thing which he had never done before, as we were not on good terms. He and mother had a good time for a couple of hours, telling again the stories of their various past experiences. But I sat there glowering, thinking of how Kaahtenny had beaten up innocent Apache women recently, for no reason at all. So I spoke up and said, "Kaahtenny. You are supposed to be a great man on the warpath. You have fought many battles and you have the reputation of being brave. But this day you have attacked peaceful, helpless, poor women. You are a full warrior while I am only an inexperienced and unrated young man. But I tell you straight, these women are my kinsfolks. I am not going to stand around while you mistreat them. If you try it again I will straighten you out myself."

Kaahtenny turned to me, replying, "You make me ashamed of myself. Hereafter I will not act like that again."

But I think that he held it against me.

So in 1900 when we were together again at Fort Sill I had the duty of subduing him and putting him in arrest for violating the rules concerning drinking, gambling, and dancing. Once I had to throw him in the guard house. As a result of all this he sent several other Apaches to tell me that he would "get" me. I considered this to be mostly a bluff but I had to be on the lookout just the same. Once he pulled a knife on me. At another time he came in where I was working, pulled a gun and waved it around with loud talk. I told him if he didn't quiet down I would arrest him again, that I was a scout in uniform who had a sworn duty to perform, and had the authority to do it. I told him further that if he didn't put his gun away I would smack him in the face with my sledge, which would probably take the starch out of him. He wouldn't look so pretty, either. I had no more trouble with Kaahtenny.

Naiche was a different proposition. In addition to being the hereditary chief of our tribe, he was a much older man than I, with a lot of experience back of him. He was a heavy drinker, dangerous when drunk. He was a smoother talker, not such a bluffer as Kaahtenny, but capable of violence. I had to put him in arrest on at least one occasion.

One night when I was riding my horse home from a church meeting at the mission, I encountered Naiche in the moonlight. He was sitting on his horse in the middle of the ford over Cache Creek. In his hand was a pistol and I felt that he was waiting for me. I knew that he was drunk. I rode straight up to Naiche but passed him to my right instead of my left. This gave me the opportunity to seize his right (pistol) hand as I passed, instead of having to reach my arm across. This did the trick. I had no further trouble.

Another Indian whom I had to arrest caused a funnier situation. This was Caspar Calisay (or Calise). Hearing that he was at the dance, drunk and causing a disturbance, I reported it to the officer in charge, who detailed me to go out and bring the man in. When I got there Calisay was indeed in an obstreperous mood. He offered to wrestle me, making various threats and challenging me to take him if I was able. Now Calisay was a champion wrestler in the tribe, and a strong man. But I was strong too. So I grabbed him, threw him to the ground after a short, violent struggle, then tied him up like a hog with my lariat. I left him lying there for some time while I went about my other duties of observing the dance for other trouble makers. Finally Calisay begged for mercy.

"Let me up, Jason," he said. "I'll be good."

In later years after we were both old and he had become nearly blind, this became a standing joke between us. Usually when I encountered Caspar he would greet me with a grin, saying, "I'm being good, Jason."

For a time Captain Sayre and his Troop C, 8th Cavalry were the only military personnel at Fort Sill, the other units having gone off to the Spanish-American War and the Philippine Insurrection leaving their families behind. At one time during this period some ignorant Indian started a rumor to the effect that Geronimo and his Apaches were going to rise up and massacre the women and children at the post. There was nothing to this. No such thoughts occurred to any Apache. Geronimo was especially disturbed over this incident, being, as he said, a U.S. soldier and wearing the uniform.

Chatto and Naiche, by smooth talking, and keeping their gambling and drinking secret, made a better impression on the whites than Geronimo did. Personally I always felt that the latter, who was perfectly open with his roistering, was actually the better man. Certainly he had been a much braver warrior and abler leader than the rest of them.

Captain Sayre during the four years he was our officer in charge did a great deal to build up the Apache fund. Under his careful management we accumulated enough to pay off our indebtedness incurred for the purchase of implements and stock as well as build up a reserve. He was also firm in holding down gambling and winter dancing.

Lieutenant Purington

Sayre was succeeded by Lieutenant George Purington, whose main interest was in the Apache cattle raising project. He even took part personally in the roundups, branding, and shipment of the stock. Through his efforts the fund grew even faster than before. Because of this most of the Apaches missed him when he was gone. But the lieutenant did not, at first, continue Captain Sayre's policy of preventing dancing during the winter. The Apaches resumed this vicious practice, with the result that two young men got pneumonia and in a short time were dead. I told Lieutenant Purington that a rule had been established permitting dancing only from the first of May to the last of September. He agreed to enforce this rule, sending me and other scouts out to the camps to control the dance as well as arrest bootleggers and cut down on the gambling. But owing to the country being opened to white settlement in 1901 the problem of keeping liquor from the Indians was difficult and serious.

Is the Indian a moderate drinker? I should say not! In all my experience I have never seen an Indian drink who didn't keep it up until the last drop was gone and he was either lying in a stupor on the prairie or was in a fighting, dangerous mood. An Indian who is drunk is a creature entirely devoid of any good desire and completely incapable of self control.

Major George L. Scott

A very nice old retired officer, Major George L. Scott, succeeded Purington. Everyone liked him, for he had a great sympathy for the Indians. Unfortunately the bootleggers were extremely active while he was in charge of the Apaches, so that the Indians were quite troublesome. In spite of his gentle nature Major Scott went after the scouts vigorously for neglecting their duty of controlling gambling and drinking. But because of poor health this fine old gentleman was soon relieved from his position.

Major George W. Goode

Major Scott was replaced by Major Goode, another retired officer who stayed with the Apaches until they were released from their status as prisoners of war in 1913. He then remained only long enough to wind up the financial affairs of the tribe and dispose of the property. Major Goode was a stout, well-built man who seemed to be well qualified for his job. Some one had fully informed him as to the problems which he would face, especially the drinking, gambling, and dancing on the part of the Indians. He had the strength of character and the determination to do something about these evils.

In carrying out his responsibility Major Goode called in the scouts and placed squarely on their shoulders the task of carrying out his orders.

Some of the Indians, when detailed to ride the range to look after the cattle or repair the fences, would whine, "I have no horse," or "I have no saddle." They had sold the horse or pawned the saddle to get firewater. Major Goode solved problems like these with an iron hand. As a result most of the Indians were resentful and disagreeable in spite of the fact that the Major was working for their own welfare. This didn't stop him. Conditions improved. Bootleggers were kept off the reservation. Gambling was controlled. Even attendance at the church services at the mission picked up. The church was well filled.

I thought well of Major Goode even though he got mad at me one time. This was when we were having a tribal conference (to be discussed later) to decide whether the tribe would be moved to Mescalero. I opposed this plan from the very start. But Goode was committed to it. At this conference, though I was sitting at the back of the room, and had no authority to express myself, I got so worked up that I interrupted the discussion to shout my views, briefly as follows: "In 1886 I was living at Fort Apache, where I first learned to do a little farming and cut wood. Then you Army people took me away as a prisoner. Now we have just got another good start in farming and cattle raising, and you want to stop it all and put us back on a reservation. This will set back our progress a hundred years!"

Major Goode got very red. He told me to be quiet, that he had a good notion to put me in the guard house.

I replied, more quietly, that I was simply talking and working in the interest of my people.

We both subsided and in later years I have felt grateful to him for his strong efforts to keep liquor and other bad influences from my people. Even though I disagreed with him strongly on the subject of moving the Apaches from Fort Sill out west.

Chapter 20

THE PROMISED LAND

During the summer of 1901 the Kiowa-Comanche reservation, the last big tract of land in Oklahoma to be taken away from the Indians, was opened to homesteading. The method was by a lottery in which those white men who were fortunate in drawing winning numbers were permitted to select quarter sections of land. Of course the Apache prisoners of war, being native Americans but not United States citizens, were not allowed to participate in the drawing. We stood by as spectators of this interesting performance.

The Kiowa-Comanche country had been used as grazing land for a number of years, mostly by cattlemen from Texas who paid the Indians grass rental. A small portion of the reservation of some 3,000,000 acres was also farmed by the agricultural tribes such as the Caddoes, Wichitas, and Delawares, small bands who lived along the Washita River north and northeast of Fort Sill. A few of the Comanches and Kiowas also did a little intermittent farming.

We had never witnessed such great excitement as was stirred up by the white man in grabbing for all this free land. Multitudes of people of every description rushed upon us in the Fort Sill area. They came in wagons, buggies, and on horseback. Many who had no other means of transportation walked, and by the time they arrived most had very sore feet from trudging through the burning sand. For this was during the hottest, driest, and dustiest part of July. Some poor homeseekers whose wagons had broken down moved in slowly with improvised log sleds replacing a broken wagon wheel here and there.

The whole area, many miles in extent, contained not a single town, only scattered Indian camps and huts together with the small military post of Fort Sill. The site selected for the new county seat was a few miles south of Fort Sill, eventually to be named Lawton in honor of our old friend General Henry W. Lawton, who had been killed in the Philippines. In the meantime the throngs camped along Cache Creek just east of the post while awaiting the opening day when the lottery was to be held. In addition to farmers, migrants, vagrants, and landless people, there were doctors, lawyers, druggists, bankers, and merchants of every variety—all with their hands out to catch custom-

[185]

LAWTON, OKLAHOMA SHORTLY AFTER THE OPENING OF THE COUNTRY IN SEPTEMBER, 1901

ers. Some healthful products such as medicine were offered for sale but for the most part these were too expensive for the poor homeseekers. A matter of special interest to me there were blacksmiths of all kinds, good and poor. They brought their tools and portable forges but some of the smiths were entirely without experience, very few being able to weld. There were also gunsmiths and locksmiths, anticipating a thriving business among the numerous outlaws, robbers, and deputy sheriffs. I am sure the locksmiths did a lot of work keeping handcuffs and jail locks in repair.

Other artisans who did a big business were the barbers. There was much long shaggy wool to be cut, and a great deal of hair to be shaved from bristly chins. We Indians, who had never seen so many hairy people, stood wondering what caused the white man to grow such luxuriant facial shrubbery. Numerous barbers were there sharpening their scissors and razors and fattening on the great trade which now came their way. Even a few Indians, mostly out of curiosity I suppose, and to enjoy the good smells, patronized the barber shops.

Here and there among the crowds might be found another type of citizen, not always welcome in more refined society—the gambler. Here was something which the Indians could really enjoy, not realizing that the professional gambler employed methods which insured that his victims never won. Filled with a burning motive for getting rich quick, the gamblers brought with them all manner of devices and machines. In a short time they had all of "Poor Lo's" money, as well as that of many of the supposedly more sophisticated white brethren. The gambling wheels set up in tents, and later in shanties, were kept running from early morning through most of the night, shearing all comers. This was golden fleece but not the kind which I sought all my life.

There were a number of doctors, always ready to answer emergency calls. We Indians were fascinated to observe that, whereas the Indian medicine man always started his treatment by burning feathers or shaking a gourd rattle, the white medicine man always said to his customer, "Open your mouth and stick out your tongue." Truly the different races have their own queer customs! The white doctor was never held up, day or night, by bad weather or poor roads. He was always on the job. And he never forgot to render charges based on the number of miles he had traveled. But, more seriously, he is a good man to have available when there is sickness in your family.

One tradesman or professional man who was never without work was the undertaker. He came in with the homeseekers, standing by to take charge of those who fell by the wayside. What malaria, smallpox, measles, and dysentery did not accomplish for him, bad whisky and gunshot wounds did. So trade was brisk for the undertaker. That this business was profitable was indicated by the fact that the undertaker was always well dressed. He brought with him ample materials to care for those who had departed this world, and usually was very nice to the dearly beloved who were left behind. This was one booming industry in those hectic days. We Indians, who had never given our deceased such fancy interments, generally only piling on rocks to keep off the coyotes, realized that we had much to learn.

Someone had to be on hand to fight sharpers and to protect all good people who were in trouble. This was the lawyer. The legal adviser saw a great opportunity for himself in this new country. Though he didn't always win his case in court, the lawyer could be counted upon to put up a strong argument in favor of his client, which was something. And we must remember that he had to earn his bread and butter too, so the fees which he charged should not cause eyebrows to be lifted too high.

Well, well! Here come the big fellows, the bankers! They arrived in fine new wagons carrying strong iron boxes full of money which was guarded by hired gunmen. These were truly the greatest of all who came to the new country, for they controlled the wealth of this land of opportunity. Surely their expectations of doing an enormous business would be gratified, for the people, trusting the bankers, put their life savings in their hands. This money was then loaned out to other less fortunate souls. One thing we soon noticed: If you did not put your money in this particular banker's vault, he would not recognize you when you next passed him on the road.

But we must not forget the real homeseekers. Who were they? We would say that they were mostly the hard-working people who tilled the earth and toiled early and late to earn their living. Many of them were intelligent and experienced farmers attracted by the chance to get free land or the hope of improving themselves. They came in old wagons, buggies, and sometimes dragging a few farm implements. They were not interested in preying on their fellow men or in getting rich quickly by some clever scheme. They were the ones who were going to build this new Promised Land of 1901. They found a fertile soil on which they confidently expected to raise rich crops of corn, cotton, and other products. Little did they realize that great wealth was not possible, that the climate of this part of the southwest was too uncertain for very successful agriculture. In the summer the corn and cotton were apt to burn and shrivel under the hot sun and to fail to sprout during the extended droughts. There would be some good years which would encourage them to believe that farming would be a great success, but these would be succeeded by several poor years. Grazing in those days, however, was always good. The country would have made an excellent cattle range had it not been fenced and broken up.

Still other men, riding in buggies and wearing black suits, also arrived. These were the preachers, moaning for the unsaved souls of the numerous lawbreakers. The preachers were continually sad because their good work seemed to have no effect. They too had heard of the Promised Land so they came with their Bibles under their arms. Typically they were thin men, their faces all drawn up with wrinkles because of the thought of the many lost souls and the widespread suffering.

As a scout I often rode along the edge of the homesteaders' camps on Beef Creek, hearing the forceful preaching from the thin lips and drawnup faces of these bringers of the Gospel. Camp meetings were often held near my village where I had the privilege of listening to this religious instruction which to me was impressive in the midst of all the greed, turmoil, and wickedness incident to the opening of the country.

These devoted preachers knew that it was mighty hard for the young people of their congregations, faced as they were daily by many evil devices and much temptation. I am sincere in saying that these good men did a fine work in saving many persons and keeping them on the straight road.

Chapter 21

OUR CAPTIVITY IS ENDED

In 1902 the Apache heads of families met with General Fitzhugh Lee* in the post headquarters building at Fort Sill. The Indians discussed the oft-repeated proposal to send them back to New Mexico. They were dissatisfied that they were still held as prisoners, even though they were now making money in the cattle business.

Naiche expressed the opinion of most of the group somewhat as follows: "We want to go back to Arizona or New Mexico, where we can live like we used to. Here at Fort Sill the water and the climate do not agree with us, and we don't like the grass and the timber, either."

Since the other Apaches nodded their heads vigorously, General Lee seemed to be impressed. Through the interpreter George Wratten he assured the Indians that he would recommend to the Government that their wish be granted.

I was opposed to the idea of leaving Oklahoma. In my opinion these Indians had right there within their own grasp all the good and useful things of life. By leaving Fort Sill and Oklahoma they would throw away all that they had gained and possibly much of what they stood to gain in the future.

Some of them had been saying, "They are working us to death here," not realizing or not caring that work is good for man, that in earning his bread and butter by the sweat of his brow man nourishes his health and gains long life, prosperity, and contentment. I have always worked hard. It has never hurt me.

So, as the meeting was coming to an end and while the Indians were still standing in the back of the room and leaning against the wall, I stepped one pace forward and asked to be heard. Trembling

---

*General Lee was the nephew of General Robert E. Lee. While serving with the cavalry in the western prairie before the Civil War he had been wounded by a Comanche arrow, the scar of which he bore all his life. During Civil War he was a famous Confederate cavalry leader. At the height of the Gettysburg campaign he had attacked and burned Carlisle Barracks, but returned there in 1896 on invitation of Captain Pratt to address the graduating class. During the Spanish-American War he was received back into the United States Army, and in 1902 was commanding the Department of Texas.

at my own boldness I told Mr. Wratten that I wanted permission to speak to the Commanding General.

General Lee, looking at me in surprise, asked, "Does that Indian speak English?"

When I replied that I did, the General said, "Young man, **you can** talk directly to me. You don't have to go through the interpreter. Speak right up. Pay no attention to the other Indians, who in any event probably do not understand us. What we have to say is between the two of us."

I spoke as follows: "I was born and raised among these Indians. I lived just like they did—a hard life, homeless and hopeless. But through a Government school I had a chance to better myself. I learned about the good and useful things of life. I learned to be a blacksmith. I worked in a steel mill. I learned farming. Now I am being forced to choose between this new, good life and that of the old primitive life o   west. If I go west to live in a camp as a reservation Indian, all that ı have gained, all that I have learned, will be lost.

"Here in Oklahoma, in spite of what these other Indians have told you, the water, the grass, and the climate are good. Where the health has been bad it is due to the Indians' own foolishness. My wish this day is that the Government should give me a house and land and permit me to remain."

General Lee responded, "Young man, what you say makes sense. Not one of the other Indians has talked to me as you did. I am going to recommend that your wish be granted. I am going to send this recommendation to Washington."

This made me feel so good that the trembling went away. But I stood alone until General Lee asked if any other Indians would like to remain in Oklahoma. Then two other young men stepped forward and came to where I was.

This meeting was the beginning of a long drawn-out agitation to remove the Apaches from Oklahoma and send them back to the desert.

A Delegation To Washington

Some time later Rogers Toclanny and Alfred Chatto received authority to spend some of the Apache fund to make a trip to Washington on behalf of the project of being removed from Fort Sill. They intended to see the Secretary of War, under whose jurisdiction the tribe was being held. George Wratten was going along as interpreter. About this time Lieutenant Purington, visiting my shop, said, "**You have been talking about getting a home in Oklahoma. Now is the chance for you to go with this delegation to Washington to present** your views to the Government. Your group has as much right as the others to use Apache funds for this purpose." With this authority from our officer in charge, I prepared to accompany the other three men to Washington.

Our mission was to see Secretary of War William H. Taft and not waste time with some under-official who had no authority to act.

We left Fort Sill via the Frisco Railroad, changed trains at Oklahoma City, arriving next day in the beautiful new Union Station in St. Louis. How different were our accommodations from the old tourist cars on which we had come east as prisoners in 1886! On our way east from St. Louis via the Pennsylvania line we were delayed twice by wrecks on the track ahead. At Pittsburgh we took the New York Flyer, the fastest train on which I had ever ridden. Mr. Wratten was told by the conductor that we were running at seventy-two miles per hour. Soon we had made up the time previously lost.

The day after our arrival at the Capital we went in to see Secretary Taft. Toclanny and Chatoo spoke feelingly to him of their desire to be returned to their old Warm Springs reservation.

"How long," asked Mr. Taft, "since you have seen that reservation?"

"It has been more than forty years," they replied.

"Well," said Mr. Taft, "if you haven't seen it lately, the wise thing is for you to make a trip out there and report to me and to your people, the condition in which you find the land. Note particularly the availability of water, timber, and grazing facilities. Also find out whether the land is suitable for farming. Then if you still want the Warm Springs reservation I will see what I can do to help you get it."

While the two Indians were listening to Wratten's interpreting of these remarks, Secretary Taft added, "There is no law in the United States that can take the land away from you."

Mr. Wratten then spoke up: "This other young man has different plans which he would like to discuss with you."

"All right," said the Secretary. "Let us hear what he has to say."

I told Mr. Taft that although most of our people wanted to go out west, a few of us preferred to remain in Oklahoma. I reminded him that the Kiowas and Comanches had donated some of their land so that each Apache would have an allotment of 160 acres, but that so far none of it had been turned over to us. I wanted his help in getting some of this land released to those of us who had chosen to remain.

"I am a homeless and landless Indian," I went on. "I have been driven from my reservation and harried from place to place. Now I am living very comfortably on the military reservation at Fort Sill. I am engaged in the blacksmith trade and am well experienced in farming. While I am still strong in body and young enough to work I would like to settle down on my own farm and build myself a home. I need your support in this."

Mr. Taft said that he would try to help me. We knew, however, that he favored building a large modern post at Fort Sill, which would require the use of the reservation for military training, so that the Apaches could no longer live there. So I felt some doubt that I would get my wish.

After we had finished our business with the Secretary of War we went across the Potomac to Fort Myer, where we had a nice visit with one of our former officers in charge of the Apaches. The following day we took up our homeward journey, taking the Big Four through Virginia, West Virginia, and Kentucky to Cincinnati. From there we went via Indianapolis and St. Louis to Fort Sill. For some time thereafter I was depressed and pessimistic over the outlook. For many months it appeared that nothing would be done in Washington for any of the Apaches.

Congressional Opposition

A bill was introduced in Congress to release the Apache prisoners of war and resettle them on the Mescalero reservation in New Mexico. News of this excited the Indians and made them restless. Tribal councils were held at which the situation was discussed, together with possible ways to help the cause along. But difficult days lay ahead. The bill had encountered opposition from both of New Mexico's senators. They voiced the fear of the citizens that Apache depredations would break out again. These people forgot that the blame for the Apache troubles had sprung from the fact that the Indians had been driven from their reservation by the whites, with no protection from the Government. The Apaches had not been wholly at fault in fighting for their rights.

Things looked dark for us. But even in the midst of general discouragement and disillusionment I did not lose hope. Then it seemed that Providence intervened. Mr. L. L. Legters, a missionary to the Apaches and Comanches, hearing of my struggle came to offer his assistance. This was gladly accepted. Dr. Roe also offered his services. The aid which these two churchmen could give was not inconsiderable. Through their connections they were able to exert influence on religious groups and other well-minded citizens throughout the United States. Public opinion in our behalf was aroused. Furthermore Dr. Roe counted several influential congressmen among his friends. Altogether, through the powerful efforts of Dr. Roe, the tide turned in favor of the Apaches. Dr. Roe was a frail man but possessed of a brilliant intellect and a strong spirit. With his help and that of our other friends in the the church we won out.

A Delegation Inspects Western Reservations

Washington having finally decided to release the Fort Sill Apaches from their status as prisoners of war and resettle them some place other than on the military reservation, a delegation was sent west to select a new site for the tribe. Colonel Hugh L. Scott and another colonel were in charge. Six Indians were sent, five of them representing the group who wished to move to New Mexico, while I went on behalf of those who preferred to stay in Oklahoma.

It was October, 1911. First we went to Mescalero, New Mexico, where we were given a cordial welcome by the Mescalero Apaches. Some of our delegation had relatives there, who made things especially pleasant for us. It appeared that the Mescaleros would be happy to have us come to their reservation to live. When we stated our desire to ride over the country they provided horses. But not for me. Being one of the opposition party, they left me out in the cold. Luckily a missionary came along about that time with a horse and buggy. He very kindly offered to take me on the trip with him. But we weren't able to go everywhere that the mounted Indians did.

The trip led over mountains and through canyons, mostly in a zigzag route. The object was to find timber, grass, water, and land suitable for cultivation. There was timber which could be used for building houses, as well as good grazing land. But the fields available for agriculture were small, being only a few acres in extent and located at a distance from the small existing springs. Irrigation would be difficult.

The Mescaleros told us that there was excellent hunting on the reservation, deer and wild turkeys being abundant. They also said that, as the reservation contained three million dollars worth of timber, we would get rich quickly. So in spite of the disadvantages of inadequate land suitable for cultivation and a scanty water supply, all the delegation except Betzinez expressed themselves as being well satisfied with the Mescalero reservation. They decided to return to Fort Sill with a favorable report to the tribe.

Next we went via El Paso to the Warm Springs reservation. At El Paso we had a long stopover while waiting for a train to take us to Engle, where we would detrain. We spent the afternoon visting Juarez, across the line in Mexico. The other five Indians spent all their money for a few Mexican trinkets which they had to leave at the customs office, as they had no funds with which to pay the duty. What fools the Indians were, thus to spend money which was not theirs, but which had been entrusted to them to pay their expenses on a trip for the benefit of the tribe.

Late that night we boarded the train for Engle, which was the only rail station then near the site of Elephant Butte Dam. We got off the train in the darkness and spent the rest of the night sitting in the depot waiting room. In the morning I was sitting in the restaurant with the two Army officers, eating breakfast. Colonel Scott, looking out the window, saw the other Apaches standing disconsolately on the platform.

"What are they doing there?" he asked. "Why don't they come in to breakfast?"

"They have no money," I replied.

"Why not? Didn't you turn over to them the expense money?"

"Yes, sir," I said. "I gave them each their three dollars, which was to last them for meals and lodging for two days and nights."

After breakfast the foolish five received the scolding from Colonel Scott which they had earned.

As we drove west in a stage I looked at the mountains, hills, and plains. This sight of my native land was inspiring, it looked so beautiful. But we all were due for a severe disappointment.

We crossed the Rio Grande at Elephant Butte Dam, then under construction, and stopped for the night at the village of Cuchillo, named after our old Apache chief, I suppose. While we were at the post office and general store one of the other Indians called to me that Colonel Scott wanted to see me at once. With some anxiety I walked over to where the two officers were talking with the proprietor.

"I want you to tell those other Indians," he said severely. "That I have found out about their trying to buy whisky here. Tell them that I am very angry with them. They are out of favor with me entirely."

When I had passed this on to the other Apaches they began to insult me and make all manner of hateful remarks. They claimed that I was the cause of their getting into trouble. But I didn't fire back at them, knowing that they knew that I had only been filling my duty faithfully while they had been acting like children.

In the morning we resumed our journey to Monticello. This was where the Apaches had made their first peace with the Mexicans. We did not stop, because we all were anxious to get on to our old reservation. From Monticello the route led up the dry creek bed which previously had been such a nice little stream. Now it was all filled in with gravel, which made it twenty jumps wide instead of the one jump which it had been before.

We arrived at the old agency after dark but got up early next morning in our eagerness to look around at our old homeland. What a depressing sight it turned out to be! The whole country, once so fertile and green, was now entirely barren. Gravel had washed down, covering all the nice valleys and pastures,* even filling up the Warm Springs, which had completely vanished. The reservation was entirely ruined. Looking around bitterly, I said to myself, "Oklahoma is good enough for me."

The others continued to stroll around, for a couple of hours, dispirited and downcast. Then we went on back sadly to Monticello, where we spent the night. I was considerably cheered to find some of the members of that Mexican family who had been such good friends of my parents. We had a very happy reunion. Monticello had many good memories for us, having been a friendly trading post where the Mexicans had been kind and hospitable.

The next day we returned to Engle where we entrained for Belen. At this point the two colonels left us. Before they departed Colonel Scott turned over to me the rest of the money for traveling expenses, charging me with handing it out in proper amounts to the others and seeing that it was used for meals and not trinkets or liquor. I felt honored to be given this responsibility.

On our arrival at Fort Sill a tribal council was called to listen to our reports and recommendations. On the basis of what the other five had to say, the leaders decided that the Apaches would request that they be assigned to the Mescalero reservation.

The Apaches Are Divided

Some time elapsed while arrangements were being completed to transfer the Indians from Fort Sill. Those of us who wanted to remain in Oklahoma notified Dr. Roe of the situation and asked for assistance in obtaining our wish. He made arrangements for me to attend a large church convention at Lake Mohonk, New York, the following October, at which time I could present my report and secure assistance in getting the Government to settle some of us on allotments in the Fort Sill area.

At Lake Mohonk the general committee in charge of the convention approved my report, in spite of the poor English in which it was worded, which gratified me very much. Adopting some of my suggestions they set to work on our behalf. Full success resulted.

The Commissioner of Indian Affairs called for me to come to Washington to straighten out the affairs of those of us who were to

---

*Jason doesn't know whether this resulted from placer mining, or natural causes.

stay in Oklahoma. The results of my trip were satisfying to our group and particularly so to me, because I had faced much opposition and unpleasantness from my own people in doing what I was convinced was right.

Back at Sill another tribal council was held, presided over by a new board of four Apache leaders. A roll call of the entire tribe was held at which each member over eighteen years of age was required to state whether he or she desired to go to Mescalero or to remain in Oklahoma. The decisions made at this time were to be final. One hundred and twenty-seven Apaches chose to go to Mescalero and eighty-seven to remain. Most of the former chiefs and warriors went to Mescalero, including Naiche, Chatto, Martine, Kay-i-tah, Kaahtenny, Noche, and Toclanny. Geronimo, Nanay, and Chihauhua had died at Fort Sill.

Death of Geronimo

I had lived in the same band with Geronimo on several reservations, had been with him for two years in Mexico while we were on the warpath, and had been his close neighbor on the Fort Sill reservation for nearly a decade. I got to know him intimately. Though Geronimo

APACHE POW-WOW AT FORT SILL

Jason is third from left in center.
Building is No. 435, Old Post

GERONIMO'S GRAVE

was a great wartime leader, after he surrendered he lived at peace and never thereafter caused trouble. Much had been written about him, a great deal of it being exaggerated or completely false. By any standard his greatest weakness was liquor. Whisky got him into difficulties in Mexico, in Arizona, and New Mexico, and finally was the indirect cause of his death.

While we were living in villages near Fort Sill, Geronimo was a scout in charge of his village. He performed his duties faithfully and was proud of his uniform. His last wife bore him two children, one of whom, Robert Geronimo, survives him and is living at Mescalero today. The old warrior did some farming at Fort Sill, raising melons and other vegetables. Being a celebrity he was in demand at various fairs and pageants or parades in different parts of the United States. He also was visited and interviewed by numerous white journalists, some of whom were far from accurate in writing up what he told them about his life. If they couldn't get enough fire and bloodshed out of his account, they used their lively imaginations.

For example, one day I acted as interpreter for a writer who asked to see Geronimo's coat made of ninety-nine human scalps. On hearing his question Geronimo was speechless. He had no such coat. It never was his custom to scalp his fallen enemy. He didn't know what to say to this man. Finally he just turned and walked away.

This great war leader came to his death in an ignominious manner. He went to town one day, bought some liquor from a bootlegger, got drunk and started home after dark. He fell from his horse in a stupor, lay in the weeds all night. Being in his nineties, the exposure was too much for him. He was stricken with pneumonia and died in the Fort Sill Indian hospital on February 17, 1909. His relatives and fellow tribesmen buried the old man in the Apache graveyard on Cache Creek. His grave is still to be seen there, being marked by a stone pyramid erected through the efforts of the then post librarian, Master Sergeant Morris Swett, a warm friend of all the Fort Sill Indians.

The Apaches Are On The Increase

It was in the spring of 1913 that the Apaches were released from their status as prisoners of war and that a large group were transferred to the Mescalero reservation. Major Goode and Sergeant Allen Branch had charge of the arrangements. For some time they were busy at the Fort Sill railroad station loading horses, mules, and personal belongings of the Indians who were going to New Mexico. Then under Major Goode and Sergeant Branch the Apaches departed on April 1, 1913 from Oklahoma.

Miss Henrietta Hospers, one of the missionaries, had been given the task of seating the Indians in the railway cars. Since she was well acquainted with the Apaches, she tried to make them happy by seating them in family groups. Unfortunately she was ignorant of the old Indian taboo that a man may not look his mother-in-law in the face. She seated some families so that this awful situation existed, with some resulting commotion before everything was straightened out.

Then before the train pulled out, the conductor discovered that the Indians had loaded their many dogs into the baggage car, and quite a few lively dogfights were developing. With little regard for separating the redmen from their pets, he threw the dogs off the train, so that the Apaches had to go dogless to Mescalero. Except for one old woman who managed to hide her pup under her blanket.

Since 1913 both groups of Apaches, those who remained at Fort

Sill and those who went to Mescalero, have done fairly well. In the latter group the death rate had gone down somewhat, so that their numbers are increasing slightly. Those of us who remained in Oklahoma have done a great deal better. Originally there were eighty-seven of us, now there are one hundred and eighty.

I think I have an even sounder reason for claiming that the Apaches would have done better had they remained in Oklahoma and settled on allotments of land. In New Mexico they probably have been fairly well taken care of by the Government, and I understand that some of them, especially the younger Apaches, have made a good start in cattle raising and farming. I have been gratified, too, to be told that quite a number who joined the church during the mission days at Fort Sill have remained firm in the Christian faith. Eventually all these Indians, like other reservation Indians, will reach a higher state of culture. But my point is, they still are *reservation* Indians. As long as the Indian remains on the reservation he will develop only very slowly. He is, if anything, too well taken care of today. He doesn't learn to stand on his own feet, to earn his living entirely by his own efforts. The future of the Indian lies in getting out and settling down like any other American citizen, in supporting himself by agriculture, a trade, or a profession. All over the world, the tribal life is disappearing. It is archaic. As I have said many times, man must earn his bread and butter by the sweat of his brow. I have done it. So can the other Indians, and the sooner they start the quicker will they attain a more satisfying and useful life.

I just want to add one thing. At the time the removal of the Apaches from Fort Still was under consideration in Washington, one of the Senators from Arizona said, "You can no more tame an Apache than you can a rattlesnake." I think that you will agree that the recent history of our people flings those words back in the worthy gentleman's teeth.

Chapter 22
A HOME AT LAST

The month following the departure of the Apaches for Mescalero our herd of ten thousand cattle was sold to the highest bidders. The activities connected with this involved much hard work for the few of us who remained at Fort Sill. Prior to the roundup we had to camp continuously on the west range and patrol around the herd day and night to prevent cattle rustling. A number of shady drifters and others were staying around the edge of the reservation watching with greedy eyes for a chance to enrich themselves at our expense. We didn't mind the long hours in the saddle, for it was pleasant on the range in the springtime, especially at night. The air was mild and filled with the scent of millions of wildflowers and fragrant sage. Indians love to be outdoors and close to nature.

We received some greatly appreciated help from a number of cowboys who were in the employ of the several cattle buyers who had come from Texas and elsewhere to bid on our stock. If the cattle brought a fair price we would have a substantial fund to be divided up among all our people.

After the cattle were rounded up in the big western part of the range we drove them east of the railroad where a large enclosure had been fenced in. From then on it was relatively easy to collect batches of cattle as they were sold. The animals were run through a chute, counted and marked, then turned over to the purchaser. One of the latter was Mr. Tom Burnett, a distinguished and wealthy cattleman from Texas who with his cowboys enjoyed the roundup as much as we did. There is always something fascinating and even exciting about this kind of work, strenuous and dusty though it may be.

The last day of the cattle sale was marred by an accident in which one of my relatives by marriage was killed. His horse fell with him while he was chasing a steer, the horse rolling on him. This Apache, Clay Domeah, was a fine young man, one of our most dependable scouts. The authorities at Fort Sill gave him a military funeral and a burial in the post cemetery.

During the rest of the summer our little band of younger Apaches who had remained in Oklahoma were busy cutting hay on the reserva-

LAST ROUNDUP
Apache cattle being rounded up for final sale

tion. It was to be sold for the benefit of the Apache fund as well as for our own use in feeding the few horses and cows we had retained after the sale. By fall we began to get restless, a feeling which increased as the winter dragged on. Our houses, still under construction, would not be finished until the following summer. Having looked forward for a long time to the day when we would have our own homes, we could hardly wait. Finally as spring approached I went to Major Goode with the suggestion that we be permitted to live on our allotments in tents until the houses were ready for occupancy. That would enable us to get our spring planting done. This being satisfactory to the Major, we all moved to our farms.

Free To Live My Own Life

In March, 1914 I moved into my own house at last. It was a frame cottage with only four rooms and no inside conveniences but it was wonderful to me who, at age fifty-four, had never had a home.

At this time I was honorably discharged from the Army as a sergeant in the Indian Scouts. I had served thirteen years, five enlistments, all with character *Excellent*. I am sure that each of my five commanding officers would testify that I served loyally, always placing duty before personal considerations.

My allotment of eighty acres was fourteen miles north of Fort Sill, on Cache Creek and three miles south of the little town of Apache. On the north and east my neighbors were Indians, on the south and west they were white men. The latter proved to be friendly and always ready to lend a helping hand when need occurred. I have been very fortunate in having such good neighbors.

When the Apache common property was being disposed of and the Government equipment either turned in for re-issue or salvage, the officer in charge wanted to give me the blacksmith tools and forge which I had used for so long. But I said no. If I received these items as a gift the other Indians would feel jealous and also consider that they were entitled to a share of them. So I bought them. Nevertheless the post authorities did give me one of the windmills, tower, tank, and pipe which had been used by the Apaches. I sank a 75-foot well near my house, which always has provided a stand of forty-five feet of good limestone water.

In partnership with another Indian I bought from the surplus property a harvesting machine. This deal did not work out satisfactorily. My partner left to me all the expense of operation and upkeep. So, although he wanted to continue this arrangement, I put my foot down and insisted that he sell out his share to me. I had to give him some plain talk.

At first I didn't do a great deal of farming, because my blacksmith business was quite good at that time and left me no spare hours in which to plant and harvest crops. In those days there was a great deal of horseshoeing to be done as well as repair of wagons and farm implements. White people for miles around used to bring me work. They said that my work was excellent and my prices never high.

General Pratt's Last Visit

During the first World War our old Carlisle superintendent made his last visit to Fort Sill. Several of his faithful former students went to Anadarko to meet him at the train.

The train arrived very late but we waited there patiently for it because we were as anxious to see General Pratt as if he were our own father. When the cars rolled in and the General stepped on the platform the Indians stood there with the tears rolling down their cheeks, overcome with happiness to see their old friend. As usual he came

JASON REPAIRING HIS CORNBINDER

up to me and clapped me on the back, saying "Jason, my boy!"

General Pratt said that he wanted to visit Fort Sill to see what improvements had been made since he was there in 1870-76. I said, "General, you will go by my farm on your way. It is right beside the highway. Please stop and see my home."

Next day when his car drove up in front of the house, I walked up to him. He looked around behind me with a smile, saying, "I am certainly happy to see you in your fine new home. But where is Mrs. Betzinez?"

I replied that she would be coming along some day. Actually, though I didn't know it then, she was to arrive a year later.

That was the last time I saw General Pratt.

Marriage

Though I had reached middle age I still was a bachelor. This was not through lack of desire to get married but because I had been too occupied with trying to make my way in the world—the years slipping by before I knew it. Also I suppose I wasn't much of a bargain, if my one unsuccessful courtship of the Apache girl is any indication. I'm afraid that humiliating experience set me back and gave me an inferiority complex so far as women were concerned. Or maybe my slowness was because "the right girl" didn't come along for many years. I prefer to think that the last reason was the real one, for romance overtook me at last.

This is how my future wife and I had met. One day in October of 1907 I had gone over to the mission. On my way I passed a new missionary who had just arrived. I noticed that she was a very attractive young woman. A few minutes later I was in the building talking to Miss Hospers, when the newcomer approached the building. I expected that she would come into the room and visit with us but instead she went right upstairs to the living apartments without saying a word. As I saw the lady through the open door that first time, a tremendous thrill went through me. I said to myself, "That is the girl for me!"

I asked Miss Hospers who the new missionary was, and she replied that it was Miss Anna Heersma, from Chicago, who had come to take charge of the Apache orphanage.

Making up my mind to strike up a friendship with Miss Heersma, I presently became well acquainted with her. We liked each other from the very beginning. On many occasions, in company with some other missionary, we went on long rides into the country or on picnics, and our friendship deepened. But during the six years Miss

Heersma was at the mission I never worked up my courage enough to tell her that I loved her. A good deal of my reluctance to do so came from a natural shyness, but also because I realized that (at that time) I had no home, nothing to offer a wife. Some day I hoped to be in a better position to propose marriage.

When the Apaches split up into two groups, one going to Mescalero and the other leaving Fort Sill to settle on individual farms, the Indian school on the reservation and the mission were discontinued. Miss Heersma went to stay with an aunt in Eugene, Oregon but later returned to Apache as Field Matron to the Indians in that area. During that short time our friendship continued to deepen, but though I now had a house, I still did not feel that I was well enough off to offer her marriage. Then, her health failing from overwork, she returned to her home in Chicago.

After five more long years, during which we corresponded regularly, I finally realized that life was getting on for both of us, and that I needed a companion for the rest of my years. So I wrote to her and asked her to come down and visit one of her friends in southeast Apache. When she arrived I went to that home and straight off asked

APACHE FARMERS—THE BETZINEZ "TEAM"

Left to right: Jason, Anna Betzinez, Mary Ewing

her to marry me. With a sweet smile she said, simply, "Yes." On June 18, 1919, we were married in the First Presbyterian Church in Lawton, where we are both members. I learned then that she had brought with her all her personal belongings, that she somehow knew that she was never going to return to Chicago!

For the next nineteen years we worked together on our farm. After we were married Mrs. Betzinez had little chance to participate further in missionary work, for there was too much work in the home and, besides, she helped a lot on our farm. Her childhood experience on her father's farm stood her in good stead now. Although we never accumulated any wealth as farmers, we made a living. And we were very happy together. Never a cross word. We worked together as a team, but my wife was a better farmer than I was.

Although Anna's parents never visited us, they were always friendly. By the time we were married they were too old to travel. But other members of her family, her brothers and sisters, and especially her nieces, have visited us repeatedly. We have gone up to Chicago on a number of occasions to see the whole family. I visited with one of the nieces and her father just this year (1958).

After nineteen years of farming and doing a little blacksmithing I grew too old to work any longer. So I closed my shop and we rented most of our land to a white farmer who has been a good, honest tenant. For a number of years we lived on my small pension and the little rent money we received. It was hard to make both ends meet, but our wants were simple. Our schedule runs something like this: I get up rather late in the morning and cook breakfast for my wife and myself. Then I do a little work around the yard while my wife does up the few house chores. At 3 P.M. she cooks dinner after which we usually sit down and talk until sunset. Then we have a pickup supper of fruit or sandwiches. I wash the dishes and we sit down and talk again until bedtime. Luckily we both are great talkers. I always write a lot in the evening, too, either taking care of the correspondence for both of us, or working on this manuscript. On Sundays we always attend church in Lawton. I drive my own car—very slowly and carefully these days.

My wife's health began to fail after she had reached her eighties, but I was still pretty strong, though ten years her senior. She had to spend some time in the Government Indian hospital north of Lawton. One afternoon about ten years ago I was driving home after having visited Anna in the hospital. When I reached a point on the highway a little north of Fort Sill a military truck coming out from a side road was struck by a car speeding in the opposite direction to me.

JASON AND ANNA AT HOME

December, 1958

This knocked the truck into my car and I was badly hurt. I lay by the roadside for an hour, unconscious while passersby were trying to get an ambulance. I partially regained consciousness about nine o'clock that night in the hospital, to hear the doctor say to a nurse, "I want you to stay by this Indian's bedside. I don't think he will last out the night."

My reaction to this dire prediction was, "That's what they think! I'm going to get up." But it was a long time before I was out of bed. Both my knees were broken and my chest crushed. However, thanks to my old Apache toughness I did get out of bed after three months. I got to worrying about my house. My wife was still in the hospital, where we visited back and forth between our wards. I knew that the untended weeds around the house must have grown to the tops of the first floor windows. Now that all vegetation was dry, if a fire started my house would burn down. So when the doctor visited my room I asked him to let me go home.

"No," he replied, "you aren't well enough. You will have to stay here awhile longer."

As soon as the doctor had left the ward I got out of bed, hobbled on my crutches down the hall where I telephoned for a cab. In my pajamas I rode to Lawton, got out at a store and bought a suit of coveralls. Then I took the bus home. Here, propped up on my crutches, I cut the weeds and saved our home.

Some time later I saw the doctor when I again visited my wife at the hospital. He wasn't mad, as I thought he would be. He just laughed.

About six years after this, and while my wife was still in the hospital, I suddenly became desperately sick, I think with an intestinal obstruction. My neighbors called an ambulance in which I was rushed to the Will Rogers Memorial Hospital in Oklahoma City, 100 miles away. I made the driver stop by the Indian agency at Anadarko to let me draw and endorse to my wife my monthly check, so that she wouldn't be without funds. I was feeling pretty terrible, but I wanted to be sure that she was looked after.

At the hospital they operated right away. I think they removed some of my intestines. A few hours later, when coming out of the anesthetic, I felt so badly that I was sure my last hour had arrived. But presently a nurse came into the room, with such a kind smile on her face that I began to feel better right away. I think that it was as much her kindness and smiling face that pulled me through as any medical or surgical care. Only one who has been through an experience like this can realize how greatly the sick person appreciates gentle kindness and good will on the part of those who are caring for them.

In due course I was released from the hospital and returned home. My wife was soon released too, but still is not in very good health, so that I have to look after her most of the time.

I work when I can. Unlike most old people I never take naps in the afternoon. Somehow or other I manage to get around, driving to town and to church. I think my friends worry about me too much.

The other day someone from the Fort came to my house before I was out of bed. "Jason!" he called. "Get up. They want you down at Fort Sill right away."

"For heaven's sake," I called. "What for? Why should they want me now at Fort Sill?"

But I got up and went with him, as in the old days, always ready to obey calls from the Army. At the post I found that an actor was there, who takes the part of Cochise on a television program. They wanted me to pose for a picture with him and Mrs. Birdsong, one of Chief Quanah Parker's daughters. I was glad to do so, though I told this young man, "You are a good actor, and you take the part of Cochise almost as well as if you were an Apache. But there are a few incidents in the film that are not entirely the way things happened." Everyone laughed.

The Golden Fleece

In 1958 we had some good fortune. The city of Lawton, preparing to increase their water supply by damming up Cache Creek, bought part of my farm where the new lake would be formed. They paid me a good price for the forty acres, a total of $6,500. In addition to this, I also received another $6,500 for an oil lease on the rest of my land. As this was more than I would ever make by farming it or renting it, I was glad to accept. So now my wife and I have enough money to keep us comfortably for the rest of our days.

I am using part of the money to make some improvements to the house. We have new kitchen equipment and have installed running water and inside plumbing for the first time in our married life. I have taken down the old windmill and replaced it with an electric pump. So now we do not have to carry in water by hand. Even better, I will have enough water to plant a little garden. For years I have been wanting to grow some flowers for Anna. Next spring I expect to have some tulips and roses for her. I know she is going to be pleased as well as surprised.

These material things are fine. I am thankful for them. But above all I value the kind friends here and in other parts of the country, especially in our Presbyterian Church, where the white people are so good to us.

And now it is time to end my story. Unlike that earlier Jason, I have found the Golden Fleece. It is the solid gold of a grand and enduring fellowship with my many dear friends, both Indian and white, and the companionship of my beloved wife. Its core consists of the deep satisfaction I feel in the knowledge of a life well spent and a firm faith in that sweet Message of a better life in the hereafter.

His first trip by air. At the age of 99 Jason Betzinez flies to Harrisburg from Lawton, Oklahoma, to confer with his editor, Col. W. S. Nye.

INDEX

A

Adkisson, Maud, 171
Alamogordo, N. M., 52
Alamos, 105
Alamosa Creek, 25
Albuquerque, N. M., 21, 142
Alcatraz, 126, 129
Antelope hunt, 121
Apache Indians, archery, 6; attacked by artillery, 42; battle preparations, 7; butchered by Mexicans, 3, 10, 14, 17, 20, 43, 53, 71, 78; cattle ranchers, 168-200; children's school at Sill, 173; clothing, 27; customs, 10; decide to move to Mescalero, 195-6; endurance and strength, 6, 20, 52, 75; faults and virtues, 10, 38; fondness for liquor, 3, 10, 17, 38, 55, 80; food, 27, 29-35; fund at Sill, 182; hunting, 27, 29-34; heroism, 73; last-ditch outlaws, 145; leave Sill, 198; longevity, 10; marksmen, 107; marriages, 18; moccasins, 28; names forgotten, 8; outbreaks, 44, 47, 50, 56; preparations for battle, 63; prisoners of war, 141-8, 165-99; raids into U. S., 102; runners, 98; shelter, 29; story telling, 55; stratagems, 131; superstition, 13, 32, 35-7; taboos, 14; taught to work, 168; under military control, 122; vengeance, 4, 8; villages at Sill, 166; war methods, 55, 57-8, 65-7, 131; weapons, 5, 77, 88
Apache, Okla., 53
Apache Pass, 40, 42
Arizona, 2
Armadillo incident, 106
Army War College, 153
Atrocities, 43

B

Baishan (Cuchillo Negro), 4, 7, 8
Band divides, 83
Bascom, Lt. George N., 41
Battle of canyon, 111
Baviacora, 99, 102
Bavispe, 89, 100, 106
Bavispe River, 86, 87, 89, 97, 99, 112, 118
Bedonkohe Apaches, 14, 15
Beneacitney, 88, 97, 107
Benito, 9, 102, 107, 117, 129
Betzinez, Jason, apprentice warrior, 63, 82; acquires land and home, 201; at Carlisle, 149-59; at Ft. Marion, 145-9; at Fort Sill, 164; baseball, 163; blacksmith, 163, 175, 178, 201, 205; birth, 25; childhood, 26; Darlington employment, 161; delegate to capital, 160, 190, 195; farmer, 125, 129, 140, 156-9, 201, 205; fight with cavalry, 69; fight with Mexicans, 78, 83, 87; goes to Steelton, 159, 160; government employee, 162-4; injured, 156, 206; learns Christianity, 156, 161; learns English, 154, 157; learns trade, 154; leaves school, 159; marriage, 203-5; military record, 201; named, 31, 154; operation, 207; opposed to reservation life, 199; parents, 25; prisoner of war, 145-9; romances, 158, 203; sells some land, 208; sister, 25; trouble with Calisay, 182; trouble with Kaahtenny, 180; trouble with Naiche, 181; victory dance participant, 100; warpath, 84, 94
Birdsong, Neda, 208
Black Mountains, 2, 11, 14, 39, 45, 51
Black River, 123, 130
Bootleggers, 183-4
Bourke, Lt., John, 141
Branch, Sgt. Allen, 198
Brooklyn, N. Y., 152
Buenavista, 87, 98, 99
Buffalo hunt, 33
Burnett, Tom, 200

C

Cache Creek, 166
California
  Gulf, 11
  Lower, 11
Caddoes and Wichitas, 163, 185
Campbell, W. P., 154
Calisay, 182
Capron, Lt. Allyn, 165
Captive members of Apache band, 77
Carasco, Gen., 17
Carlisle Indian Industrial School, 149-59
Casas Grandes, 1, 8, 19, 20, 52, 68, 77, 78, 79, 81, 94, 96, 112, 113, 121, 122
Chapo, 106
Charleston, S. C., 151
Chattanooga, 145
Chatto, 24, 58, 70, 102, 107, 117, 129, 130, 140, 167, 190, 196
Cheyenne and Arapaho Agency, 163
Chihennes (see Warm Springs Apaches)
Chihuahua, Chief, 73, 74, 83, 97-9, 100, 102, 107, 129, 135, 140, 145, 167

[211]

Chihuahua, Mexico, 1, 2, 10, 15, 16, 20, 52, 112
Chihuahua, Ramona, 118
Chiricahua Apaches, 4, 39, 42, 46-8, 56, 88, 135, 145
Chiricahua Mountains, 4, 29, 39, 64, 66
Chiricahua, Tom, 167
Christian Endeavor, 171
Civil War, 5
Clifton, Arizona, 14
Cochise, 4, 9, 24, 39-42
Colony, Oklahoma, 164
Colorado River, 11
Columbus, N. M., 1
Commissioner of Indian Affairs, 161
Cooper, Edward, 156
Coronado National Forest, 42
Crawford, Capt. Emmett, 131, 132, 133, 166
Crook, Maj. Gen. George, 54, 57, 75, 115-24, 129, 133-5, 141
Cuchillo Negro (see Baishan)
Cuchillo, N. M., 194
Cut through the tent affair, 41

D

Davis, Lt. Britton, 123, 126, 128-31
Decoration of buffalo hides, 34
Delegation to Mescalero, 193
Delegation to Warm Springs, 193
Dick, Harold, medicine man, 172
Dilthche, 10-14
Domeah, Clay, 200
Douglas, Arizona, 10, 66
Dragoon Mountains, 42
Duncan, Arizona, 26
Dutch Reformed Mission, 163, 170

E

Eighth Cavalry, 182
Elephant Butte Dam, 24, 194
Ellen, sister of Jason, 25, 48, 125
El Paso, 21
El Reno, Oklahoma, 162
Engle, N. M., 194
Esqueda, 10
Ewing, Mary E., 173

F

Fernandina, Fla., 151
Fire dance, 93
Fire in camp, 110
Fires, Apache method of starting, 13
Fording Black River, 123
Forsyth, Lt. Col. George A., 63n

Fort Apache, 118, 121, 122, 129, 131, 141
Fort Bowie, 40, 42, 64, 65, 135, 139
Fort Craig, 25
Fort Cummings, 19
Fort Marion, 140, 145, 146, 147, 148, 150
Fort McRae, 25
Fort Grant, 122
Fort Sill, 149
Fort Thomas, subagency, 46, 47, 49, 54, 122
Four Mile Crossing, 175
Fourth Cavalry, 63n, 131
Free, Mickey, 41
Fronteras, 88, 121
Fuller, Herman, 159

G

Galeana, 20, 52, 93-6, 113-14
Gallup, N. M., 142
Garcia, Col. Lorenzo, 75
Gatewood, Lt. Charles, 131, 137-8
Geronimo (Goyakla), ability as warrior, 6; character, 182; death and burial, 196-8; family killed by Mexicans, 1, 14; farmer, 125, 129; in battle, 95; joins Juh, 16; leader, 58, 72-4, 88, 97, 100, 101; liquor craving, 47, 77, 107, 129, 135, 196; lives with Chiricahuas, 17; lives with Chihennes, 17; mentioned, 50, 63, 75, 83-6, 88-9, 92, 99, 110, 114, 116, 118, 121; outbreaks, 24, 47, 48, 56, 130; prisoner, 148; prophet, 90, 113, 115; raids, 82; surrender to troops, 121, 122, 132-6, 138; wife captured, 80; youth, 15
Geronimo, Arizona
Geronimo, Robert, 48
Geronimo, village, 167
Ghost Mountain, 163
Gila Mountains, 57
Gila River, 11, 46, 56, 58
Gila Valley, 47
Gil-lee, 55
Goode, Major George W., 183-4, 198, 201
Goyakla (see Geronimo)
Grazing privileges, 168
Great Canyon, 81, 91
Guadalupe Mountains, 1
Gymnasium at Carlisle, 158

H

Halley's Comet, 18
Harris, 155
Harrisburg, Pa., 160
Heersma, Anna, 173
Hessian Guardhouse, 152

[212]

Holbrook, Ariz., 141
Hospers, Henrietta, 198
Huachinera, 110
Hudson River, 152

I

Indian agents, 54
Indian scouts, 49, 50, 56, 62, 92
Indian Territory, 148
Isleta pueblo, 23

J

Jacksonville, Fla., 145
Janos, 1, 8, 17, 68, 121, 126
Jersey City, 152
Jornado del Muerto, 52
Juarez, 21, 52
Juh, 15, 16, 19, 46, 48, 49, 76, 83, 84, 91, 92, 95, 101, 110, 112, 122

K

Kaahtenny, 49, 53, 70, 83, 126, 129, 167, 180, 196
Kansas City, 143
Kawaykla, James, 53
Kay-i-tah, 75, 136-38, 139, 196
Killing Mexicans with rocks, 91
Kintal (see Ramos)
Kiowas and Comanches, 149, 165, 168
Kiowa-Apaches, 166n
Kronenbergs store, 155

L

Lake Mohonk Convention, 195
Lang, Walter, 161
Las Cruces, N. M., 24
Lawton, Capt. Henry W., 137, 139, 185
Lawton, Okla., 185
Lee, Maj. Gen. Fitzhugh, 189
Legters, Rev. L. L., 192
Life at Carlisle, 153
Lock, Frank, 154
Loco, 6, 24, 25, 33, 44, 49, 58, 69, 129, 167
Lordsburg, N. M., 19, 109
Low, Flora F., 154

M

Magdalena Mountains, N. M., 23
Mah-ko, 2, 14, 15, 39
Mangas, Charles, 148, 167
Mangas, Colorado, 4, 9, 43, 50
Martine, 136-9, 196
Massai, 143-5
Maus, Lt. Marion P., 133, 166
Medicine dance, 172, 175-177
Mescalero Apaches, 43, 113

Mexicans, bounty for Indian scalps, 3; enslaving Indians, 10, 20; fights near towns, 1-9, 10, 93-6; greed, 43; hatred, 52; kill Crawford, 132; kindness, 11, 20, 26; liquor to Indians, 3, 10; massacre Apaches, 3, 17, 71, 78; troops, 25; women captured, 113, 121
Miles, Gen. Nelson A., 135, 136, 139, 165
Mimbreno Apaches, 4, 43
Missionaries, 170
McComas, Charlie, 109, 118, 120
Moctezuma, 87, 98, 99, 106
Mojave Indians, 12
Mother-in-law taboo, 14
Monticello, N. M., 24, 25, 26, 194
Mount Vernon Barracks, Ala., 165

N

Nah-de-ga-ah, 126-128
Nah-thle-tla, 10, 18-24, 26, 48, 130
Naiche, Dorothy, 53
Naiche, 40, 58, 70, 135, 167, 181, 196
Namiquipa, 19, 20
Nanay, 6, 24, 44, 48, 50-54, 70, 133
National Geographic Society, 49
Navajo Indians, 23, 54, 77, 92, 142, 166
Negro troops, 25, 44, 46, 149
Netdahe, 15, 47, 55, 76, 123
New Mexico, 2
Night the stars fell, 18
Noche, George, 167, 196
Nonithian (see Tudeevia, the younger)

O

Opening of Kiowa-Comanche country, 185
Oputo, 89, 97, 99, 100, 106
Outbreaks, 126, 130

P

Parker, Quanah, 208
Paul, Miss F. G., 154
Peaches, 116, 117, 118, 120, 121
Pecos River, 33
Pensacola, Fla., 148
Perico, 138, 167
Philadelphia, 152
Phoenix, Ariz., 12
Pinos Altos, 45
Powder Face Crossing of Canadian, 163
Pratt, Capt. Richard H., 149-151, 158, 159, 174, 202
Pueblos, 166
Purington, Lt. George, 183, 190

Q

Quakers, 156

[213]

R

Raid into U. S., 88
Ramos, 1-9, 10, 39
Red Moon, Okla., 163
Reeder, Chilyan, 158
Rincon, 21
Rio de Janos, 71
Rio Grande, 4, 21, 23, 33, 142
Robertson, Wash, 163
Roe, Dr. Walter C., 164, 170, 172, 192
Rush Springs, Okla., 165

S

Safford, 46
Saint Augustine, Fla., 140, 145, 152
Saint Louis, 145
San Andres Mountains, 52
San Bernardino Springs, 134
San Carlos Apaches, 40, 46, 88, 123
San Carlos, Ariz., agency and reservation, 42, 44, 48, 49, 54, 65, 76, 88, 93, 118, 122, 126, 131, 141
San Carlos River, 46
San Francisco River, 60
San Miguel River, 1
San Simon Valley, 62
Sante Fe, N. M., 21, 24
Santa Maria River, 20
Santa Rita del Cobre, 1, 4
Scalping, not practised by Apaches, 8, 86, 101
Scouts, 131, 133, 136, 166
Scott, Gen. Hugh L., 165, 166, 168, 193
Scott, Maj. George L., 183
She-neah, 92, 95
She-sauson, 95
Shnowin, 18
Sierra Huachinera, 70n, 71
Sierra Madre Mountains, 49, 70, 76, 83, 89, 91, 97, 100, 106, 110, 118, 121, 135
Silver City, 45
Sixth Cavalry, 68n
Slavery, Indians sold into, 10
Smallpox, 45, 47
Smoke signals, 13
Solomon, Ariz., 46
Sonora, 15, 16, 17, 21, 85, 103
Sonora River, 102
Southern Pacific R. R., 64
Spanish-American War, 182
Speedy, 118

Stein's Peak Mountains, 62, 66
Sterling, Albert, 56-7, 122
Swett, M/Sgt. Morris, 198

T

Taft, William H., 191
Tenth Cavalry, 149
Toclanny, Rogers, 69, 167, 190, 196
Troup, Harry and Abe, 160
Troup Music Co., 160
Tsoay (see Peaches)
Tudeevia, the elder, 9, 24, 39
Tudeevia, the younger, 24, 26, 27, 31, 38, 50
Tupper, Capt., 68n
Turkey Creek, 125
Twelfth Infantry, 165
Twin Buttes, 53

U

Ures, 86, 97, 98, 102, 105
U. S. Government dealings with Apaches, 25, 44, 54
U. S. troops, 6, 49, 52, 60, 63, 66, 68, 71, 74, 115, 133
Utes, 166

V

Victorio, 6, 24, 44, 49-53, 95
Victory dance, 89, 77, 100

W

War dance, 4
Warm Springs Apaches, 2, 3, 4, 9, 15, 17, 21, 23, 48, 49, 50, 56, 72, 135
Warm Springs, N. M., agency reservation, 4, 6, 24, 25, 46, 50
Water tanks (ponds) at Sill, 169
White Mountain Apaches, 60, 126, 137
White Mountains, 128
White Sands, N. M., 52
Wichita Mountains, 165
Womanhood ceremony, 60
Wratten, George, 138, 166, 168, 189
Wright, Dr. Frank, 164, 170, 173

Y

Yaqui River, 81, 82, 86, 90
"You can't tame an Apache," 199
Yuma, Ariz., 11
Yuma Indians, 12